THE SAGA OF IRON ANNIE

NOVELS BY MARTIN CAIDIN

AQUARIUS MISSION

MAROONED

CYBORG

OPERATION NUKE

THE LONG NIGHT

HIGH CRYSTAL

CYBORG IV

THE LAST DOGFIGHT

DEVIL TAKE ALL

NO MAN'S WORLD

THE GOD MACHINE

ANYTIME, ANYWHERE

WHIP

THE LAST FATHOM

THE MENDELOV CONSPIRACY

FOUR CAME BACK

THE CAPE

ALMOST MIDNIGHT

MARYJANE TONIGHT AT ANGELS TWELVE

WINGBORN

THE LAST COUNTDOWN

THREE CORNERS TO NOWHERE

STARBRIGHT

JERICHO 52

SELECTED BOOKS BY MARTIN CAIDIN

The Saga of Iron Annie
Kill Devil Hill
The Tigers Are Burning
The Fork-Tailed Devil
Zero!
Samurai!
The Ragged, Rugged Warriors
Black Thursday
Thunderbirds!
The Long, Lonely Leap
The Long Arm of America
The Mighty Hercules
Let's Go Flying!
Cross-country Flying
Test Pilot
Hydrospace
The Winged Armada
Air Force
Golden Wings
Thunderbolt!
This Is My Land
Everything but the Flak
A Torch to the Enemy
The Night Hamburg Died
Barnstorming
Boeing 707
Flying Forts
Flying
Messerschmitt Me-109
The Zero Fighter

The Mission
The Silken Angels
When War Comes
Its Fun to Fly
The Power of Decision
Ju-52/3m Flight Manual
Rendezvous in Space
Man-in-Space Dictionary
Spaceport USA
The Astronauts
War for the Moon
I Am Eagle!
Rockets Beyond the Earth
Red Star in Space
Jets, Rockets, and Guided Missiles
Rockets and Missiles
Planetfall
Destination Mars
Vanguard!
Countdown for Tomorrow
The Greatest Challenge
Aviation and Space Medicine
By Apollo to the Moon
Man into Space
New World for Men
Why Space?
First Flight into Space
Worlds in Space
Overture to Space

etc.

The SAGA of IRON ANNIE

by Martin Caidin

DOUBLEDAY & COMPANY, INC.
GARDEN CITY, NEW YORK
1979

LIBRARY OF CONGRESS CATALOGING IN PUBLICATION DATA
Caidin, Martin, 1927–
The Saga of Iron Annie.
1. Junkers Ju-52 (Transport plane) I. Title.
TL686.J8C34   623.74'65
ISBN: 0-385-13350-2
Library of Congress Catalog Card Number 78–1189

First Edition

CONTENTS

For

PETE AND GLYNES

One week after this book was completed, only two days after we flew an air show of the Valiant Air Command for the U. S. Air Force and NASA at Langley Air Force Base, in Virginia, our Lockheed P-38L Lightning fighter, with Pete and Glynes Sherman in the cockpit, crashed and killed two wonderful people with whom we had flown many hours and shared wonderful moments. From all of us who knew and loved them, this book is dedicated to Pete and Glynes—may their wings take them to heights yet beyond our own vision.

THE SAGA OF IRON ANNIE

PART ONE

The Beginning

What the hell am I doing in this corrugated condominium?

That's a good question. Or it would be if I had selected another time and another place. Like relaxing on a wooden porch with a cool mint julep in one hand and a good cigar in the other, and contemplating the curves in a pair of beautiful legs. *Then* it's a good question, because there's plenty of leisure time to think about it, and it's tough to get in trouble with that mint julep. But not when you ask the question and your left hand grasps a huge control yoke and your right hand is on a brace of three engine throttles, your feet are pressed hard against the rudder pedals, and you're advancing those three throttles. And your eyes are scanning the gauges for the green light on for fuel pump, and you're checking the manifold pressure, revolutions per minute, carburetor air temperature, cylinder-head temp, and oil pressure, oil temp, and fuel pressure, fuel selector, and fuel flow. Don't forget that umpteenth check of the fuel-flow knobs and hydraulic-pressure and the vacuum-pressure gauges, and always that extra glance at flap setting and trim set. The yoke's full back, and you steal another glance at the directional gyro and the flight gauges. Right outside your ears, left and right and in front of you, the props are screaming and the tail wants UP, and it wants it NOW, so you keep the full back pressure on the yoke, because you want it full bore, balls to the wall, when your feet pop the brakes, because you're crazy.

The machine you've got by the tail is screaming and snarling and it wants to move, it wants to run, right now, baby, and ahead of you is thirty-six hundred feet of macadam airstrip. Well, not quite. Between you and the edge of that runway there's about eight hundred feet of grass. The ground is bumpy and the grass is too high, because it hasn't been mowed for a while and with all the thunderstorms in summer, Florida grass is thick and wet

underneath, so that it promises to do a beautiful job of slowing down an airplane trying to get into the air. And I'm crazy enough to try to lift this monster off the ground *before* we reach that beautiful paved strip.

Well, what the hell! Why not? I'm at the controls of *Iron Annie,* a three-engine corrugated-skin monster of slab wings and angular bends, of right-angled turns and knobs, and of all sorts of protuberances, and God knows what else jutting out into an airstream. An airplane is a flying machine that is supposed to be smooth-skinned and streamlined and sleek. Not *Iron Annie.* She scorns the gentle touch of the designer. She looks like a battlewagon with the wings added as an afterthought. The cockpit is a boiler factory of noise, of screaming prop blades and thundering exhaust stacks and howling engines, and she trembles all through her frame. She wants to cut loose, to *fly.*

This is the only Junkers Ju-52/3m remaining in the world. The *only* one left remaining out of thousands and thousands that were built in Germany. Her number is N52JU, and Merritt Island Airport, in Florida, is a hell of a long way in miles and years from the plant at Dessau where she first rolled from her factory into daylight. When I first got my hands on this relic of aviation history, she was a basket case, a bedraggled phoenix desperately short of even her own ashes for a revival. Yet, in a long, adventure-filled journey of time and effort, she was brought back to life again and her strengths and weaknesses revealed. But it happened, it really happened. *The* resurrection.

When they first saw her bone-battered carcass, in 1976, the men who were going to try to give her new life wept openly. There was great gnashing of teeth and battering of foreheads against the nearest wall, but they went at it anyway, and now it's the summer of 1978. The born-again *Annie* is about to fly again.

3

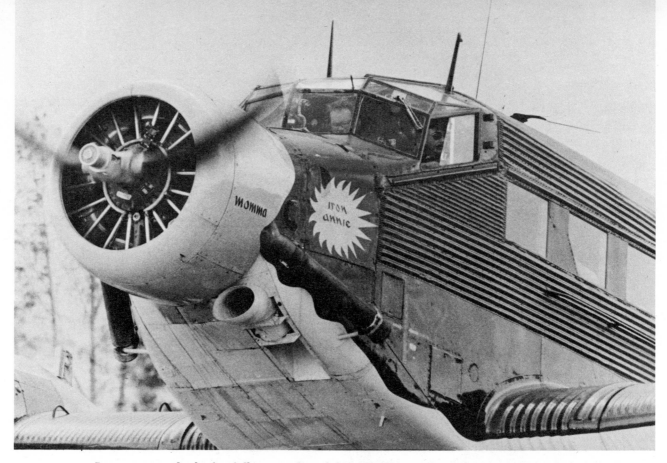

Last-moment checks for full-power short-field takeoff from the grass overrun at Merritt Island. Martin Caidin in the pilot seat is visible in the cockpit. KEN BUCHANAN

Only a short distance from this soggy grass (and that inviting stretch of paved strip) is the enormous sprawl of a place known world wide, the Kennedy Space Center, from where men sailed to the moon and where massive shuttles will boom on naked flame and Thor-thunder into high orbits about this interesting globe we call Earth. But it's silly to think of things like that when more pertinent questions are at hand in this shaking front office of a 23,100-pound iron creature from the winged past, such as: *What the hell am I doing here?* I've been flying for thirty-five years and I've caressed yoke and stick in more kinds of winged shapes than I can remember, but most of that flying has been in small and friendly airplanes of one and two engines. Nice airplanes, with the curved lines and sleekness of a woman's body, and sensible controls, and—

But what am I doing here? I've asked that question of myself so many times, so I suppose that to lay the truth naked the answer would have to be the lure, the siren call of this incredible iron monster. I remember when I first saw her and walked along her rotting floorboards and touched that great wooden yoke, and all the questions that spilled through the wonder I felt. The cockpit of the Ju-52 was filled with strange levers and dials and knobs and switches and handles and rods and things you turned and pushed and pulled and dialed and rolled and twisted. I stared at the fuel-flow start and the wobble pump and a central-ring quadrant, and the spark advance, and switches all over the damned place with metal-engraved signs in four languages. I couldn't identify half of them, but that was mitigated by the fact that they didn't work anyway.

I blinked the sweat out of my eyes. Got to remember that *Annie* will mesmerize you, sling you right back through a time tunnel so you forget which end of the calendar is up. It was almost time to go. Well ahead of us, beyond the grass, on the paved runway where the antiseptic Cessnas and Pipers and Beeches fly, a single-engine spam can was turning off the active and we were about clear to go. Last-moment checks. Tail wheel locked, directional gyro on 110 degrees, another glance at the trim indicator and I nodded in satisfaction. The needle wasn't where The Book recommended, but

4

flight manuals are musty tomes from history and are guidelines and not bibles, and practice now dictated where that needle rested on this sort of takeoff.

I glanced to my right. There, in the copilot seat, prim and comfortable in shorts and a halter, attentive to every detail, impish grin proclaiming her delight, Dee Dee looks at the world directly before her—the bulk of which is occupied by the mass of the nose engine. With the yoke full back, a job to which she contributes, Dee Dee can't see very much except engine and sky. She will stay with me on the controls through the takeoff run and climb-out.

John Glenn, an old friend, once said that having 120 pounds of recreational equipment aboard a spacecraft—especially if it was warm and lovely and soft and *very* friendly—was just about the best way to go, and it didn't matter where you were going. A beautiful young copilot is that way. . . .

Standing between Dee Dee and me, his bulk favoring a gorilla rather than a skilled crew chief, is Larry Urback. Larry and I have been through a lot together, belted down a few in our unsavory past, and remember motels in faraway places where we kept a baseball bat handy for the mosquitoes and a .38 in one hand for nocturnal visitors. Well . . . there are trees and buildings on the grass end of this field, and Larry heaves himself up through the hatch for a fast look to our rear, the blast of noise and air from the nose engine just about slamming his head back. He drops down, nods, shoves the top hatch mostly closed. His look tells me it's clear to go.

One fast glance again. You look for needles in precise rows, and what's out of place jumps at you. Larry is scanning the panel like a hawk out for revenge. I gesture with my right hand and he nods again. The gauges are his and it's time to come off the brakes. I have a fleeting reminder. *This machine was designed just about fifty years ago, and this particular airplane, the last German-built Ju-52 in existence in the world, is more than twice the age of my wife, in the copilot's seat.*

I make a last-moment change in plan and instead of popping the brakes I keep my toes hard on the brakes and ease forward on the yoke. The corrugated monster is like a ballet dancer and that fast: before you can believe it happens, twenty-three thousand pounds of airplane are perfectly balanced. The tail is up at once and I snatch a hair

of back yoke to keep her level, *and we're standing still, engines and props screaming, the airplane in level flight and we haven't moved an inch.*

I'm off the brakes and, at once, moving straight ahead, *Annie* accelerates with astonishing speed. It's like watching a locomotive lunge forward from a standing position. You know it's too big and heavy and clumsy to do anything fast, but no one told this airplane and so she does her own thing, roaring and bellowing. Thirty-six inches manifold pressure with three needles pegged smack on. The props at twenty-two hundred and fifty revolutions per minute. Out of the corner of my eye I see Larry's thumb stab upward. It's all in the green and we're rushing forward and *damn* but that's a *short* patch of green. The softness of the ground clutches at the big tires and holds her back, but I keep her exactly level. One eye is on the air-speed indicator and the other on the space between the row of runway lights. If we can't get up in time it means bouncing onto the paved surface and there's barely enough room to squeeze between those lights and I don't want one of them stabbing into a tire. We're at forty, then fifty, and then sixty miles per hour and she feels light, but at this speed you need right rudder to compensate for torque and propeller downwash and you need rudder to correct the bouncing movement, and it's fast on the feet. *Annie* demands a lot of rudder at this speed, but that big barn door way behind me does what it's supposed to and the response is immediate. We are running out of grass now. A better wind would have helped. It's about eight miles per hour but quartering from 40 degrees to my left, and the temperature is ninety-six, which does not help, no sir. The pavement is ahead, so I ease back on the yoke. She's so finely balanced with 25 degrees of flaps and the trim set *just* so that the problem is over-controlling, so I do it easy, very easy indeed, and the impossible happens again.

A hundred feet of grass remaining before us and *Annie* is flying. The nose has come up hardly at all. It's an amazingly flat-attitude climb with this flap setting, and the air-speed needle is swinging past 75 as we're over paved surface. Because of the temperature, I let her build to 85, then come back some more on the yoke, and by the time she's accelerated to 90, those props screaming at the world, we're going upstairs at a thousand feet per minute. I ease her into a 30-degree bank and those great wings come around as if we were on a pivot, just as smooth as a satin nightgown against cream-white skin, the nose swinging through the horizon as if it were on rails.

Beautiful. Just plain beautiful. The cockpit's an absolute bedlam of engine noise and howling props and the wind beating in through the overhead hatch and the open side windows. At 500 feet above the ground, Larry flicks off the fuel pump and the green light winks out and we both, through practice and association, glance at the three fuel-pressure gauges. Right where they belong. We don't want much altitude for this flight, so I let the nose drop down, and at once the air-speed indicator shows 100 on the button and I nod to Dee Dee and her fingers have her yoke now and I hold up my forefinger. She nods; she'll keep the iron bird at the 100 indicated.

The uneven rumble of unsynchronized props is gone and she's honey smooth. Normally we bring back the power in level flight to 26 inches manifold pressure, the nose engine at 1,875 rpm, and the wing engines at 1,850 rpm. No one knows why they read slightly off in this manner, but at cruise you can forget what the gauges say and set everything by shadow synch through the mirrors. They're more reliable than the fanciest electronic gadgetry ever invented. But, for the moment, I decide to hold the higher settings of 32 inches and 2,100 rpm, because we're turning in the direction of Patrick Air Force Base, where on the beach seventy thousand people are waiting for our appearance.

I reach down to my right, where there's a huge wheel they must have removed from some ancient zeppelin. It's time to start cranking up the flaps.

Jack Kehoe, of the Valiant Air Command (VAC), holds position off the left wing of *Iron Annie* in his meticulous T-6, headed for the big air bash at Patrick Air Force Base. PAUL BROWN

I bring the throttles back to 32 inches, and as soon as they're steadied down I come back on the three props. Instantly the sound changes, the harsh screaming of paddle-bladed props is gone to a deeper and much more pleasant rolling thunder. Nose prop at 2,100 rpm, and then I glance to my left, outside the airplane, to the polished-steel mirror on the left-engine cowl. A curving line of light moves toward me, and my hand nudges the prop control. What I'm watching is a shadow strobe effect, and as my hand moves the left prop control and reduces its speed, the curving line slows some more and finally disappears. This is visual confirmation that the left-engine propeller is now turning with *exactly* the same speed as the nose prop. Larry is doing the same to the right engine, and then the sound settles down. You can feel it.

Larry taps my hand; he'll do it. His huge paw turns that wheel as if it were greased, and we're at zero flap setting. He rolls in some nose-down trim, and I go on the yoke. Dee Dee releases her own pressure as I trim for level flight and take back control. Dee Dee and Larry put on their headsets and I grab for mine, make a final trim adjustment, hold level flight at 1,200 feet. We're indicating about 135 mph now and I know what to expect.

"Eagle One from Eagle Two," comes the voice in my headset, and I look to my left and there's Colonel Jack Kehoe of the Valiant Air Command in his letter-perfect T-6, sliding in steadily to ride *Annie's* wing. He comes in close. *Very* close, his wing actually riding over or under our own, as the mood hits the big Polack. In the back seat of the old North American trainer is his wife, Susie, a lovely, lithe

Pete Sherman brings his big Lightning fighter off the right wing of the Ju-52/3m—a perfect example of today's warbirds no longer being birds of war. STEVE ROCK, U. S. NAVY

young creature. Jack grins and Susie waves and the headset is alive again.

"Canary to Annie, coming up on the right." Rick Thompson in his bright yellow Harvard, the Canadian version of the T-6, with his wife, Marcia, in the back seat, and he matches Jack on the opposite side of the big, three-engine airplane, and I won't have to worry about these two cats, because they've glued themselves to those big corrugated wings through a lot of air shows.

That's what this is all about right now—an arrival air show for the Air Force, and the sky is filling with sights that mist eyes of old-timers and bring wonder to the hearts of their sons and daughters, because this is history on the wing. A flash of gleaming metal above and to my right; Pete Sherman in his gorgeous Lockheed P-38L Lightning that he rebirthed from a lonely death on a New Jersey farm, now with great shark teeth on each cowling. The twin-boomed killer eases ahead as more fighters come along to join up with Pete. There's a Curtiss P-40N Warhawk and three North American P-51D Mustangs and, oh ho! John Silberman and Jay Hinyub in their Beech AT-11, complete with Norden bombsight in their old bombardier trainer replete with twin engines and twin tail,

and they'll ride herd on *Annie* through the show, because they have a ball playing wingtip games with us.

High above, there's one of our own spam cans, a Comanche with four hundred horses in the nose, and inside the plush cabin, Leo Kerwin, who is the Glorious Leader of the Valiant Air Command, is watching everyone come together in the sky, and he calls out instructions and snarls at people who are a few seconds ahead or behind in their schedule, because he wants this first pass down the Patrick runway at *precisely* high noon. Four more T-6s have joined us, and the Martin brothers come thundering into the group in their North American B-25J Mitchell, and there's someone I haven't met yet in a Douglas A-26 Invader. In the cabin of *Iron Annie*, Ken Rowley and Ted Votoe and Karl Frensch are watching all the other iron birds setting up their positions. Vern Renaud is floating along in a lovely old Stearman PT-17 Kaydet biplane, and in the distance we see a formation of a Beech T-34 Mentor and two North American T-28 Trojans on a long pursuit curve to join up, and higher up there's George Baker in his Lockheed T-33 Silver Star, just jet-loafing at four hundred per, and Leo is grumbling at us again.

Rick Thompson's gleaming Harvard from Canada holds tight formation with *Iron Annie* en route to Patrick Air Force Base. PAUL BROWN

"Annie, bring it around to the Pineda Causeway. You've got thirty seconds to come around," he commands.

"Roger, over, out, wilco, and up yours, Glorious One," I call back, and you can almost hear the grins all around. Larry Urback is on the intercom. "Confirm smoke switches on," he announces matter-of-factly. He doesn't screw around when we fly a show. Everyone is in tight and a single wrong move can spell disaster. Larry's words are the signal that it's time for business.

"Annie's coming down now," I call in the open on the mike. "Curving left pass over the causeway and we'll hit the runway right on the deck."

A chorus of clicks from the other pilots who will be moving with me.

"Fighters ready." That's Pete in the Lightning, and he's speaking for the other fighters as well. In the meantime, Larry has pushed the prop controls full forward and they're screaming again. I've got my right hand on the throttles, and the nose is down and we're really zinging it now, the needle coming around to 150, 160, 170, and we're still accelerating as I start easing back on the yoke, and we're doing 190 as we cross the south end of the

Patrick runway. The big tires are about a foot or maybe six inches off the runway as we beat down the field and Pete calls it out.

"Okay, Annie, we're coming up and you can, ah, start your smoke *now*."

Larry hits the switch on the right of the quadrant and from each wing engine there's an explosion of smoke. We're pumping a special oil directly into the wing engine exhausts, and the thick smoke tears backward as the fighters scream low overhead on their run. For a moment, I think of Karl Frensch in the cabin behind me, because Karl once wore a Luftwaffe uniform and he used to fly his Ju-52 in invasions and air battles. That was more than thirty-eight years ago, and here he is in a sky full of deadly fighters putting on a warbird show and there just ain't nobody mad at nobody. Then I push it from my mind, because the end of the runway is coming up *fast* and I know Ted Anderson, microphone in hand, is spellbinding the crowd, scaring the bejesus out of everyone, shouting that *ohmyGod they're on fire they're going to CRASH and LOOK OUT and—*

Very quietly, Larry's voice sounds in my earphones. "Fighters clear." That's the signal that no

Let's smoke 'em! *Iron Annie* bends over in the start of a curving dive, smoke pouring from the left engine to start the air-show "attack." PAUL BROWN

Ken Stallings, of the U. S. Coast Guard, a brilliant pilot who flies anything with wings, holds "just short of landing" on the Ju-52 wing on the way down to the air show. KEN ROWLEY

one is above us or coming up behind us. I go to full power on the throttles, and *Annie* screams like a wounded dinosaur. I haul back on the yoke, hard back and no nonsense about it, and the great old machine leaps skyward, the sudden pullup jawing everyone down tight in his or her seat. We're pulling up tight and curving to the left in a climb that shoves the T-6s and the AT-11 away from us, and I watch carefully as the air speed bleeds away, and then it's forward on the yoke; follow the rule, never let it get below 100 mph indicated in this kind of pullup and climbout. Just like that, we're at 1,000 feet and coming off on the power, still banked over steeply, and I see a blur as the T-33 howls down the runway through the smoke trail we left, doing better than five hundred miles an hour.

"Smoke off," I call, and Larry moves the switch and suddenly we're not on fire any more.

"Annie coming around for full stop," I call to the other pilots crowding the same airspace with me. "T-6s and the AT-11 cut below and ahead. Land first."

"Roger that." A chorus of assents and we see the other iron birds moving down and below, and then it's time for us to set up for descent and landing. Back on the throttles, fuel pump on, and props moved to full forward. I hold back the yoke until the air speed's down to 100 again and Larry is rolling in 25 degrees of flaps. We're around on final now. The flaps come down to 40 degrees and Larry rolls in some nose-down trim and I let her slow to 80 indicated. A fast cockpit scan, everything in the

Flaps full down, wired in the slot on her approach, *Iron Annie* comes down the rail to land before the crowd of one hundred thousand onlookers. PAUL BROWN

Pete Sherman taxis *Glamorous Glynes* to the flight line, where he'll "present arms" in the Valiant Air Command warbirds presentation. PAUL BROWN

green, fuel pump on, fuel selector centered, mixtures FULL RICH, and *Annie* floats gently out of the sky and I let her ride on her air pillow. I'll put her down directly before the crowd, about three quarters of the way along the runway. The landed warbirds are now on each side of the long strip. *Annie* gentles on at just above 70 miles per hour, and it's yoke back and brakes applied at the same moment and we roll about eight hundred feet, just a nice touch for the crowd when she comes to a stop with her tail easing to the concrete.

People see it but they don't believe it. Just like that, the corrugated monster has *stopped*. But there are the fighters and bombers coming in behind me, and as Larry calls out that the tail wheel is unlocked I ease the throttles forward, come back on two and three, and let a quiet bellow from the left engine and a tap of right brake swing us off the active onto the taxiway.

"Ju-52 clear," I call out.

"Got it," Pete Sherman acknowledges, and his big Lightning feather-touches onto the runway, the Mustangs and the Warhawk and the other machines behind him, and then we're all lined up and Leo Kerwin grumbles some more at us and reminds us to "Look smart, you people." We get the signal and taxi back across the runway behind an Air Force truck and then, one by one, we swing into

position to face the crowd, lock brakes, set up postlanding checklist, and start shutting down. The props grind to blurs and then they freeze in their final positions and we kill the radios and the switches and follow the checklist we know by heart, and it's hot as hell in this bright burning sun and we're soaked in sweat and we look at one another and grin like crazy, because this whole thing, this entire scene, is so incredible and impossible that it can't be happening; I mean, this is a page right out of World War Two, and here we are *and it's real!*

Larry and Dee Dee leave the cockpit, and for a moment I sit alone in the Ju-52, savoring the moment, feeling the heat also from the engines and the smell of oil from the props. The guys are shoving the chocks beneath the big wheels and emplacing the control locks, and suddenly Ted Votoe sticks his head into the cockpit and hands me a cold, cold Coors. He grins at me and is gone, and I stay there a few more moments, because sometimes being alone with your iron bird is the right thing to do. I pat the big yoke, take a long slug of the cold beer, and then leave the pilot's seat. I marvel, as I do every time a flight ends, at the fates that have put me in that seat and let me come to know and love and fly this incredible airplane that is so steeped in history not only of war but of aviation

e Dee Caidin, who, with her husband, spent years saving and restor-
; *Iron Annie*. Dee Dee is a pilot, parachutist, balloonist, competition
rsewoman—and professional model. BUD PELLETIER

erst Martin von Caidin, Ju-52 pilot and instructor, chaplain of the
liant Air Command, command pilot of the Confederate Air Force, for-
r "guest" of secret-police jails, ex-parachutist—and a somewhat irrev-
nt ordained minister. PAUL BROWN

itself. This machine *is* history. It's the greatest airplane of its kind ever built and it seems so impossible that she is the last, the very last of her breed in
all this world.

— ◆ —

That's what this story is all about. THE SAGA OF
IRON ANNIE. A history of the rebirth of an incredible flying machine. A history of the machine as a
type, through all the models built and all the
places they flew and battles they fought, in wars
and out of wars. But, for the first time, we can tell
this story as it *should* be told, because it is absolutely intimate, exquisitely personal, and historical
at the same time.

We fly the truth, we fly reality every time the
yoke comes back and the earth falls away and that
sweet thunder sings in the sky and we feel in our
bones and through our bodies the essence of what I
believe is the greatest flying machine ever built.
What I share with you now is living and flying history. The reality of it.

But there's another element of which we must
speak. Those of us who have flown, rebuilt, and re-
created this machine admit unabashedly, without
hesitation, to another truth.

This is a love affair.

11

On August 19, 1909, Orville Wright and his sister, Katharine, arrived in Berlin, Germany. After settling in sumptuous arrangements made for them at the best hotel in the German capital, Orville met with members of the German Wright Company, which had been formed for the specific purpose of selling various models of the Wright Flyer to the company and training at least two men to the point where they could solo and be able to teach other men to fly. This was to launch a wave of continuous pilot growth and a new era of aircraft development in Germany—an effort carried out by private individuals upon whom much scorn and ridicule were heaped by government officials. Despite the abuse of the Prussian military, the members of the German Wright Company delivered to Orville Wright a draft for forty thousand dollars to meet their contract terms. In today's terms, that would be nearly a half million dollars.

Until 1908, almost all Europeans had considered Orville and Wilbur Wright as loud-mouthed buffoons who talked much better than they could fly. The Wrights' claims of initial flight on December 17, 1903, at Kitty Hawk, on the Outer Banks of North Carolina, were dismissed as absolute nonsense, and further claims of sensational flights at Huffman Prairie, eight miles outside Dayton, Ohio, were considered to be the unfounded mutterings of two clever bluffers. Then, in 1908, in France, Wilbur assembled an old model he had built in 1905 and shipped to Le Havre. He cleaned up the long-crated machine, set up a flight, and in the face of twenty-six doubting witnesses, shot into the air and swept gracefully through the skies in perfectly coordinated turns and figure eights that stunned his audience. Children ran screaming through the streets of nearby Le Mans with the words *"Il vol! Il vol!"*

He flies! He flies! Indeed he did, and the next day, *four thousand people* swarmed to the scene to watch the miracle repeated. Wilbur took all Europe by storm, just as Orville was doing in the United States. There was a great rush to buy the Wright designs and be taught to fly by these astonishing brothers from the United States.

The Prussian military, in characteristic form, refused to believe that they might be influenced by the capabilities of anyone save Germanic stock. The truth was that the greatest efforts of men of science and invention in Europe before the arrival of the Wrights were little more than tragicomic attempts to get into the air. Inventors hopped or stumbled about, more often collapsing in wreckage than flying, and when they did manage to become airborne, every second was so precarious that death and destruction were never farther away than the blink of an eye.

On the twenty-eighth of June in 1908, at Kiel, J. C. H. Ellehammer, another aeronautical aspirant, tried desperately to get into the air with his No. IV biplane. His crude flying machine lurched and stumbled precariously along the ground and at long last hopped piteously into the air for two separate flights, each of which lasted the extraordinary time of about eleven seconds, with the craft barely remaining in one piece and the pilot bravely but desperately hanging on for dear life. These were more hops than they were flights, and officials of the German Government rolled their eyes back into their heads and called for enough *Schnapps* to blot out the sight.

Undaunted by this effort, another German—Hans Grade—was hard at work on a triplane, his *à la* Ellehammer. During October of 1908, Grade, with admirable wisdom, restricted his work to ground tests until he might accumulate sufficient meaningful data to take to the air. In January of 1909, Grade's triplane struggled off the ground, again with breath-holding lack of control and unsettling brevity, but still within the embrace of what could be accepted as true flight. It was obvious to Hans Grade that his triplane—for a whole variety of reasons including insufficient power, poor wing design, lack of understanding of camber, and above all terrible instability and lack of proper control—had only a cloudy future and would be far better off left lying unattended and forgotten on the ground. Grade turned to the center of aeronautical activity in Europe and swallowed his pride, for the Germans little liked to admit French superiority in *anything*, and copied a Demoiselle design but with sufficient changes so that it could be called a modification or improvement. Whatever, in September 1909, at Borck, Hans Grade got into the air for Germany's first true flight. It proved that the French design was, in very calm air, manageable, that a German could copy the design of another, but most important that Hans Grade knew how to fly.

But what really mattered in Germany was the historic flights of that diminutive genius from a far-off land. Orville Wright commented in a letter to his brother Wilbur: "On September 23, I finished on the Tempelhof Field. . . . I was compelled to stop after an hour and 46 minutes on account of the water supply being exhausted. The little drive on the water front had broken. As a result, the water had all boiled away."

Now, there is an incredible difference between staggering through the air in home-built machines, or even fluttering along in German copies of the Demoiselle, and flying in an older American machine through turns and circles and swooping along at the slightest whim of its pilot for an hour and forty-six minutes. The former was of little or no interest to the rigid thinking of the German military, but the latter was clear evidence that such a machine could cover great distances for long periods of time, and in a single stroke strip away the concealment enjoyed by great military forces on the ground.

On October 2, 1909, Orville Wright's flying machine climbed to 1,637 feet above Tempelhof, and he enjoyed a grand view of the entire city. That not only was too much to ignore but brought on an unexpected consternation among the general staff of the military. It was also a shock when Orville Wright took aloft as a passenger none other than the Crown Prince of Germany.

The more Orville Wright flew at Tempelhof, and the longer he trained German pilots, the more intensive grew the observations of his flights. The Germans also discovered that, right in their own back yard, there were geniuses who had performed brilliant work on aerodynamic theory that was already recognized as some of the more important bedrock of practical aviation. Ludwig Prandtl had completed an astonshing presentation in airfoil sections, drag analysis, and boundary-layer theory. The great mathematician Wilhelm Kutta had produced his own outstanding work on airfoil sections. But such efforts were overshadowed by the dazzling performances of Orville Wright. A frantic search ensued for Germans who understood the vexing problems of improving aircraft designs to where machines of a practical nature could be built in quantity.

In the meantime, the number of qualified observers—"qualified" representing men of clear thought and open mind—at Tempelhof continued to increase. What they saw would inspire them to efforts they could never have believed possible, for Orville Wright was proving that a flying machine did not need dead-calm air in which to operate—and if this was so, then it would also not be restricted in its use in the field. The words of Orville in another letter to his brother mark well what was seen and so carefully noted by the German observers at Tempelhof.

"I never passed through so many and such severe whirlwinds as in the flights here," wrote Orville, "but they are usually in certain parts of the field, and I can keep out of the worst of them if I choose. I would be flying along very nicely when all of a sudden the machine would begin to quiver. And in looking at the tape [with which Orville would judge sudden shifts in wind direction] I would see it swerve to one side and angle 45 degrees, and in a few seconds, without any change of the rudder, it would swing an equal amount to the opposite side."

———◆———

Through this fledgling stage of aviation, the Germans were excelling in lighter-than-air craft. The great zeppelins were being developed, the huge rigid airships, with which Germany had no competitors worthy of note anywhere in the world. Zeppelins are impressive creatures, swollen gasbags though they may be, stuffed into rigid shapes by their metal framework, and they only obliquely fit into this history of iron birds that fly with rigid wings and without the lifting power of hydrogen. Yet they must be brought into the context of our own avenue of interest, for they help explain the stiff-necked and rejective attitude of the German Government toward airplanes that lurched and hopped about like grotesque parodies of creatures that truly are capable of flight. In their simplest form, the airplanes were feeble humor, and the zeppelins were an astounding, even an overwhelming, success. Between 1910 and 1914 alone, German zeppelins, in commercial service with five machines, carried more than thirty-five thousand passengers across one hundred seventy thousand miles of routes without so much as a single injury of *any* kind to crew or passengers. The zeppelin was king and the airplane a wraith of a buffoon.

———◆———

When Orville Wright amazed his German audience at Tempelhof, an obscure engineer was delving into the flow of fluids at varying speeds and, more specifically, was developing a new calorimeter (a device for measuring heat). The engineer determined that as the velocity of the flowing fluid increased, any object in the stream of the flow created a parasitic drag. The greater the size or resistance of the object the greater the drag in the gas stream until it became so severe as to wreck any smooth flow.

At this time, the engineer who probed so deeply into fluid stream flow discovered his interest piqued by the news stories of the Wright Flyer performing its aerial ballet over Berlin. Mild interest developed into a deep frown and then serious thinking. The machine flew on airfoils. *All* the lifting power of the device came from the airfoils, which shaped the flow of air across its surfaces.

Ah, but what is that flow? There lay the key. To an engineer working with fast-moving air—such as air flowing past a wing—the atmosphere *is not a gas*. It is a fluid, and it behaves like a fluid, and its behavior may be anticipated under many possible conditions. Until this moment, this obscure engineer had evinced little or no interest in aviation, but the Wright Flyer tugged his imagination to serious thought. The wings—the airfoils—provide the lifting force by shaping the flow of atmospheric fluid as it races above and below the airfoil.

Anything else is so much waste. Struts, wires, braces, mounts, seats—whatever—all produce parasitic drag. The greater the drag (all such objects being considered parasites to the goal of smooth fluidic flow) the less the efficiency of the total device and the greater its loss in flight efficiency. Out of curiosity, the engineer sketched out his ideas, mused over his concepts, prepared detailed drawings, and submitted them to the government for issuance of a patent. It was this man's concept that the obvious goal of an aeronautical engineer was to reduce parasitic drag to its minimum and thus gain maximum efficiency in flight. Since everything other than the wing produced such drag, why not design the flying machine *entirely as a wing?* The patent, drawn up in 1909, was issued on February 1, 1910, for "an aeroplane consisting of one wing, which would house all components, engines, crew, passengers, fuel, and framework."

Strangely enough, this same engineer never brought to its ultimate shape the design he patented, but he did launch a revolutionary concept to the burgeoning world of aviation: the thick wing that would contain as much of the aircraft's payload and requirements as possible. It would also be a fully cantilevered wing; that is, its entire structural support would be obtained by so constructing the wing that it would not need external braces, wires, and other supports—which, in those days, wasn't just revolutionary but naked heresy. Ah, but there was more. The wing would be made of metal, and it would be built like the truss construction of a bridge, which meant, in its final form, a thick wing of unprecedented strength.

This was the beginning of what would become known in aviation circles as the *deep cantilever wing* and which would emerge also as the strongest large airplane wing ever to go into production. While it would often be compared to the wings that went into Fokker, Ford, Stout, and similar products, especially where corrugated metal was concerned, the others would all follow, *not predate,* this patented design.

Now let's move forward to 1912 and the Technical University of Aachen. It was at this highly prestigious facility that Professor Hans Reissner designed a canard aircraft—one which, like the Wright Flyer, mounted the tail in front of instead of trailing behind the wings. The canard was, therefore, old hat by the time Reissner got around to his home-grown Erector-set construction, but what was new was found in the corrugated aluminum Reissner built for his wing surfaces. The

Reissner canard was a braced monoplane, and its wings were technically described as "corrugated aluminum sheet of no profile." Surprisingly, it managed to fly although it was intolerably heavy for the engine power available, but, lacking needed refinement of design, it passed quietly from the ever more active field of aviation.

———◆———

"Why is he telling us all these things?"

I can hear the voices rising in the background, eyes peering beadily across the top of the pages of this book. Patience. It fits together neatly, and it shows us in a way we have never before seen the intricate and enchanted webs by which we have moved from the past to the awaiting future.

We saw how Orville Wright captured the imagination of all Germany with his sensational flights at Tempelhof, and how his swooping and graceful flight brought furrows of deep thought to the brow of an obscure engineer who took out a patent for a thick wing for an airplane, and—

Hold it. That obscure engineer? This is where it all begins to fit together in the unbroken chain from 1909 to this very moment.

For he was a professor. *The* professor of thermodynamics at the Technical University of Aachen, *and his name was Hugo Junkers.*

It begins to fit *now.* For that same university also hosted Professor Hans Reissner, who developed the canard design with corrugated aluminum for wings. Those names fit together. There is yet another name that carries all the way across the years: Kurt Weil, today the professor emeritus of the Stevens Institute of Technology's Department of Mechanical Engineering. How does Kurt Weil fit into our myriad of names and details? For starters, Kurt Weil was a student at the Technical University of Aachen, where he had met and worked with Professor Hugo Junkers. Later he became one of Junkers' most trusted engineers, who would lay down the design requirements for an airplane that would become internationally acclaimed as the Junkers Ju-52/3m.

The *same* Professor Kurt Weil who in 1978 joined me in N52JU, the last remaining German-built Iron Annie in the world, in an emotion-racked encounter that none of us who were present will ever forget.

I take the liberty of crossing decades to strengthen this extraordinary linkage of events with an unbroken, if at times obscured, chain from Tempelhof in 1909 to this moment. In 1978 I flew the Ju-52 south along the Florida coast to Pompano Beach Aircraft, where Red Gargaly and Jake Bixby, of the Federal Aviation Administration, were waiting, with Kurt Weil, eighty-three years old, for the arrival of the airplane Kurt had not seen for some forty-odd years. The day was beautiful and the tower cleared me for a low and fast approach, and at a thousand feet we went full bore on the rpm and throttles and rolled a wing into the sky, down with the nose, and we came whistling from the sky, flattening out at the last moment and going to the smoke generators for the wing engines. *Iron Annie* moved within inches of the runway surface, and at the end of the field I horsed her into what I hoped would be a splendid demonstration of how to make a grand old iron lady look as if she were spanking new, by hauling up in a steep climb and rolling out into a downwind leg to land. The wind punched straight down the runway and we touched on the numbers and went to brakes and back yoke, and well before the first turnoff, at eight hundred feet from the numbers, we released the tail-wheel lock and were taxiing.

That visit is for later pages, but it is appropriate here to share with you the letter that emerged from that visit as I received it from Kurt Weil:

———◆———

I want to express to you again my gratitude for your generous gesture of bringing yourself and your magnificent crew with the Iron Annie to the Pompano Beach airfield where I could enjoy such a splendid bunch of men, radiating the joy of living and demonstrating with justified pride the Old Tante Ju—the product of your brain and your handiwork. The emotional experience, which I did not mind admitting to you, emanated from the spontaneous impression of genuine comradeship and friendship for you who re-created my brainchild of fifty years ago into yours of our days now. Certainly, this Ju-52 never before "had it so good" as under your hands and enthusiasm—not to speak of skill, understanding, and piloting art. Many thanks again to you all for an unforgettable experience.

Best wishes for all of you. *Keep her flying!*
Kurt

Digging through musty history is fascinating. Being directly involved with living history is rapture and total enchantment, and I have long and marvelous chapters filled with things to say about Hugo Junkers and Hans Reissner and an incredible variety of aircraft that emerged from the drawing boards of Hugo Junkers and Kurt Weil and so many others. But this is not a book about the Junkers lineage or the company or even the fascinating development in aeronautical and adventure-crammed stories of such machines as the F-13 and the W-33 and the three-engine G-24 and the G-31 and the monstrous G-38 that finally brought to life the original patent of Hugo Junkers from 1910—in which the greatest airplane in the world for its time offered luxurious passenger seats with picture-window views in the nose and the leading edges of the wings!

Those are other stories and the subject matter of another book, and it is only with difficulty that I tear myself away from the all-steel airplanes Junkers built in World War One, and the revolutionary fighters he built with wing skin-stressed construction so rugged that the machine went into the air *without any spars in the wings.*

By 1917, pressed by Germany's needs for revolutionary military aircraft, Hugo Junkers produced the first low-wing cantilever monoplane fighters, mostly of metal construction and scorned by most of the Kaiser's hierarchy because they lacked the *obvious* struts and braces and wires an airplane needed to keep its wings from breaking away from

the fuselage. No matter that they flew like no other machines or that their promise was so stupendous; the J.7 and J.9 fighters of 1917 never overcame the myopia that so affects high-ranking government officials.

But our interest begins with the Junkers J.10, of 1918, for this was the machine that was the beginning of the design that became the world-renowned F-13 and began the direct line of ascendancy that would lead to the Ju-52.

This story, which remains directly along the lineage of the Ju-52, is where we will track our course from this point on. Before we do so, however, I wish to share with you a conclusion by Charles H. Gibbs-Smith, respected internationally as a brilliant historian of our air age, who in his magnificent work *Aviation: An Historical Survey* refers to Hugo Junkers and the world he altered:

The influence of Junkers was to affect the whole course of aircraft evolution. He may be fully and fairly credited with the design and construction of (a) the first practical cantilever-wing aeroplanes, (b) the first practical all-metal aeroplanes, and (c) the first practical low-wing monoplanes, all of which he continued to develop successfully over the years.

And now join me in a conversation with the grand old man of the Iron Annie clan: Professor Kurt H. Weil.

The sense of unreality grew stronger as the day waned. Here we were at the manicured expanse of Pompano Beach Airport, along the southeastern coast of Florida, on a bright and sunny day, surrounded by a colorful variety of airplanes that ran the gamut from tiny Pitts biplanes and Cessna 150s to Beech King Airs and Piper Navahos and Bellanca Vikings and—it commanded the entire field —the great, three-engine shape of the Junkers Ju-52/3m I had just flown into the airport. But that wasn't the unreality. It was the man walking with me, eighty-three years old, white-haired, small of stature, and seemingly tireless as he bounced along, waving his arms, gesturing an animation of hand signals and excited words, and it seemed so bloody difficult to accept that this diminutive giant was in the main the one man more responsible than any other for creating the Iron Annie.

It was also an opportunity that could not even be labeled simply as priceless, because it was more than that. Obviously, a good part of my time and an overwhelming part of my earnings had moved in an unbroken line to N52JU, gleaming on the ramp and surrounded by a swarm of disbelieving and open-mouthed spectators. Kurt Weil and I had decided on a few moments of our own, for I knew that the way to capture the lineage of the Ju-52 was to do it *now*, with *this* man, as a part of living history. Our paths might not again cross, for neither of us would dare tempt the fates for the future with the exception of our mutual promise to make such a meeting an annual event.

What I wanted to know—and I did not want the information from official histories or biographical studies or any other works prepared by those on the sidelines—was the proper ancestry of the Ju-52, and the man who walked with me, smiling with delight and waving his arms in a human imitation of a helicopter winding up for imminent flight, was the Rosetta Stone of all I sought.

"Well, there is no question," Kurt said emphatically. "There is always a starting point, but we want one with meaning to it, no? Then, we must dismiss everything up to the end of the First World War, in 1918. Everything that happened before then was bastardized by military needs, by men who were both intelligent and stupid but who shared high powers. And it was they who decided what would be designed and what would be built. So we forget all that, no matter how important, and we turn to that moment when we all made the transition from fighting to not fighting.

"Let us consider what was the situation when the war ended. We had at that time what we can describe, and properly so, as the standard configuration of airplanes. No matter where you came from or anything else—and we forget strange, individual machines—the airplane the whole world knew was the biplane of wooden structure. You could never mistake such an abortion. There were struts, bracing cables, fabric covering, open cockpits, machine guns, and God knows what else sticking out in all directions. Some were even beautiful airplanes, but when a war is over, a beautiful military airplane turns almost at once into a dog. People should never forget that airplanes are subject to the rules of life by which we all live, no? That includes profit and loss. It includes the ability of a machine not only to pay its own way but to make a profit so that the company that owns the machines and the pilots who fly them and the crews who maintain them all remain doing just what they are doing. If the airplane cannot do these things, then it must be subsidized, which is its own admission of failure, or everybody goes out of business and you start thinking about bread lines. I—"

He paused and we stopped to look up, a timeless expression on our faces, as an old Apache snarled its way into the air with mock severity. Far above and beyond the old Piper twin, several thin contrails sliced the deep blue of the stratosphere.

"*Ach!* Back to the end of the war, all right? Those of us in the business of airplanes began to understand the word: *business.* Airplanes could carry mail and cargo and people faster and better than anything else. So we must use these machines for a commercial enterprise. But it is a difficult thing to be commercial with a machine designed to be so inefficient it must lose money. That was the problem almost everyone faced. They needed airplanes, and the fields and the woods were absolutely overflowing with airplanes, and all of them were those terrible strutted and wooden military clompers. They were no good for commercial air work, but what else was there? So for a while they filled the skies, but never forget—the years make so much nonsense romantic, I suppose—that the only reason they stayed in the air was that they were free for the asking, because they were everywhere, and because big government subsidized the pilots, the fuel, the maintenance, the ground crews— everything. That sort of good thing lasts only for a little while and everyone knew it and. . . ."

He sighed, a tremulous touch back to some ancient marker in the fledgling days of history. "The new thinking was going on in the back rooms. The only reason, as I said, for the old military planes to be used is because they were free, they were there. But there was another point to make, you understand?" His eyes lit up brightly. "There was nothing else with which to replace those terrible clunkers. And that is the key, the beginning to the future."

He smiled again and took my arm and we walked along slowly in this gentle forest of wings and propellers; *home,* really. "We needed a revolution, and it was Hugo Junkers who made it all possible. He had already put Otto Reuter to work for him. Otto was a brilliant man, far ahead of his time, and he designed for the Junkers Company the machine the world would come to know as the F-13. As quickly as possible, Junkers put the airplane into flight testing, for he believed it was the machine the world *needed* to make sense out of commercial flying. It was an airplane with a formula of design that set the standards for design we still use today: it was all-metal, featured a low-wing design, and was a cantilever monoplane. Not only that, it carried its four passengers in a completely enclosed cabin, including space for their baggage. The pilots flew in an open cockpit. It could have been closed, but you must understand pilots from that time. Most of them did not like closed cockpits. They had to hear the sounds and feel the wind and things like that to keep them happy. The passengers did not care. They were comfortable and their cabin was heated, they were out of the wind; well, it was quite a design.

"The point is that the F-13, in aerodynamic terms, was really a very advanced design, very highly developed. Everybody did not agree with Junkers. They were so propagandized with their struts and braces and biplanes and things sticking everywhere into the airstream that to them the F-13 was literally an 'ugly, naked machine.' Do you realize we put an entire engineering and public-, or customers-relations, force to work to salvage it? Not in terms of flying, but an aesthetic salvage job! Gropius, Van der Rohe, Breuer, and many others invented—that's as good a word as any, right?—the concept of 'functional beauty' to educate the public away from those biplane monstrosities they all believed in so much.

"Now let us get down, as you say, to brass tacks. It is a philosophy of design, of concept, that is everything, and you must understand this about the F-13 if you are ever to understand evolution in machinery *and in the successful use of that machinery in flight.* So we had this little F-13, which we first flew in 1919 with its one engine. It was made by BMW and gave us 185 horsepower, which really was not very much for an airplane that weighed almost five thousand pounds. Later the power went up to 310, when we used the Junkers L5, but these are details. We could cruise better than a hundred miles an hour, the airplane could endure almost any kind of weather, it was so strong, and it could operate from fields so rough they were filled with small rocks. That is actually the kinds of fields from which F-13s flew in China, as one example. I mean hard ground covered with loose dirt and rocks, but nothing seemed to bother this airplane. As to what its real potential was, a few months after the initial test flight, the prototype, the very first one built— and we are still talking about 1919—climbed to an altitude of 22,140 feet. *Ach,* that was *flying!*" He smiled and shook his head, pushing dreams away from our conversation.

The company with which Weil would live as an integral part manufactured about 320 of the small F-13 monoplanes, and Lufthansa (known in those

The start of a legend and an aerial empire: the Junkers F-13 in this picture *is still flying today* some sixty years after it first took to the skies. KURT STREIT

days as Luft Hansa) flew about fifty of the corrugated wonders as the mainstay of their fleet for many years. Above all, the F-13 established completely new concepts *and realities* of strength, reliability, endurability, and brilliance in its functional capacity. Or, to state it in other words, it was a tough iron bird on which you count—no matter what. And that is the stuff from which legends are made.

"Because it is so long ago," Kurt went on, "and so close to the end of the first world war, the memory of what the F-13 was able to accomplish never really went into our history books." He made a sour face. "If only we could license historians the way we do engineers, history would read very differently from what most people know. So!" He laughed heartily and slipped back through the years. "It is hard to believe that the F-13 was the best known, the most famous commercial airplane in almost every country in the world. Even in the new Soviet Union, by order of Lenin himself! and this is in 1922, the first airline from Moscow to Nizhni Novgorod, which today they call Gorki, was opened with an F-13. But do not try to find such facts in the history of Aeroflot, because what Russian in his right mind would openly admit the first airline of the Soviets used the best machine in the world—a German airplane?"

His arm gestured to take in our own area. "Here in the United States, too, much the same thing happened," he continued. "Have you ever heard of the Larsen JL-6? This was an airplane, a number of them, controlled by John M. Larsen of New York and intended to set up a reliable airmail operation in the United States. The JL-6 was a remarkable machine, and in December of 1921 it set a world record for endurance. Edward Stinson and Lloyd Bernard took it up over Long Island, outside New York, so they could circle the town of Mineola, and they flew without a stop for twenty-six hours and nineteen minutes. I do not forget these numbers because they were such a part of me. And that airmail they were supposed to fly? Oh, they did, they did; they made the runs from New York to Omaha and San Francisco. By the way, they also flew those machines from Central Park in New York. Right in the heart of the city. I cannot prove that, but I was told this was so."

He laughed. "Now for the best part of the story. There never was a Larsen JL-6. What there *really* was, well, this Larsen fellow formed the JL Aircraft Company, and he bought a bunch of F-13s from Junkers, from the Dessau plant, and imported them to the United States. Then he changed F-13 to JL-6, claimed to have designed the machine, further claimed also to be the builder of it! He was quite a crook, this fellow. One of the funniest parts of all this was when Larsen went to General Billy Mitchell of your Air Corps to sell him production quantities of his JL-6 to be used as an armored attack plane. He told Mitchell they would replace the German BMW engine of 185 horsepower and, with a new designation of JL-12, equip it with the 400-horsepower Liberty engine. He was a smart crook but not a smart man, because the moment he told General Mitchell he would put thirty machine guns on the airplane Mitchell recognized him for the scoundrel he really was. There is another side

The direct ancestor of the Ju-52—the Junkers G-23/G-24 series, which gave Lufthansa its first reliable scheduled airliners, the strongest machines of their day. JUNKERS ARCHIVES

A rare photograph of Adolf Hitler—his rise to power still in the future—in a leather flying helmet, studying charts with the crew of a Junkers G-24 in which he toured Germany. CAIDIN ARCHIVES

to this," and here Kurt Weil smiled, "that Larsen did not know. After the Armistice, in 1918, Mitchell had met with Hugo Junkers in the Dessau factory."

We stood in silence for a while. Then I had questions to ask. Kurt had known Junkers and Von Karman and the other engineers when he was a student at Aachen. In 1923 he joined the company as an engineer and received an immediate assignment to analyze the new transports that were to be built. Should they have two engines or three? Should the company push further development of their three-engine G-23 model? Which way should they go? The same year Weil joined the company, Junkers produced the prototype G-23, with a 195-hp L2 engine in the nose and two 100-hp D1 engines in the wings. Flight tests soon showed their inadequacy, and the replacement was the new G-23, with three 160-hp Mercedes D111A engines, and although the G-23 entered service it continued to give the company's flight operations division, and other airlines, serious headaches. One of the jobs to which Kurt Weil devoted himself, along with other engineers, was to bring forth from the essentially sound design of the G-23 a machine that would be operationally reliable. The result was the G-24, a tri-motor airliner that weighed about thirteen thousand pounds and offered its nine passengers cabin lights, reclining seats, toilet facilities—comfort that mattered. It was so strong that several G-24s that

A Lufthansa G-24 being prepared for a scheduled flight. Note the heavy flying suits of the crew and the massive wooden propellers. JUNKERS ARCHIVES

crashed banged up the airplanes severely, but every passenger and pilot walked away. Any other airliner in the world would have killed all aboard.

"There's an interesting sidelight to all this," Kurt went on. "I'm sure you have people asking all sorts of questions about the Ford Tri-Motor and how it compares with your Ju-52 and that sort of thing?

OPPOSITE PAGE:
Published here for the first time are these pictures of the three Junkers G-31 transports that performed a miracle of air logistics that even today would seem impossible. The G-31s were modified to take uncowled Pratt & Whitney radial engines, the pilots retained their open cockpits, and the job was on. The job? To fly the disassembled parts of that enormous dredge (left) and all the buildings and structures and equipment in that picture, piece by piece, from a jungle dockside airport into a high rough strip at Bulolo, New Guinea, where it would all be reassembled into the working dredge shown in the pictures. The entire operation, including support, required more than seven thousand flights into steaming jungles, through terrible weather, under primitive conditions—without a single accident or injury. A perfect job with a perfect safety record for the G-31 fleet of three airplanes! PHOTOS FROM CONSOLIDATED PURCHASING & DESIGNING, INC.

Of course, of course. But let me tell you an aside to the Ford about which few people know. Almost everyone understands the Ford came before the Ju-52, but what they *don't* know is that, long before the first Ford ever flew, there was in commercial service in many countries *an entire fleet* of three-engine commercial Junkerses. By 1925, our European Junkers network was flying about one hundred F-13s, as well as some fifty 3-engine G-23 and G-24 models. Remember that I am talking about regular daily scheduled service all over Europe. Also remember that this was 1925, a full year before the Ford ever showed up. And in 1925"—he smiled—"Henry Ford sent his envoy, Dr. Edward Rumely, to Dessau. Rumely had one goal in mind, which was to find out how much truth there really was about this fleet of planes we had roaring all over Europe, especially the three-engine models. Because, with the exception of some engine-mount problems on the G-23 series, we were operating with really an astonishing schedule and reliability. At any rate, Rumely reported back to Henry Ford that all the stories, no matter how astonishing they might seem, were true.

"Here we come to the interesting part. As soon as he had read what Rumely reported, Ford personally invited Hugo Junkers to visit with him at Dearborn, Michigan. *They had that meeting.* Did you know that?"

I hadn't. . . .

"And what happened was that Ford wanted to make an agreement to build Junkers machines in the United States, but he demanded that he do so with a royalty-free license. In other words, Mr. Ford was so puffed up about himself that he figured Junkers would be honored to let him build —for free—all the Junkers designs he wanted to in the United States. You can imagine what Junkers told him, but in any event what happened was that after Junkers left, Ford told Bill Stout to build him a tri-motor design. The airplane that resulted had the Fokker configuration, with a high wing, but still used the Junkers all-metal structural design."

Kurt looked at me with his bright, open eyes. "And that is why there is so much that is similar between the Junkers design and the Ford Tri-Motor. The first Ford came from William B. Stout and—"

I interrupted. "That was the 4-AT model," I said. "It had the three engines of 220 horsepower each and carried ten passengers. Um, it was listed with a top speed of 105 miles per hour, but that's storybook time. You got a hundred and five if you were at the best operating altitude and had plenty of power and the temperature was right, you know, that sort of thing. Ninety-five miles per hour would have been more accurate."

Kurt nodded. "It made its first flight in June of 1926. And I feel compelled to repeat that this was long after we were operating a great fleet of three-engine airliners in regular service."

"What about the G-31?" I asked.

Kurt positively beamed, and he clapped me on the back. "I was hoping you would ask, finally! Because it is an even better comparison. Well before the Ju-52 came into being, in fact while we were still working out the basic philosophy of what would be a completely new design, we decided to build an interim machine that would improve on the G-24. And in 1926, the same year that the Ford 4-AT showed up, so did the G-31. It was an astonishing airplane that carried passengers or freight. As an airliner—and we can compare this to the Ford—it had three engines of 450 horsepower, had a crew of two, and carried sixteen passengers. Its *honest* speed was ninety miles an hour, and on the European flights, the passengers enjoyed stewards serving food and drinks. As a cargo machine it was incredible. Three G-31s made marvelous history when they operated in New Guinea. Here was the most backward region in the world. Among other jobs, they flew a monster mining dredge, piece by piece, into a clearing in virgin forest in the mountains to help develop the Bulolo gold fields. They operated under the worst weather you could imagine, with the most primitive maintenance, but with a reliability that is still hard to believe.

"So there are two more points to make about these trimotor planes from Junkers. By the time the first Ford Tri-Motor appeared, it had been preceded by large *fleets* of three-engine Junkers in much of the world, and even then it was eclipsed by that incredibly rugged G-31. My second point?" Again that smile. "Why, the best was yet to come. We were about to create the design philosophy for the really new plane."

He pointed across the field, where *Iron Annie* gleamed in the sun. "There. *Her.* We were about to create the Ju-52."

The philosophy.

The philosophy of design. That was the heart and soul of the Ju-52 success story, the bedrock of the production program, the deep-rooted foundation of design. The philosophy of an aircraft's design emerges when the demands and requirements are known. First you establish the best standards of performance in the world and accept the challenge that you must exceed these by a staggering margin. But you watch yourself carefully, for the key is not miles per hour or cargo load or service ceiling or range or passenger seats or so many of the elements that are trumpeted in the sales brochures. The key is to *think* in unprecedented terms.

Think in terms of total lifetime in flying hours for the machine. Not simply strength, but durability. Think in terms of thirty and forty and fifty thousand hours of operational and productive lifetime. Compute so many hours of flight operation per year, and enter the computations with consideration for flying in good weather and bad, on short flights and long, and in daylight and in darkness, so that a reliable estimate may be made of an average flight time in hours per year. That means new instrumentation and radio and navigation systems and *their* reliability. It means an ability to function in severe weather, which in turn means duplicate gyro instrument panels.

Now, this introduces yet another oblique design element. Inclement weather means more than instruments and navigation aids. It directly affects the performance characteristics of the machine. It requires a large ratio between cruising speed and the speeds for takeoff and landing. It also demands a severely reduced time for ground layovers caused by maintenance requirements. Reliability becomes paramount so that the airplane spends as little time as possible *being forced* to remain on the ground because of poor engines or lack of parts or tools or equally maddening weaknesses in planning. Project

into future commercial situations; if there is less time required for overhaul, repair, and inspection, then operational cost goes down, insurance rates go down, maintenance costs go down, *and profits go up.*

The machine will operate from large, city-centered airfields and remote strips. But it must be equally simple to load and off-load both passengers and cargo at *any* facility. This reduces the effort and time spent in such operations, increases the potential value of the machine, improves its revenue position, and again adds to its revenue profitability.

Now there is the matter of the engines. This involves far more than simply available horsepower, which produces the performance figures so sacred to the public relations office. Engine horsepower is rarely in proportion to the true requirements of a successful machine. Are the engines available in quantity? Do their parts stand up under long hours in the field? Are they equally versatile for short hops, when temperature and operational cycles are at their worst in terms of engine wear? Can they handle long-range flights, when they run for six or nine hours, or even longer, and still prove reliable? Can they be repaired in the field or must they have the services of elaborate ground facilities to attend to small problems that *should* be easy of repair?

There is another critical element to be considered in terms not only of engines but the number of engines per aircraft. There were new engines available with the horsepower necessary to produce a viable and successful twin-engine airliner. These were expensive power plants, and their use would also determine just how *inexpensive*—or costly—it would be to maintain operational status in the field. When you select engines for the production of an airliner, you not only buy the engines that go onto the airplane, but you buy spares, and you buy replacements—all of which adds up to a staggering investment.

Now, if the machine has but two engines, an engine failure of one at takeoff with a full load can turn instantly into a catastrophe, because fully half the power has vanished. That is a fact of life. But if there are three engines, and we can select a model that is available in quantity, meets the cost criteria, and has proved its reliability, and we lose one on takeoff, it means a loss of only one-third power. Which means the airplane can continue its climb-out on its remaining two engines and *safely* complete a circuit or whatever maneuvers are necessary to land all in one piece.

"There was much more to this design philosophy than met the eye," explained Kurt Weil. "There is always the matter of continuing a takeoff with one engine out, but we went further than this in our thinking. For example, we made certain to design this airplane so that it could fly on any two of its three engines. If it was in the air and an engine failed, the airplane would simply keep on flying until it reached a main terminal. No matter that the gear was down. It was fixed and it meant drag, but that didn't matter. Neither did the fact that the production machines would be using fixed-pitch propeller blades. Simplicity and reliability were the sacred watchwords, and we intended that this air-craft—committing the cardinal sins of other air-craft—would *still* continue to fly with an engine out. It was more than safety; you must understand this. If the engine failed on the ground, the air-plane must be able to take off on any two engines and fly to a major center where spare engines were kept. This way, we would reduce to the minimum the major places for maintenance and replace-ments, and our costs would go way *down*. It is the key, that philosophy I keep talking about.

"We were using every ounce of experience from Junkers-Luftverkehr and most especially of our Persian section, Junkers-Luftverkehr Persien, with which I was in a controlling position. Now, Ernst Zindel was placed in charge of the detailed en-gineering. He ran the team of men who would do the detailed design, the machine work, the piecing together of all the elements that grew from the design philosophy.

"There has been a lot of conversation through the years, and you will find this in many books and magazines, that we designed this machine to be used both as a single-engine and as a three-engine machine, depending upon the customer's needs. This is silly. If we would design it with one engine

only, or three engines only, why not a *two*-engine version? It makes much more sense to provide all three areas of performance, no?"

Kurt Weil laughed gently. "That one fact seems to evade all historians. Why we would build a sin-gle-engine machine and another with three en-gines, but never one with two engines. *Ach!* Histo-rians sometimes make up their histories.

"The fact of the matter is that Ju-52 was in-tended from the outset as an aircraft of three en-gines, for all the reasons you know as well as these others I have given you. Let me explain just a bit more what I harp about so much, this design phi-losophy. I told you how we planned that the air-plane must be able to use *any* fields, anywhere, no matter how simple or primitive the facility. We carried this a step further and based our opera-tional requirements on the ability of the airplane to perform in commercial, scheduled service from just open fields. Not even the maintenance centers would have runways or taxiways. Just open fields and places to start and stop and park, no matter what the need. If ever there was an airplane in-tended to be free from required ground services, then it was the Ju-52 more than any other machine ever built.

"Now, let me explain another point that is not so obvious. The design requirements were such that all these demands meant giving up certain ele-ments. We could not build what people wanted now to see: a sleek, streamlined aircraft. Oh, we could build those at Junkers and we did, with per-fect aerodynamic lines and enough curves to bring an artist to delirium. But that wasn't our intent with the Ju-52. We went the route of all these elements we have discussed because we were absolutely de-termined to build a heavy airliner that would oper-ate profitably *without any subsidies*.

"Listen, more airplanes are designed in calm sur-roundings than in all the drafting rooms in the world. I used to take long walks in the Austrian Alps at Bad Gastein in the summer of 1929 with Hugo Junkers, and it was during such moments that we finalized the philosophy of the Ju-52. Be-cause we had to agree on a violation of the rules that Junkers himself had laid down for his earlier transports. Then the requirement was always to in-crease the ratio of payload to the takeoff weight. We reversed this trend with the Ju-52. We actually *reduced* the ratio of payload to takeoff weight. As mad as this seems, it was—when you considered all the other design elements—the key to the incredible success of the Ju-52. It took even me several years, close as I was to everything that was happening, to truly understand what Hugo Junkers had conceived on his own.

"The key to commercial success was to concentrate on achieving not the highest payload per flight—*but the highest payload per plane per year.*"

Clearly this point had simply been missed by historians, who never recognized this most fundamental element of Junkers. So think about it, that basic design, the astonishing ruggedness of a structure that could almost repair itself, the ability to fly engine-out to any repair facility, and— Listen, *it adds up.* If a competitor carries twice the payload of a Ju-52 for the same power but spends only a third or a fourth the time in the air, and its operational expenses are three or four times as high, what's your winner?

Now, think of what you've read so far and then think of the wing engines of the Ju-52/3m. They aren't standard in their *configuration.* Oh, they're as common as any old radial engines you'll find almost anywhere in the world but not the way they're stuck onto those wings. If you stand directly before or behind or directly over the Ju-52/3m, you'll see that the wing engines do not point straight ahead. They're not in line with the fuselage. In fact, they're mounted six degrees outward of the fuselage datum line. It looks pretty awkward when you think about it.

So why did they do this? Why slant those engines outward? Because they are always throwing air directly back into the area of the tail: the big vertical fin and the barn-door rudder and the stabilizers and the airfoil-shaped elevators. Which means that it doesn't matter what engine you lose, you're *always* going to get a good airblast across that tail, and that means better control at low speeds, most especially at *very low speeds.* Remember one of the design tenets of the aircraft as an operational item of equipment: it must be able to make a normal takeoff, fly, and land at its intended destination with one engine shut down through the entire flight.

This is an inherent value, and it sets up the operational secret of the aircraft: its unbelievable strength and ruggedness and its ability to fly under conditions, weather or mechanical, that flatly ground most other machines. Equally as important:

the onboard systems must be as trouble-free as it is humanly possible to make them.

Maintenance-free. That's another good term. It means you have the least possible quantity of bugs and disorders in your aircraft systems to keep you on the ground when you should be flying. Also, when you consider that the Ju-52 was birthed in 1929, it's a good idea to think about the state of the art of aircraft systems (hydraulic, electrical, and goodies like that) *at that time.* Hugo Junkers and Kurt Weil thought a long time about that matter, and they told one another to vary nary an inch from the golden rule of the Ju-52: keep it simple and make it stronger than anything else.

Picture an airliner in a maintenance shop—and what you see is a small army of specialists and technicians and engineers and mechanics crawling all over and under and atop and within the airliner brought to that shop for inspection, maintenance, repair, and possibly overhaul. There is a great intricacy of hydraulic systems and gear-movement mechanisms and vast amounts of wiring and—well, it's been known to bend eyeballs out of shape with one long, hard look.

Picture now the Ju-52/3m in that same shop. *No hydraulic lines of any kind.* That's right; there simply *weren't* any. The gear was down and welded, so that took care of that. The early Ju-52s used a compressed-air system for oleo struts to absorb landing shocks. If the system was low, you simply pumped up your strut just as you did your automobile tires. If the system failed in flight, so what? You landed a bit more carefully and the landing roll and taxi might be a bit stiffer until you could get more air into that strut. There wasn't anything else to it. There were no hydraulic lines to break, none to clog, *and none to burn in the event of a fire.*

In other words, the key to everything was to stay manual instead of using power systems, as much as possible. The brakes in the original ships were also compressed-air, and they could be refilled (or pressured up) by using oxygen or nitrogen bottles on the ground, or simply using ram air when flying, to repressure the system. Now, this had some drawbacks. Using the brakes in the old Ju-52 required feats of dexterity and swiftness that could shame a circus acrobat. They really weren't that great. If you wanted to use left brake you didn't bother with your feet. Oh, no; none of this left brake with left rudder pedal. You pulled all the way back on the left throttle, past a detent. This put the left engine into idle to kill thrust on that side, and it also applied left brake. Since you had more than dead idle on the right engine, and you would, in fact, increase right-engine power to help in a left turn, the damned system *worked*.

If you wanted to turn to the right, you simply reversed the procedure. What happened if you wanted dual braking? You grabbed the center throttle—and this explains why it stuck up higher than the wing-engine throttle knobs—and hauled full back on the knob. Your airplane came to a stop.

Okay. Let's make it clear that hydraulic systems such as on the DC-3—which are now in my Ju-52—are better and in practice much more efficient. But hydraulic systems today are a hell of a lot more reliable than they were back in 1929, and that had a lot to do with making final decisions. Other decision-making points? *If you use compressed air, you don't have to store a lot of hydraulic fluid.* You can always produce all the compressed air you need in the field or use in-flight pressuring to get what you need. Then, too, Junkers planned for the machine to be operated from large grass or dirt fields, and braking requirements under those conditions just ain't the same as at all those huge, concrete-paved runways we have today. Just as the tires that went on the Ju-52 were bald. That's right. No grooves and no treads that you could see. Bald. Smooth as a baby's backside when they were brand-new. They were intended to operate from grass and dirt and gravel, and treaded or grooved tires didn't mean a hoot under those conditions!

No one in his right mind builds an airliner the size of the Ju-52, especially with monster flaps, without adding electrical or hydraulic boost to operate those flaps. The systems, especially in the Ju-52, broke all the rules. *They were left out completely.* In other words, you went manual and you stayed manual. To the right of the pilot's seat is the Mighty Wheel. It has a ball joint at the end of a handle. If the handle is down, then only the trim operates when you move the wheel. If the handle is pulled up, then the flaps and the trim operate together *and you're never out of trim.* The flap system is tough to move. It takes muscle and a lot of it, because your arm is turning huge coil springs that run back through the fuselage to the flaps. Okay, it makes for sweaty armpits and bulging forearm muscles, but there's virtually nothing to

fail and absolutely no power systems to crap out.

By now I'm sure you're getting the idea. Utter simplicity, unprecedented strength, and maximum reliability.

It works. There's more to this design philosophy, but it comes later in this story, because it fits into operational situations where events as they happen tell the story better than a flat recital of equipment. And as the Ju-52 emerged from concepts and ideas and operational experience of other aircraft, it became obvious that the Junkers company was on the edge of what could well turn out to be the greatest airplane of its kind ever built.

———◆———

In the summer of 1929 Kurt Weil and Hugo Junkers were at Bad Gastein, in the Austrian Alps, where they were finalizing their design philosophy for their new, three-engine transport.

Their development program called for the airplane to be produced as the Junkers Ju-52/3m series. Unfortunately there rose in their midst a nasty problem. They had planned to use three Junkers L-88 engines for each aircraft, but there was an awful mess in the engine development section of the company, and one day everyone threw up his hands and said, "Screw it," or words to that effect, and aborted the engine test program. The engine was a blah: it failed repeatedly in tests and promised to be a permanent imminent catastrophe in flight.

However, the decision was made to start immediately "on the design, engineering, and wind-tunnel work, and the building of the first prototype," Kurt Weil explained. "We would go to a single-engine airplane, with only one engine in the nose and no wing engines, because the originally specified L-88 engines had to be aborted. But the test flights could be started in 1930 with the single-engine version. We could use other engines for testing, until we received the engines on which we had decided for full mass production: the Pratt & Whitney Wasp radial engines from the United States, which Germany intended to put into mass production through the Bavarian Motor Works. BMW had worked out a license agreement with Pratt & Whitney, and we all felt this was the most rugged, the most reliable, and clearly the best radial engine existing anywhere in the world."

At this point Kurt Weil departed from the local scene at Dessau, where the Ju-52 was being shaped and formed. (In fact, Weil from 1927 on had been in Iran, proving out the pioneering operational concepts for Hugo Junkers, and had, in fact, been called home to establish the design and performance parameters for the Ju-52.) The test was the worst possible. Junkers told Weil to work in a country that was economically barren and then form an airline and operate it at a profit but absolutely without any government or private subsidies. *Kurt Weil did it.* He started off with four old F-13s that had been abandoned and were slowly deterio-

rating in the Soviet Union, and from 1927 to 1932 slowly increased his fleet of aircraft, ran on schedules, operated with the most primitive maintenance and support, and ended up with a successful, profitable undertaking that in five years never suffered so much as a single accident.

And while Kurt Weil returned to distant places to eat Iranian dust, metal was being cut and shaped and the first Ju-52 began to emerge from the engineering shop.

They rolled her through the factory doors in late September of 1930, and there had been nothing like her squared shape ever to be moved into daylight from the Dessau plant. The first of the line to carry the designation of Junkers Ju-52, known more specifically as the Ju-52ba, listed on the production line as *Werke* Number (which corresponds to Serial Number) 4001, and given the registration code of D-1974. Her initial history would prove as complicated as her changing coding, and in one of those baffling omissions of historical record, after her period of flight testing and one engine change after another, the first of the line would be purchased for commercial service—*after which every trace of the airplane disappeared!*

However, let us follow its trail for the moment. The factory records indicate that the Junkers L-88 engine, of 800 horsepower, was to be fitted to this prototype machine. Several sources indicate that this engine did indeed lift the first Ju-52 into the air for its test flights. Other records indicate that the engine was mounted to the aircraft but, faced with the dismal performance of the power plant up to this time, Hugo Junkers ordered the engine, with its four-bladed fixed-pitch metal propeller, removed from its mount, to be replaced with a BMW VII aU engine of 755 horsepower. The VII aU engine, unlike most of the power plants from this company, was not the expected radial but in fact a twelve-cylinder, in-line, liquid-cooled engine. The horsepower from this machine is again one of our bits of wry humor, since its rated output varies from 600 to 755 horsepower, and you may have your choice, depending upon your source. *However,* I do have in my possession a very rare document that was produced by the Junkers Company,

The "immortal first of the line"—the very first Ju-52 built, *Werke* Number 4001, registration D-1974. After being sold to Luftfrako, the airplane vanished into thin air without a single trace of its subsequent life. JUNKERS ARCHIVES

The front office of the first single-engine Ju-52—stark simplicity and maximum usefulness, the mark of the Junkers Company. JUNKERS ARCHIVES

which lists the results of a series of test flights and, following those tests, offered the machine as a commercial product with a buyer's choice of two engines: the BMW VII aU with a clearly specified rating of 685 horsepower turning a four-bladed wooden propeller, and the Armstrong-Siddely Leopard fourteen-cylinder, two-row radial engine, which was available in various versions from 720 to 800 horsepower.

In any event, after its first flight tests and the compulsive engine changes, the prototype (*Werke* Number 4001) was redesignated Ju-52be (from the original Ju-52ba), equipped with the BMW VII aU engine of 685 horsepower, and sold to International Luftfracht und Makler Kontor Air Express. More popularly known as Luftfrako in the interests of time and the endurance of the human jaw, the cargo line placed *Werke* Number 4001 in service. After that . . . *pouf*. No one knows a thing about the machine. It was scrubbed from all official records, it seemed to disappear from photographic negatives, and Luftfrako appeared incapable of remembering anything about the machine except

that it had been bought and dispatched to operations.

There remains one other minor mystery about the single-engine Ju-52 line. It would seem that since this group of machines—prototype and immediate commercial products—led off the vast number of Ju-52 aircraft to be produced, we would know precisely how many were built, to whom they were sold, and what was their history subsequent to leaving the Dessau plant. Strangely enough, we are to be denied this gleaming of numbered accuracy, and all we can say for certain is that at least five and no more than seven of the single-engine models were built!

John Stroud, of Air International, is a competent, thorough, and very solid British citizen who wades through technical and historical material with all the skill and aplomb of an albatross feathering its way along uplifting ocean breezes. One of his favored projects has been a reckoning of the civil (commercial) version of the Ju-52. Alas, even John Stroud groped helplessly in this mishmash of plagued historical data and finally admitted that

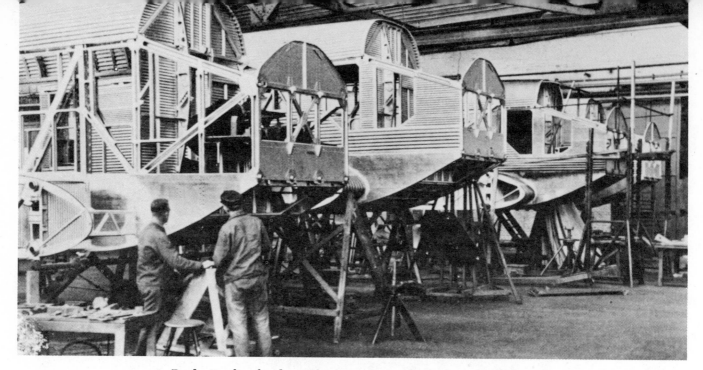

Production line for the single-engine Ju-52/1m series. JUNKERS ARCHIVES

"there are gaps in the knowledge of Junkers aircraft history and some may now never be filled. Secrecy and distortion under the Third Reich, compounded by the destruction of war, has exacted its toll, while many of the people who knew the facts are now dead. The first of the mysteries is how many single-engine Ju-52s were actually built . . . five can be substantiated [but] this still leaves open the question: was there a sixth aircraft, and if so, was it the second built and was it a Ju-52ce, or is the answer that changes were made on the production line?"

———◆———

There was no question at Dessau, either in the factory workshops or the conference rooms of Hugo Junkers and his staff, that they had a thoroughbred on their hands. The single-engine Ju-52, despite its shortcomings in power enforced by only a single engine, already exhibited flight and performance characteristics with enormous appeal for commercial operators, and as fast as these groups discovered the details of the new Ju-52, they were standing in line to buy the airplane.

Its boxy and angular shape misled the casual observer as to the performance intrinsic in the design. Certain elements of its lines were unmistakable—simple, strong, practical. That the lifting power of the wings was enormous would never be questioned, for the ninety-seven feet of wing also featured a remarkable design by Junkers known as the double wing, which performed its own small miracles of lift and controllability for the aircraft. The only question that leaped immediately to mind was one of power. Could *one* engine provide the energy necessary for operations with heavy cargo loads—an assignment Junkers stated implacably could be handled with more efficiency by this airplane than any other, including his own line of enormously successful transports?

Hugo Junkers addressed a group of businessmen with just these key points in mind. "The need has become manifest for larger units," he told his audience. "There is need in civil aircraft for a larger cargo space which must, moreover, be entirely unobstructed. This means a cargo space that will not be bothered with the arrangements of the internal structure, so that the most bulky and unwieldy goods can be carried, and so designed to permit loading and unloading, again even of bulky crates and packages, easily and rapidly. Last and not least, all this must be performed under a more favorable economic relationship between payload and running expenses, and into this final cost we also consider the initial cost of the aircraft itself.

"All our accumulated practical experience with the numerous air transport companies operating their services with Junkers aircraft has gone into this Ju-52. We have succeeded in producing an airplane with a large cargo space and yet with outstandingly good aerodynamical qualities. This means that in spite of the very large fuselage of the

30

The only way to make money hauling cargo was maximum utilization of all available space—in a picture worth a thousand words. JUNKERS ARCHIVES

The first of the line—*Werke* Number 4001—coming in to land after a test flight. Note the flaps and drooped ailerons. JUNKERS ARCHIVES

Ju-52, it is eminently suitable for long-range flight."

A neat, concise, impressive address to an erudite audience, and all the more remarkable because the aircraft used by Junkers in his presentation was a low-powered version of the Ju-52, with the 685-horsepower BMW VII aU engine. Even more remarkable—in fact, it borders on the incredible—is that 685 horsepower was used to lift from the ground and move through the air an airplane with a takeoff gross weight of 15,432 pounds! The data sheets on the Ju-52 (which also has been referred to in Junkers Company records as the Ju-52/1m to differentiate the design from the later, three-engine models) show an empty weight of 8,558 pounds and a normal loaded weight of 14,551 pounds. It was the official German airline that permitted the

greater takeoff gross of 15,432 pounds, which they considered acceptable for the cargo version.

The more we look at the squared-off lines of the Ju-52 and its single engine of 685 horsepower (which lacked full utilization because of the fixed pitch of its propeller blades) the more astonishing becomes its performance. The normal operating procedure for the Ju-52 was to absolutely stuff its fuselage, through hatches, doors, and weird apertures above, below, and on each side of the fuselage, with everything that could be crammed into the airplane. This made a separate entry door on the copilot's side of the cockpit, through which the pilots crawled, a necessity. Getting into the cockpit through the cargo-jammed cabin was impossible.

This made for interesting numbers for the "total

disposable load" for the airplane in its maximum weight configuration of 6,842 pounds, of which the crew of two totalled 352, special equipment 55 pounds, and if the range was intended at 620 miles, 192 gallons of gasoline and a working (commercially profitable) payload in cargo of 4,895 pounds. No matter how you add it up, this is astonishing efficiency and performance.

Remember, the *European* or African staging lengths and the range of 620 miles more than meet the needs of virtually any operation for its time. Performance figures—so beloved by students of flight operations—always seem to begin with maximum speed, which has always been a mystery to those of us who fly, since maximum speed, most especially in transport aircraft, is a so-what item. Cruising speed is everything. Thus the 121-mile-per-hour top speed of the Ju-52 with its staggering payload is meaningless, since the airplane was never intended to fly at such a speed, and it would do in its engine in short order if it tried (and cut its range by perhaps 60–70 per cent because of excessive fuel consumption). What mattered was that hour-after-hour cruising speed of 99 miles per hour. In reality, of course, there is only an average cruising speed when you operate an airplane like this, with limited power, at its maximum commercial flying weight. If your average cruise speed is 99 miles per hour, then what it *really* means is that you climb with everything you've got in the power bank, balls to the wall, to your cruising altitude. Then its back with the power, lean out the mixture, and hope you'll get from 85 to about 89 miles per hour, with the airplane flying along with the nose well above the horizon. What you're doing is getting all the lift you can without burning too much fuel, and at times you even leave in about 10 degrees of flaps for extra lift. As the fuel burns off and the airplane gets lighter, your wing loading goes down and the power loading goes up. You can measure this in fractions, but it's enough to lower the nose and reduce the drag and get the flaps back into normal position, and *then* you've got your 99 miles per hour. If you're on a really long flight and the tanks get emptier and emptier until they boom hollowly at you, then you'll notice that cruise speed creeping over 100 miles per hour.

There just aren't exact figures for flight performance. This is one of the great dragons that has so long needed slaying; it's amazing to us that people still clutch so frantically at exact numbers. *There*

aren't any. When you get a specified cruising speed, *it is always open to manipulation.* You've got to specify temperature and humidity and just how well the engine is working this day, and your fuel octane, and how the airplane is loaded, because a changing CG (center of gravity) affects everything else, including crisp or sloppy control response. Maybe you're off trim in the rudder area, and that means a slight skidding or slipping motion for the flight, which means increased drag. Very little drag but enough to cut down your performance. There are some pilots who are ham-handed on the controls, and without a feather-light touch you lose performance. All these things are involved, so we go by an average, we live by an average, and we modify our needs to what averages are available to pluck from our performance hat.

Let me take this just a bit further. If you were to place two Ju-52s side by side as soon as they had entered operational service, each with a different customer, the first thing you would notice is that appearances are deceiving—and that from this day forward it is extremely unlikely the two machines would be equally matched in their flight performance, except for those averages we use. Obviously, the crew isn't going to weigh the same in each bird. The radio equipment may differ. One crew may need over-water survival gear. One crew may keep their airplane much cleaner than the other, including waxing the big iron bird, and that can make a lot of difference in performance. Fuel octane ratings may be different. The type of propeller used can change the performance drastically. And just the way the machines are flown is enough to render them quite different creatures.

Assume the iron bird cruised at its average 100 miles per hour, and again, considering all elements of its size and drag and fixed gear, getting this performance for over seven tons of airplane is really an outstanding accomplishment. But what is even more remarkable is that the Ju-52 could float to earth like a great, fat pillow, sliding down on final approach to the runway at a comfortable 55 to 60 miles per hour, and then being held in the flare until it touched its wheels to the ground, nose high, at a speed of about 50 miles per hour. The flight tests showed the airplane quite capable of dropping in at 48 miles per hour, time after time, and this is indicated air speed. It's not the same as ground speed. If the airplane touches down at 50 miles per hour and it's landing into a 20-mile-per hour wind . . . then it touches its wheels to earth at only 30 miles per hour! Landing without wind and going to brakes right off the bat from touchdown, the Ju-52 would stop easily in under six hundred feet. The pilots did this often enough that no one even raised an eyebrow at the sight of the big machine feathering to earth.

Where the Ju-52 lacked in performance was its service ceiling when it had a belly filled with cargo and the tanks topped off to their takeoff load of 192 gallons. Service ceiling is, again, a sometime number, proportional to temperature above all else, and taking off at gross weight meant the ceiling was only 9,190 feet. What this spells out is that the airplane at this altitude, or in the proximity of this altitude, was still capable of climbing 100 feet per minute. Any higher and it was hanging on the edge of a stall.

With the prototype Ju-52, the performance problem spun directly from the BMW VII aU engine of 685 horsepower, because it simply didn't produce any real power at altitude, and its own ailings were compounded by use of the four-bladed wooden prop, a great, flailing club that left much to be desired for thrust efficiency. No question but that a better set of blades up front could have added a couple of thousand feet to this first of the breed.

One of the more amazing statements I've found about the airplane is Junkers' absolute honesty in describing the machine to its customers. It was starkly apparent to anyone who knew airplanes that the engine was a stopgap measure, and even at its best was missing more than 100 horsepower from the intended design. "The excellent aerodynamical qualities of the Ju-52," stated a company representative, "find a truly practical expression in its performance figures. The smooth, aerodynamically good lines render it possible, even with the relatively low power (685 horsepower) developed by the BMW VII aU engine at present fitted, for the aircraft to put up a very fair performance."

Absolute honesty in advertising! It may also have been a very cool move by old Hugo, who knew that anyone casting a beady eye on the performance of the Ju-52/1m, with that clanking old engine, must know that a more powerful engine and a better propeller would mean a completely new arena of performance. The engine mount was designed for power plants to 1,000 horsepower. Stick one of those up front, and add a really efficient set of propeller blades, and the performance would literally jump ahead 10–40 per cent, depending upon the area in question. Certainly the rate of climb would go up, perhaps doubling, and the service ceiling would increase by at least 50 per cent. This is a favorite game pilots like to play, but it's made up from hard experience.

For example, we quoted the range of the Ju-52/1m with its 685-horsepower engine at 620 miles. But this is with everything possible stuffed into the cabin. Junkers provided space for a great variation in this performance. If the airplane took off at 8,818 pounds and flew with a cruise speed of about 103 miles per hour, then the range increased to about 930 miles in a span of between nine and ten hours. An extra 286 gallons of fuel could be loaded aboard the airplane in the wings or in the lower belly without interfering with cargo space, to increase the range to 620 miles with a *payload* (the stuff you carry to make money) of 4,950 pounds; 1,242 miles with 3,130 pounds; 1,863 miles with 1,650 pounds; or, 2,173 miles with 882 pounds. Which is *excellent* performance.

There were some other design elements in the Ju-52/1m series that did not escape potential customers. The airplane flew with the revolutionary Junkers-design *double wing*, which was patented by Junkers and had been the subject of extensive flight testing for many years before it reached the Ju-52/1m and would again be modified before the single-engine line was abandoned. Very simply, a narrow auxiliary flap runs along the whole length of the trailing edge of the main wing. This flap is divided about midway along the span of each wing, and when the flaps are lowered the camber (curvature) of the wing is increased greatly. This does a number of things, the main effect being an enormous increase in lifting capacity of the wing. But Junkers went even further. The outer portion of the auxiliary wing served as the aileron, and a great, huge thingadoo it was. In normal flight, the inboard part of this double wing remained fixed and the outer part operated as an aileron. When you went to full flaps, the inboard section lowered to 40 degrees, the outboard section lowered to 15 degrees, and a slot of nozzle shape in cross section, was formed between the main wing and the trailing wing. The result is astonishing control effectiveness and great lift at low speeds.

When Junkers tested its big, 51,000-pound G-38 transport, the second prototype was fitted with the double wing. The first machine had a standard

The largest aircraft in the world at its time, the 51,000-pound G-38 proved the validity of the Junkers thick-wing and double-wing concepts. Passengers had salon-type seating in the nose and leading edges of the wings. JUNKERS ARCHIVES

wing, and the difference between the same birds of a feather—except for the double wing—was phenomenal. *The rate of climb increased by more than 50 per cent.* The stalling speed dropped sharply and the landing roll was reduced by approximately one third. What was even more delightful was that if it became necessary to abort a landing and the pilot had normal full power, then even with the flaps full down, to as much as 45 degrees, the airplane still developed high lift, and a safe go-around could be made without changing the flap settings.

That in itself is literally astonishing and provided an element of safety no other plane in the world at that time, or for many years to come, even came close to matching.

There's more to say about this incredible double wing, but since the design was somewhat altered with the impending three-engine version already in the making, we'll wait until we get to the bird in which we have our consuming interest.

The tail-gear system of the Ju-52/1m was a strange, on-again, off-again, and let's-switch-things-

A vast sea of duralumin—the upper wing surface of the Junkers G-38. JUNKERS ARCHIVES

around arrangement. All the early-model Ju-52/3m machines, powerful, rugged, and the final intended design, featured a tail skid—*not* a tail wheel. But not the prototype of the single-engine airplane, which had a full-swiveling tail wheel. Ah, but there was more. Junkers fitted out the main undercarriage with oleo-pneumatic shock absorbers and the compressed-air brakes we've discussed. The brake handle was on the great yoke column, which was a central column between the pilot seats, and a duralumin arm branched upward at 40 degrees, so that each pilot had his own yoke. Dead center in the top of the central column was a knobbed handle. Full back on the left side and you had left brake, full back on the right side and you had right brake, but full back in dead center and you had full brakes on the main gear *and the tail wheel.* Whoever flew this prototype must have enjoyed the ground ride, for Junkers equipped the tail wheel with its own shock absorbers, which gave a cushioned ride along even rough ground. And to operate the system of brakes for all three wheels, as well as to start the single engine, compressed air was used, derived from two high-pressure containers.

Starting the engine with compressed air deserves further comment. This seems strangely archaic in light of the then modern design of the Ju-52/1m, but compressed-air starting was a feature common to many German aircraft and, considering the time, the conditions, and the equipment available, it made good sense. Batteries in 1930 were really rather cruddy, explosive, leaky, and guaranteed to be unreliable. If you were operating in cold weather, your problems compounded.

Now, I never flew the Ju-52/1m with compressed-air starting for its sole engine, but I had for several years a nifty Messerschmitt bf-108b, a single-engine job that was the forerunner of the bf-109 fighter to come. And this Taifun that I flew, in our modern day and age, still had its original equipment—including a compressed-air bottle for starting. For quite some time, I operated this machine in Europe in some movies, and then set up its permanent home at Ed Lyons' frenetic Zahns Airport, out on Long Island, New York, where it's been known to get viciously cold.

Now, starting up most engines in cold weather requires preparation, dragging the prop through a couple of times, careful priming, playing gently with the throttle, setting up every switch and con-

trol with surgical precision, kicking a tire, praying, and then hitting the starter button. If the battery isn't up to full strength, you may quickly develop blackness in your heart and gas in your stomach. If you miss the first time around, that is all, brother. I've had it happen more times than I want to remember, and so has everyone else who's flown in the cold. When batteries are not up to snuff, there is no real zap in their cells.

But, with that bf-108b, it was a matter of turning this and moving that, and setting it all up, and making sure those brakes were on, because when you unscrewed the safety grip and pulled on that compressed-air starter, just like *that*—faster than you could see at all—that prop was a blur and the engine was turning and you were running full steam. It was beautiful. After takeoff, you left the intake valve open for a while until the gauge showed the bottle was fully recharged, you sealed off the system by screwing in the grip again, and you were set for your next time at starting. (A gift was also provided in this system: The old engine in the bf-108b would sometimes quit just for the cantankerous hell of it, and diving the bird wasn't enough to get it restarted without plunging hellbent for leather for the ground. But you cleaned up your act, set the systems for starting, and just pulled on that compressed-air system and you were off and running again as soon as it takes to tell about it.)

There were some other elements about the old Ju-52/1m worthy of comment before we progress to its successor. The greenhouse—the see-through part of the cockpit—was probably the best in the world for a large transport, and if it didn't quite make the top of the list, it was as good as anything ever put together. (Even today, the visibility from the Ju-52/3m I fly is better than *any* large airplane I've ever seen.) There were also enough windows and sliding ports to do two things: turn the cockpit into an absolute bedlam and also provide a half dozen odd places for cooling air to come blasting into the front office.

Junkers referred to its Ju-52/1m as a machine of "robust construction," and this has got to be the grandest *under*statement of all time in aviation. There were some modifications to the basic design that found their way into the final, Ju-52/3m so that it was considerably improved over the single-engine model, but the idea of breaking a wing on even the first, Ju-52/1m series was patently absurd.

No one ever knew the full strength of the airplane, because no one ever tested it all the way. You just knew, when you crawled through the wing, amid this enclosed forest of thick spars and heavy metal braces, that you were inside the main structural member of a massive trussed, cantilever bridge—and that was just about the way the thing was built. It was a stirring, magnificent confidence builder—and it got better as newer models of the machine came along.

About the only really disappointing aspect of the Ju-52/1m is that not enough were built, and the type wasn't around long enough, to have built up the kind of interesting history one expected from so glorious a start to a whole new line of sterling machines. But even the handful of 1m models set the stage clearly for what was to come. The single-engine monsters operated as land planes and as seaplanes with great big floats, and it is a wonder how they ever got off the water—especially loaded with freight or carrying two pilots *and sixteen passengers!*

As stated earlier, the prototype was engined and re-engined and finally sold off to Luftfrako and then disappeared in the mists that enshroud all Flying Dutchmen—wherever they may be.

The second airplane in the line was modified with a greater wingspan and went through a series of rapid engine changes, which started with a BMW water-cooled engine, then a Leopard radial engine, and finally a Junkers Jumo 204 diesel engine of 750 horsepower. The diesel was a smelly but reliable power plant that was great for cruise operations but prone to sag badly if a pilot wanted or needed full power *right now.* To fly through emergencies, you had to learn to anticipate your needs well ahead of time. One of the markedly different aspects of the second airplane was that the four-bladed propeller was replaced with a two-bladed wooden prop, which somehow turned in better performance, and the airplane went on to quiet glory as both land plane and seaplane in its Jumo-powered model as the Ju-52do.

By the time the third airplane rumbled along under its own power, it was showing the signs of modification. The taper of the leading edge was modified for better lift, and general strengthening of the structure was carried out where some less-than-perfect signs had been noted in the first two models. With initial testing completed, it went off to Sweden to serve as an airliner, alternating between wheels and floats as conditions and areas dictated.

The fourth off the line (*Werke* Number 4005) had its role cast before it was purchased, as a fifteen-seat airliner powered with a 780-horsepower BMW IXu and blessed with one of those head-wracking designations, this time as the Ju-52cai. It went to the tongue-twisting Reichsverband der Deutschen Luftfahrtindustrie for commercial service. Its pilot may have been frightened by the name of the company for which he flew, for he messed up one day and managed to drive his airplane at high speed into rough ground. It would have been a crash from which the machine could have been rebuilt, but the fuel cells were ruptured, the switches were still on, and the result was fire, which closed out the history of the bird, in the spring of 1931.

No two of these aircraft were alike, but the modifications were essentially in the individual requirements of customers for cargo or passenger service. The hatches, windows, and loading system of each aircraft were modified drastically from one machine to another, and remodified when the aircraft went into field service. The fifth airplane in the line received the registration of CF-ARM and was ordered by (and delivered to) Canadian Airways in 1931. It had a weird profusion of loading hatches and ports, and was also distinguished by the fact that it flew over wheels, giant floats, *and* skis. It came into life as a Ju-52ce with the old BMW VII aU engine and the meat grinder of a four-bladed wooden propeller, but in 1936 the designation went through its magic change to Ju-52cao when a Rolls-Royce Buzzard engine of 825 horsepower was fitted to the airplane. As an indication of what a good machine can do, given half a chance (such as the power being increased from 685 to 825 horsepower), we might note that the original maximum payload was 4,895 pounds. At St. Hubert, Quebec, with the Buzzard screaming away in the nose, the airplane took off in a run of just under eighteen seconds with a payload of 7,590 pounds.

CF-ARM was the most successful of the entire single-engine series. It flew under extremely harsh conditions in the Far North, was bought in 1942 by Canadian Pacific Airlines, and was still flying in 1947. Finally, its owners decided there were plenty of much newer and better machines in the vast quantities of DC-3 and other types available as ex-

The Messerschmitt bf-108b, with compressed-air starting system—owned and flown by Martin Caidin (standing) with ace flying buddy John Hawke. HOWARD LEVY

military aircraft, and the grand old CF-ARM was deliberately broken up. Strangely enough, somewhere up in Canada, the fuselage of that machine remains in a grove of trees, forgotten and whiling away the years.

We're back now to the mystery of the total number of single-engine models built. *Werke* Number 4003 was never assigned to any known aircraft, and *Werke* Number 4006 was the fifth Ju-52/1m to be built. But then the numbers jump one space to 4008, which was a three-engine airliner ordered even before it was built by Lloyd Aéreo Boliviano.

And what of *Werke* Number 4007? Was it the original 4003 with its designation changed on the production line to 4007? No one knows, but 4007 emerged from the Dessau plant with three engines and was the first of the line to be identified as Ju-52/3m. It made its first test flight in April of 1932.

What happened to the great ancestor of the line? *No one knows.* It was never given an official registration, there was never seen a photograph of the airplane outside the factory, and of its history—beyond the fact that it first flew in April of 1932—everything is a complete blank.

Little matter. For it was only the end of the beginning.

PART TWO

The Machine

They say thirteen is *the* unlucky number. Could be. Of course it's only a superstition. Ask any pilot. What the hell difference does a number make? Now, what really counts is a rabbit's foot. . . .

Well, once upon a time there was this airplane, see? And its number was *4013*. It was a Junkers Ju-52/3m*ce*, and when it came into existence it had a really tough act to follow. The first of the three-engine Ju-52s had gone off to Luftfrako and, like the original Ju-52/1m, disappeared. Two more of the new Ju-52/3m airliners rolled out of the factory, bought well before their delivery by Lloyd Aéreo Boliviano and christened with the names *Juan del Valle* (*Werke* Number 4008) and *Huanuni* (4009). Strangely enough, these two airplanes were never given a registration number or coded letter series but were painted with their new names, outfitted with special, rectangular windows, sliced and cut and angled with cargo and passenger doors on both sides of the fuselages, and splashed with the red, gold, and green colors of Bolivia. There was another, *very* important difference. The Bolivian airliners were powered with American engines, for the long-awaited Pratt & Whitney Hornets had finally arrived. They were wrapped within narrow-chord cowlings and fitted with two-bladed propellers, a power-plant arrangement that greatly appealed to the Bolivians, who had unwavering faith in the Hornet engine.

Right behind these two iron birds destined for future life in South America came *the* airplane, *Werke* Number 4013 and registered as D-2201. The airplane was given the name *Oswald Boelcke* and painted up in the colors and insignia of the early Luft Hansa and prepared for immediate passenger-carrying service. There was little to compare the characteristics of *Oswald Boelcke* with its *Juan del Valle* and *Huanuni* predecessors, since every Ju-52/3m being built was really an individual machine. These were commercial airplanes being sold by a company in business with the hope of turning a profit, and Junkers stood ready—and proved itself able—to turn out machines with astonishing individuality without interfering with the production line. Despite the sales that came quickly from Bolivia, Romania, and other customers, Hugo Junkers held his greatest pride in *Number Thirteen,* as D-2201 quickly became known as. This was, after all, the first of his great new airliners scheduled for regular carrier service with a *German* airline, and Junkers was much more interested in hearty toasts from his countrymen than slurred grunts from that distant land stuck in the South Atlantic.

Thirteen was a bird that sang a close, yet vitally different, song of power. On its first test flight, in May of 1932, *Boelcke* took off to the thundering snarl of BMW engines encased in Townend speed rings to reduce drag. Now, those engines were of special importance. They were known as the Hornet A-2 series and—well, you see the rub, don't you? The engines were American in design, and the Bavarian Motor Works had signed a license agreement with Pratt & Whitney to build the American engine, modified to metric measurements, in Germany. That's why the paradox is acceptable when we identify the engine as the BMW Hornet A-2, even though the German engine manufacturers spent as little time as possible pointing to Pratt & Whitney as the originating genius for their new BMW radial engines.

Number Thirteen had a pioneering role cut out for her. As the first of the Luft Hansa airplanes, she was assigned to "route proving." The airplane was fitted out with standard Luft Hansa equipment, loaded to the weights that would be flown on actual scheduled runs, and then sent along the routes of the German airline, so that every detail of operation could be recorded. In this fashion, stage lengths would be accurate, ground maintenance,

The famed *Oswald Boelcke*—the Ju-52/3m that pioneered the Lufthansa Ju-52 fleet for "route proving"—and survived a devastating head-on collision with a training plane. LUFTHANSA

crew turnaround, baggage loading and unloading, and fueling and other servicing would all be well known by the time the growing fleet of Ju-52/3m airliners would be moving into scheduled flights.

Less than two months after *Boelcke* began its proving runs, a great event in commercial aviation took place in Europe: a thumping get-together at Zurich of manufacturers from all over the world, where they would do their best against one another in what is officially described as an "international meet." One of the major events was known as the Circuit of the Alps, and the contest was to decide on the basis of performance the best new airliner in the world.

Number Thirteen, alias *Werke* Number 4013, Registration D-2201, and bearing its name of *Oswald Boelcke*, ran away with the competition. All Europe—and much of the world, in fact—looked with intense interest at the gleaming Ju-52/3mce as

it swept across mountainous terrain, exceeding every other machine in the Circuit of the Alps competition. The news was flashed to the Dessau plant and to Berlin, and at Luft Hansa and Junkers offices toasts were offered to the new wonder of the commercial airways. August 1, 1932, would go down in the record books as indeed a memorable day.

But not the way the crew of D-2201 figured, and certainly not in the manner in which the Junkers Company, or Luft Hansa, or anyone, for that matter, had anticipated. Returning in triumph from Zurich, Ju-52/3mce cruised directly over Schleissheim Airfield. Small planes with newsmen and well-wishers drifted nearby, and from the cockpit of the Ju-52, Flugkapitan Polte smiled at the growing celebration.

His smile froze in horror as an Udet U.12 Flamingo biplane swept down toward the bigger airplane in a curving turn. A Ju-52 always seems to be flying slower than it really moves through the air, and the Flamingo pilot badly misjudged his speed and distance. Polte had a terrifying look at the biplane as it swelled in size and smashed directly into the Ju-52.

The explosion was heard for miles, and the big tri-motor staggered, lurched crazily to one side. The blast sent pieces of the Flamingo in a sputum of wreckage along the wing and body of the Ju-52, after which it sprayed wildly in a fan-shaped pattern, carrying the bodies of its two occupants. Everyone watching from the ground waited in despair for the Ju-52 to tumble out of control. Polte was doing an incredible job of hanging onto his airplane, for the Flamingo had torn into part of the cockpit, the landing gear was twisted and broken, the left stabilizer and elevator, as well as the vertical fin and rudder, were badly damaged, and wreckage of the biplane had ripped into and gouged a great tear in the side of the airliner. The left engine was ripped from its mounts, tore away, but did not fall from the aircraft, as it was held dangling from the wing by restraining safety cables.

Unbelievably, impossibly, Polte found that the Junkers responded to the controls. The left wing had also taken damage in the trailing wing, lift was messed up by damage to the leading edge, and there was no way the Ju-52 could remain flying. But Polte did the impossible, fighting the big airplane all the way to the ground, leaving the flaps up, and wisely flying straight ahead into a large cornfield—*and landed successfully!*

No one aboard *Werke* Number 4013 had been killed. Of a sudden, thirteen was a very *lucky* number. . . .

———◆———

Meanwhile, the disassembled parts of *Juan del Valle* and *Huanuni* had been dispatched by merchant ship to Bolivia. They would be followed in the very near future by *Chorolque* and *Bolívar,* and later another three Ju-52/3m airliners would be on their way to South America. But those first four aircraft, three owned by the Bolivian Government and the fourth "donated to the cause" by the industrialist Simón Patino (this was the *Bolívar*) and used by the Bolivian commander-in-chief, General Hans von Kundt, were to become the first four of the famed Iron Annie line to enter combat—a role

that had never been intended by either Kurt Weil or Hugo Junkers. That lack of intention stands as one of the greatest shattered hopes of all time, since before it reached its final zenith in mass use, it was the military Ju-52 that would endear the machine to its users and set standards of ruggedness and reliability under "impossible" conditions still unmatched by any other airplane ever built.

Now, before moving any farther into the use of these Ju-52/3m types that were so early in the history of the airplane that they were officially listed as *pre*-production models, it seems wise to explain this so-called combat role of the fledgling Iron Annies. The terrible border struggle in the late twenties between Bolivia and Paraguay is little known to most Americans and Europeans. The Gran Chaco War was its official name, but to the pilots who flew for Bolivia and Paraguay—and many of the pilots and other combatants handling technical equipment were hired mercenaries from throughout the world—it was known as the Green Hell Air War.

The area in dispute, where the fighting waxed and waned from pure savagery to near unconsciousness on both sides, is a vast green hell of thick jungle, sucking marshland, deep forests, and vicious terrain. The Gran Chaco covers some three hundred thousand square miles, and most of the area, even today, except for aerial reconnaissance, remains unexplored and unmapped. But there is one section in particular, the Chaco Boreal, which has long been a thorn in the mutual side of Bolivia and Paraguay. Fighting for its possession went on sporadically until it escalated suddenly in the late 1920s, and then, in 1932, it exploded into the most costly and bloody combat ever known in South America.

The fighting raged for three years and literally exhausted both sides. The place was hardly fitting for a war, with its killing climate, a thriving infestation of poisonous insects, all manner of reptiles, and countless strains of virulent diseases and sudden fevers.

The first two Ju-52/3m transports ordered by Bolivia arrived in that country in time to be impressed immediately into combat service, and they were the largest aircraft used in the entire Gran Chaco War. No one had ever expected the German-built machines to be thrown into a military support role, as their future was planned for Bolivian commercial service. But, with the wildfire spread of fighting in 1932, the unique ability of the Ju-52/3m was recognized at once by Bolivian authorities—and the Germans who were running the war for Bolivia.

In short, the Ju-52s were used for "anything and everything" roles. As the fighting increased, the third Ju-52 arrived in South America, and soon the fourth plane was added to the unique roster of transports. Their job was to get men, supplies, arms, or whatever was needed from the major centers of Brazil into the isolated combat areas, where roads were virtually unknown and the only transport that did not require weeks was by air. Other planes that were used carried only small loads and could not withstand the gruesome and primitive conditions under which the Ju-52s operated matter-of-factly. Maintenance was horribly inadequate, and only the enormous strength of the Ju-52 airframes and the faultless reliability of the 550-horsepower P&W Hornet radial engines gave the airplanes the slightest chance of staying operational. There were few smooth landing strips, and in fact, the Ju-52s were touching down on high mountain slopes where airstrips had been gouged and clawed from precipitous mountain flanks. The worst fields were those deep within the forests and the jungles, for any clearing immediately was filled with sucking mud that could wipe out an airplane on its first landing try. The Ju-52s would often land with supplies and weapons, be loaded up with wounded whose only chance of survival was to be flown out to a hospital, and find the field a quagmire.

On one occasion, the pilots refused to take off from such a mud-soaked field, which was a wise move indeed, especially in view of the fact that the airplanes could not even taxi. Orders were shouted to the Bolivian soldiers, and local tanneries and butcher shops were raided, and when these were found to be short of supplies, cattle by the hundreds were killed and the hides spread over the muddy fields to form an incredible patchwork runway of cowhide!

Against all odds, under the worst maintenance, fueled always by small cans in the hands of soldiers, flying in terrible weather, attacked by enemy fighters, the four Ju-52s did yeoman duty and survived the conflict, which ended in 1935. There were other Junkers planes in the battle, including aging F-13s and even a trio of W-34 single-engine transports that were hastily modified as bombers. One of the best indications of what the Ju-52s went

through is found in the experience of a Ford Tri-Motor, the *Cruz del Sud*. The airplane went into service in September of 1932. Its crew, noting how the first Ju-52s operated by simply stuffing them absolutely full and flying them away, refused to be outdone. On October 26, 1932, they loaded the Ford with artillery shells and fuel drums, and should certainly have paid more attention to the landing gear, which had begun to sag from the heavy weight. It was a short flight: the airplane failed to get off the ground in the high and hot air and ended its career in a terrible crash.

T. Wewege-Smith was a mercenary pilot under contract to the Bolivian Cuerpo de Aviación, and he would always recall the Gran Chaco War as a battle that raged under the "perpetual and maddening sun, which gave place to an intolerable hot-house atmosphere during the wet season, the malaria-bearing mosquitoes that bit by night and, the *marihuis* that bit, stung, and drank by day, the scorpions that infested the bedding, the million and one other discomforts, but worst of all, the loss of friends: one would go down with fever, another in flames, but it amounted to the same thing in the end."

By 1935 both sides were almost paralyzed by their losses, they were economically devastated, and they had endured a terrible slaughter. Sixty-seven thousand Bolivians died, another ten thousand threw away their weapons and deserted, fleeing across the border to Argentina, and yet another twenty-one thousand were taken prisoner and interned. Paraguay took casualties of thirty-six thousand dead (no number is available for the wounded) and another thirty-eight hundred men captured.

It seems almost too much of a story to be true, but one of the Ju-52/3m transports that fought in the Green Hell Air War *survives to this very day*. After the fighting ended, in 1935, the fourth Ju-52 of the Bolivian forces, which had been donated by the industrial magnate Simón Patino, was returned to its owner. The airplane was given a thorough overhaul, updated with new equipment, and placed back in business flying. Later it was sold to Argentina, with a registration of LQ-ZBD, where further modifications were made, including installation of a tail wheel instead of the tail skid, fitting NACA (National Advisory Committee for Aeronautics) full cowlings to the wing engines, and other technical improvements. The first Argentinian operator was Aeroposta Argentina. Later the machine was transferred to the Ministerio de Agricultura y Ganadería de la Nación, where it was further modified to become the biggest damned crop duster ever seen in South America. Finally, after a long and grueling career, the original *Bolívar* was retired, cleaned up and put into presentable shape, and transferred to where it is today: the Air Force Museum of Argentina.

The spectacular durability of the airplanes in the Gran Chaco did not go unnoticed in Germany. The first machine for Luft Hansa—D-2201—had already demonstrated the astonishing structural strength of the machine. But the Gran Chaco fighting, with its primitive and intolerable conditions, with its ulcer-producing *lack* of facilities, made it stunningly clear to the members of the German Government, and especially the burgeoning Luftwaffe, that here was a machine that could operate in the field with all the dependability of a simple and rugged truck. The very philosophy that had been expounded by Hugo Junkers and Kurt Weil for commercial success had been carried a vast step farther: the Ju-52/3m loomed suddenly to military planners as the perfect transport, for its logistics demands in the field were clearly less than any other airplane, and lessened logistics demands could be spelled out another way: greater freedom in the arena of battle.

While such planning was under way, however, the commercial line continued in both its development and its production. As the airliners rolled from the Dessau plant and then began to be built in other factories, the changes and improvements continued as well.

Overnight, the Ju-52/3m had become the measure by which all future airliner success would be judged.

There's nothing like hearing from a satisfied customer. One of the groups that purchased the Ju-52/3m transports, and launched commercial operations with their big airplanes on both wheels and floats, was DNL Airlines, better known in their local area as Det Norske Luftfartselskap, the national air carrier of Norway. After several years of service, the Norwegian Government issued the following statement:

———◆———

While Norway had been linked up with the European air system as early as 1931 by a route from Copenhagen via Gotenburg to Oslo, it was not until 1935 that a national air company was formed.

Det Norske Luftfartselskap, a company established by the largest Norwegian firm of shipowners, started in with two modern Junkers Ju-52/3m seaplanes on the Oslo-Tromsø line, which runs along the coast via Bergen and Drontheim, and later extended that service southward via Stavanger and Copenhagen as far as Amsterdam. Upon making the projected connection with London, the Norwegian company will have a system of airlines that does justice to the importance of its long-standing economic relations with Western Europe and Great Britain. Some years ago, a third Junkers Ju-52/3m machine was put in service to cope with the large volume of traffic on the DNL lines.

Those who are familiar with the North Country, its countless cliffs rising sheer from the sea, its fjord-rent, steep shore, and the veil of mist and cloud that often overhangs it, will readily understand that safety of flying in those regions depends in the first place on the reliability of the machine. That DNL place every confidence in the Ju-52 is clearly proved by the fact that they have this year decided to fly direct from Oslo to Bergen *across the mountains* instead of following the coastline.

———◆———

That's a tough act to follow with any airplane. DNL not only operated in violent weather but in terrain even worse than the weather, and when you mix in all the ingredients of howling and treacherous winds, low clouds, instant fogs and mists, turbulence whipping off the craggy shoreline, steep mountains where engine failures meant going down in impassable terrain . . . the more you think of the conditions existing and the manner of service of the Ju-52 the easier you can appreciate the glowing pride of the Norwegians that their Ju-52/3m aircraft turned in nothing less than superb performance. The practice in the North Country was to use wheels when weather permitted, and when the winter closed down the airfields, the machines were equipped with the great duralumin floats built by Junkers so that operations could continue year round without interruption.

Now, as we move into the civil versions of the Ju-52/3m, we can better relate to the essential structure of the machine and how this affected its entire history. We have already learned enough of the airplane to appreciate its great structural integrity, but we need now to go more than skin deep.

So we return to the fundamental philosophy of design: a thick-winged cantilever monoplane built along the same strength characteristics of a steel bridge. Understand that it is the elemental design with which we are concerned, not minor modifications to suit a particular environment. Thus we sustain in the evolution of the Junkers philosophy the use of corrugated-duralumin skin to bear some of the flight and structural loads of the machine. This was used in early Junkers airplanes, and its strength and efficiency were improved through

Lufthansa's *Kurt Steidel*, registration D-AVUP, on takeoff for a scheduled flight. Note the spatted main gear wheel pants and the unusual tail-skid arrangement. The Ju-52 started out with a tail wheel, went to the skid, was modified later back to the tail wheel.

the years, culminating in the Ju-52 as the best example of all that Junkers had done.

The essential design emphasized the wing construction in the form of the extremely strong, all-metal girder, with center sections built as an integral part of the aircraft, which itself was built up as a series of metal frames with considerable reinforcement in the cockpit and cabin areas. The result is a complete structure covered by both smooth- and corrugated-surface duralumin that bears the major load, but various bulkheads throughout the machine also contribute to that ultimate goal of enormous structural integrity.

If we take a closer look within the wing, we find that the airplane has eight main spars made of tubular duralumin. These are arranged in the form of four double-tubular spars, arranged in pairs vertically and braced with short struts, which adds even more wing strength. At the wing roots there are extremely strong transverse bracings. These combinations of the design were added to by the corrugated surfaces, since they did not transfer transversal loads, and absorbed torsional forces.

In effect, the thing kept getting stronger and stronger the more its basic structural elements were joined. The middle portion of the wing was built into the fuselage proper, so that it formed the direct undersurface of the aircraft, and the wings were joined to the aircraft by what were described as "typical Junkers screw couplings."

The fuselage itself was of a rectangular section, with domed decking. The construction was of du-

47

ralumin frames and bracing of simple channel section, together with four *longerons,* to compose the frame—simple, neat, supporting of each element from one to the other, and possessing enormous strength. The outer fuselage surface was of stressed skin of corrugated light-alloy sheeting. Now, the doors and hatches in the Ju-52 are a matter of one airplane to another, to meet individual customer needs, so for this identification we'll use N52JU as a major example. In our airplane we have three main fuselage doors. The main cabin door is on the left side of the airplane, just aft of the trailing edge of the wing, and this is used for normal entry and exit, via ladder. The door itself has a quick-release jettison system so that it may be removed, literally, within seconds, and is so removed for skydiver or paratrooper or cargo drops. *Before* flight, by the way.

Directly across the cabin from the main entrance is a huge, rectangular cargo door. On N52JU this is larger than on earlier aircraft and results directly from World War II military requirements. The door splits horizontally, the top half held by wires, while the bottom half becomes a platform (using pipes wedged into notches on the wing or reaching to the ground) big enough to load barrels, drums, kegs, stretchers, and even entire aircraft engines. The third door is at the front side of the cabin on the right, directly behind the copilot bulkhead, and opens out to the right wing. There is also a sliding hatch in the cockpit between the two pilot seats, large enough for easy movement from the aircraft. And in the belly, reached through the Number One floor hatch, which leads to the storage compartment, is another door, which hinges downward. This is used only rarely, as some strange body convolutions are necessary to use it at all.

The cockpit is separated from the main cabin by massive framing and metal-and-wood paneling—and in our airplane there simply is no way of knowing how many modifications have been made to this area through the years. But since we're talking about the basic framework, there really isn't much change between one aircraft and another except for equipment detail. The cockpit proper provides for two pilots, with a foldable (hinged) center jumpseat directly between the cockpit bulkheads, so the engineer is seated behind and between the pilots. The airplane came off the production lines with two small hinged doors closing off the cockpit from the cabin in order to afford privacy for the crew in flight, keep the cockpit dark

for night flying while cabin lights were on, and also to lower measurably the storm of noise from the cockpit into the cabin. The windows on either side of the cockpit slide back and forth, the top hatch opens in flight, and there are forward windows on each side of the windshield that can be opened—forward—in flight so that a cooling small hurricane can be set up for the flight crew.

Which also provides an excellent source of water smashing into the cockpit during rainstorms. As an aside, I cursed this airplane that provides such high levels of dew in rain, until I spent time with many DC-3 pilots, who were amazed at how *little* water came in the Ju-52 cockpit. "In heavy rain," explained Vern Renaud, captain for Eastern Air Lines, "we used to wear rain aprons on our laps so the water would have a place to collect and then run off onto the floor. Later we got smart. Wherever the flight crews stayed at motels, the shower curtains would disappear, and we'd sit in the cockpit with the shower curtains about our necks like giant bibs, covering us completely, with our hands beneath the curtains working the flight controls."

Annie, I take it all back. . . .

The pilot's seat in N52JU can be raised and lowered, and it slides fore and aft. The copilot seat is hinged by cable to lift up to storage space beneath but lacks the means to adjust. There are full controls on the pilot's side, including toe brakes of the DC-3 type. The copilot has only a rudder bar instead of pedals. This stems, of course, from the original airplane, with the brakes of compressed air operated by pulling full back on the throttles, so that either pilot had full access to the braking system—which is not the case with N52JU.

Seating is on both sides of the cabin, and seating arrangements depend upon individual aircraft and intended use. But the airplane could carry seventeen passengers in reclining seats of surprising roominess and comfort.

Dual controls were featured in all the early production models and retained through the later ones, with each pilot provided a control yoke that might have come from the bridge of the *Titanic.* In most of the early service, however, the radio operator most often occupied the right front seat, while the man to his left attended to flying. Later, with the addition of heavy and bulky radio and navigation gear, so much room was occupied by this equipment that the radioman's position was moved back into the cabin.

Another feature of the Ju-52 that has always en-

The front office gets more cluttered with the change from one to three engines, new navigation equipment, and the requirements of scheduled airline service. The cockpit of the Ju-52/3m with Lufthansa. LUFTHANSA

deared itself to pilots is the manner in which pilot muscle force was transmitted from the cockpit. Keep in mind that everything aboard this machine is manual—muscle power being the key. The pilot operated his controls, and this was transmitted to the appropriate surfaces by smoothly functioning pushrods, with the only control cables to be found in the tail.

The Ju-52 featured swift-control-response safety features that to this very day astonish pilots who board the time machine and find it replete with ideas they wish were incorporated into their modern steeds. For example, with the flaps fully lowered to 40 degrees the ailerons droop 15 degrees, providing an extraordinary lift component and docile control right on down to stall speed. The flaps are red-lined at 100 mph indicated air speed—

which means you are not to exceed 100 mph when the flaps are down. But pilots do such things, and Junkers built into the airplane a delightful safety gimmick in the form of an oil damped compressed coil spring package that reduced the flap settings whenever the pilot went "Oops!" and sailed through the "don't exceed" speed. Very, *very* neat.

Back for a moment to the cabin. As mentioned, it could be configured in any way the purchaser desired, with the most common arrangement being seventeen passenger seats. These were individual seats, but some models mounted a double seat on the rear of the bulkhead door, and others had a single seat on the lavatory door. Certain customers set up cabin bulkheads and partitions to create a small forward cabin for privacy. Most airliner arrangements had light luggage racks of webbing above

49

the seats running along each side of the cabin, and there were varying arrangements of roller blinds, shades, or window curtains.

The floor of the cabin ingeniously opened into storage or luggage compartments. Hatch locks were moved to the side and the hatch covers lifted physically from the floor. These gave much extra room for baggage and cargo, and also provided direct access to inspect control rods, springs, wires, and other aircraft systems. Again, a delightful touch.

Facing aft, at the rear bulkhead the left side has a removable bulkhead door that leads to another cargo/luggage compartment with a maximum allowable load of 150 kilograms—or 330 pounds. Beyond this compartment, which in the fuselage is directly to the left of the lavatory, there extend several more compartments, each separated by swinging gates that are locked in position before flight. Now, this jumps the storyline of the Ju-52/3m, since the earlier, commercial models lacked storage areas beyond the cargo hold. But when the military version came off the production line and the Germans decided to add an open gun position, some swift modifications were made: the after fuselage was greatly strengthened (one of the advantages I have in N52JU), and provision was made for the heavy far-aft weight of gunner, weapon, ammunition, and supplies, plus the effects of drag on the gun-position windscreen, the gun and the crewman jutting out into the windscreen. Which, again, becomes a singing hurrah to the astonishing versatility of the airplane.

The landing gear on the original Ju-52 line was of split and unfaired (no coverings to the big tires) main wheels, with struts connected directly to the fuselage and the wing center section. The gear struts leading to the wing were equipped with spring dampers to soften the shock of landing and high-speed ground runs.

The landing gear also went through a series of changes and strengthening as the weight of the airplane increased steadily. As the weight rose from the Ju-52/1m to the 3m series, for example, Junkers installed Faudi-type pneumatic legs made by VDM for added strength and shock-absorbing qualities. The tail wheel of the first 1m model gave way in later versions to an airplane with an elaborate tail skid, equipped with springs, bungee cords, and shock dampers, and for a while the 3m series rolled off the line with wheels or skids, depending upon

customer preference. A tail-wheel locking pin of soft metal was used; when in the locked position, it kept the tail wheel from swinging freely and thus aided the pilot in holding a steady course when taxiing. If he forgot that the lockpin was in place, and a powerful side load was exerted on the system, the pin snapped and freed the system before it suffered damage.

There were still other modifications to the gear systems. After a while, the main wheels were covered with so-called spats, or teardrop-shaped fairings to reduce drag and increase cruising speed. These did their job, and also collected mud or permitted water collected on takeoff from wet fields to freeze and jam up the wheels. They were used only for a while and then discarded as impractical for the extremely slight increase in speed.

Another improvement to the main gear came with heavier versions. It was still the fixed, divided type constructed of half axles and radius rods hinged to the fuselage, but the air system was abandoned, and oleo-pneumatic shock absorbers were attached to the upper wing root of the foremost spar. In the last production run—which we find on N52JU—another significant change was made when the air-pressured legs were discarded. These were replaced with KPZ telescopic legs in both the main and tail gear assemblies. The legs were filled with animal fat and equipped with Uerdinger annular springs and then sealed.

Again to jump the time line, when we found it necessary to check out our gear during a change to new wheels and tires, for the life of us we couldn't find any reference to this KPZ system—essentially because we didn't know the bloody things were installed on N52JU. Karl Frensch came to our rescue with a group of German engineers, and even ran up against a blank wall, since the last Ju-52 Frensch had flown in Europe was in 1940, when the system with compressed air was in use, and this system wasn't shown in the German aircraft manual. The thing to do in a case like this is to punt, and we did, with elaborate X rays of the gear legs. Lo and behold! we now had an idea of what peculiar gadgets the Junkers Company had placed in the main gear legs. There was the oleo strut, there was the animal fat still secured within the main housing, and there were the springs, and unexpected layers of spring leaves as well. Another Ju-52 pilot remembered it all. "*Ach,* you have the best," he said proudly. "They installed these because, once they were on the airplane, we never touched them again. They are very strong, they take battle damage extremely well, and you *never* have to service them. They are sealed permanently."

To all the engineers in the Dessau plant: thank you!

We've noted before that the purist who wants to know precisely what type of cowlings or fairings were fitted to the Ju-52 is in for a bad time, because the variety was not only endless, it was often on-the-spot modifications that marked many of the airplanes. The Ju-52s flew without cowlings of any kind, they flew with speed rings to smooth out turbulent airflow, they flew with bulky NACA (National Advisory Committee for Aeronautics—another nifty gift from the United States) cowlings, and they flew with a loose-ended variety of completely enclosed cowlings, with exhaust systems going in every direction according to the individual model. So, to the buff out there: tough luck, old chap, but your only success is going to be in collecting a record of as many different modifications as you might identify. If ever there was an *anything goes* airplane, this is it.

I have been particularly intrigued by the NACA cowlings that went on the majority of wing engines for the Ju-52. These were big, clumsy to the eye, bulky in shape, and seemed almost like sky anchors to hold back a machine struggling for speed. Which only goes to prove that the old-timers who dabbled in the wind tunnels in the United States knew what they were doing, because those clumsy-looking cowls (which are unmistakable in the photographs with this book) did an excellent job of smoothing out the internal airflow behind the cylinder rows. They also set up an inlet-to-outlet ratio that used the heated cooling air from the engines in a way that squeezed it from the back of the cowling, providing additional thrust to that achieved by the propeller itself!

Many of the engines fitted to Ju-52 models had frontal plates that could be adjusted to control airflow, *very* necessary for desert or winter operations, especially with the early BMW engines.

Now the propellers. It's another take-your-choice selection, depending upon the models. There were two-bladed wooden props and four-bladed wooden props, and fixed-pitch metal props of two, three, and four blades, and there were metal blades that could be adjusted on the ground for best-climb or best-cruise position, and there were propeller sys-

tems adjustable in pitch in flight by cockpit control, so that maximum thrust for takeoff could be set and, after reaching cruise altitude, the angle of the blades be brought back into a coarse position for best-economy cruise. I've flown this kind of prop on a number of planes, including my bf-108b, and it's infinitely better than the fixed-pitch system. And infinitely better than that is the constant-speed propeller, which has an automatic governing system that allows the pilot to set a desired rpm with his cockpit prop control, and that rpm is kept no matter if the airplane climbs or descends or holds level flight. The sensors within the prop governor are told what setting is desired by moving the prop control in the cockpit, and they use counterweights and other systems to maintain the intended rpm. These were fitted, in many versions and models, to various Ju-52 aircraft.

There seemed to be another anything-goes situation with fuel tanks. These were in the shape of odd-sized drums in the wings, secured in place by both metal and leather straps. I don't know where the Germans got their leather, but the straps in my Ju-52 today are still in almost perfect shape, and we haven't had to replace a single one of these items, which is some sort of incredible testimonial. In the early commercial models, the airplanes usually held about 600 gallons of fuel, with variations from 570 to 630 gallons being normal, and provision for doubling (and more) the entire fuel capacity. A hand-operated wobble pump in the cockpit got the fuel moving toward the engines, which was a complete circus acrobatic act in itself, and once it was moving in the lines, and spilling out on the ground (deliberately), you tried to fire up the old beasts. Once started, the fuel pumps (Jumbo manufacture), mounted on the rear panels of the engine fire walls, went into operation, driven by universal-jointed shafts. Certain airplanes intended for extremely cold-weather operations also had a separate tank for a special fuel used only for starting up and shutting down the engines. It was an elaborate and clumsy system, but it did help cranky engines come to life when they would otherwise have refused to budge. And any old pilot was familiar with the trick of pouring some high-octane fuel into the oil to raise its ignition point just to get his engines started—a practice as effective today as it was then.

There was another "trick" involving the tail unit of the Ju-52/3m, the details of which would never have been known had it not been for the marvelous time we spent with Kurt Weil at Pompano Beach. The tail unit for the Ju-52 is of the normal monoplane type, with a semicantilever tailplane passing through the top of the fuselage and braced to the underside of the fuselage, with a single strut on each side. The elevator is of double-wing construction, like the main wings and ailerons, and is horn-balanced, as are the ailerons. The whole unit is covered with the corrugated metal sheeting of the wings and fuselage. The horizontal stabilizer is adjustable in flight and has external position markings. That latter item, being able to see the stabilizer position for trim, is perfect for cross-checking. If the trim in the cockpit indicator is set at zero, so will be the tail unit, and you can tell with only two glances if everything is up to snuff. If it isn't, you don't take off until you find out what's messed up.

Now for that item given to us by Kurt Weil. We identified the tailplane as being semicantilever "and braced to the underside of the fuselage, with a single strut on each side." According to Kurt Weil, it isn't. Semicantilever, that is. It's fully cantilevered, like the main wing.

"But when we were making a flight test one day," explained Weil, "we encountered a problem with flutter of the horizontal tail. It was a problem with this one airplane only, but we had a government official aboard, and he was frightened almost to death by the sudden violent shaking of the tail. *He* ordered the external struts put on the machine, and nothing the engineers could do or say would change his mind." Weil shrugged. "So we did as we were ordered and built the tail with the strut."

And it would all come full circle one day—as told to us by Kurt Streit. We had been discussing with him what Weil had told us, and Streit nodded knowingly, a smile coming to his face. "And I for one am very glad about what happened," he told us. "We were flying supplies to the Russian front, dropping cargo from the air, and one of the big packages was caught in severe turbulence and it smashed into the left horizontal tail. The blow was so severe the whole machine swerved wildly to the side, and I was sure we had lost the entire tail on that side. In fact, it had been ripped loose by the impact—but was still held in place by that strut that *shouldn't* have been there in the first place. . . ."

Not *everything* about the new Ju-52/3m airliners was of the most advanced design or represented the acme of science and technology as it could be applied to commercial air service. New engines and constant-speed propellers and amazing navigation instruments and an unmatched strength of structure all suffered from design and performance failure in what can kindly be described as the *Krappenhausen*. Or, as it is termed somewhat more delicately, the water closet or the toilet and, in more contemporary terms, the john or the head. Is it really so strange to accord so much attention to this diminutive aspect of design? Should so small a volume be accorded our intense interest, as compared to the outstanding characteristics of the airplane?

Well, that depends. If you're spoiled by modern air travel and pressurized cabins and wonderful air conditioning and flush toilets and hot meals and movies and champagne, well, then I suppose it is a bit unusual. But if you can recall back to the "old days," when air conditioning in airliners was a dream of the future equally as distant as man walking on the moon, then you were *very* interested in flying on hot days. In the summertime the interior of an airliner in the early thirties could and often did become a sweltering hotbox, and one of the marks of air travel in those times was perspiration dribbling down all parts of the body.

Such flights also meant the need for passengers to answer the call of nature and retire to the water closet for biological necessity. On the hotter days this immediately revealed a weak link in the passenger-accommodation design of the Ju-52, an event marked by wide eyes and wrinkled noses and choking gasps. The toilet facilities were of the "dry type," consisting of a large metal can where everything was simply collected. The heat in the *Krappenhausen* often built up to more than 100 degrees,

and airplanes often experienced variations in air pressure inside the fuselage, especially when the *Krappenhausen* door was opened to permit its white-faced occupant to stagger back to his or her seat. But that brief opening of the door could be determined without the turn of a single head, as the ghastly stench wafted through the cabin, assaulting the hapless passengers, bringing women to breathe deeply in perfume-soaked handkerchiefs, and unleashing a flurry of activity in the cockpit, marked by a slamming of the doors closing off the cabin and violent wrenching of every window within reach to full open position.

In desperation, Junkers engineers installed a small suction valve underneath the "big bucket" to rid the airliner of its choking odors.

Of course, there was another problem in this matter of relief for the human system, especially the male bladder. The women passengers had little solace in attending to their needs, but many of the airliners provided for the male passengers in the water closet that ingenious device known as the "relief tube." The working end in the lavatory was in the convenient shape of a funnel, into which the male passenger would relieve himself, the contents then sluicing down the tube to be sprayed back beneath the fuselage. You think this is too much emphasis again? You're wrong, because you could almost always tell the age of a Ju-52, or its frequency in service, by the streaks along the after section of the fuselage and the astonishing need to replace the corrugated metal (which stood up better to jungle rot and Russian cold) where it had been eaten away and corroded in unexpected fashion. Through all the early years of flight, in fact, the greatest damage done on a steady basis to operational Junkers airliners—and which necessitated the most frequent complete replacement of the corrugated skin—was in this "splash and spray" sec-

Lufthansa put its Ju-52/3m transports into service in 1933 in Europe, then extended the early routes to eastern Asia and throughout South America. This Ju-52 is operating from a glider-training airfield. LUFTHANSA

tion of the bottom fuselage aft of the water closet.

When I first flew N52JU, we still had this same devilish equipment, and until the time we made the drastically necessary change to a more modern device, the only protest available to the crew was found when one lifted the toilet lid before use and the occupant of the *Krappenhausen* stared into a portrait of Adolf Hitler. A fitting if somewhat opinionated appraisal.

———◆———

Cockpit arrangements for the early airliners were in keeping with "only what is necessary." The crew had controls to use standard gas, another control for fuel when flying at high altitude, a control to adjust the engine cowlings, an oil-cooler control, and an oil-shutoff valve. These were considered the basic regulating controls for the engines, which were also fitted, of course, with throttles, mixture control, engine start-run-shutoff controls, carburetor heat, and a charming switch for ignition timing adjustment: SPARK RETARD and ADVANCE. Those of us who today enjoy modern avionics are quick to forget that there was a time when these electronic

miracles simply did not exist. Even the common and everyday VHF (very high frequency) radio and navigation aids were wispy dreams of some unreachable future. For radio and guidance, the crews operated with an Askania remote-indicating compass with, of all things, pneumatic transmission. The radios were bulky, heavy, and guaranteed always to be erratic, and called for the use of fixed, homing, and drag antennas. But the radios were there, and they did work (most of the time), and improvements were being made all the time. As the radios grew more powerful, it became necessary to modify the aircraft. The radios were now generating so much power that the very structure of the aircraft and its components were interfering with transmission, and finally all Ju-52s were built with every moving part, from the rudder to the engine controls, interconnected one to the other and with the aircraft structure by short wire connectors so as to prevent problems with electrostatic charges and discharges during flight. "Electrically securing" the aircraft is commonplace today but was revolutionary then.

Even changing from a tail skid to the rubber tire

in the tail wheel presented its own problems, since the aircraft could produce and discharge an electrical charge when landing. To eliminate the problem, the engineers attached a wire coil to the tail-wheel fork that grounded the Ju-52 when the tail let down to the runway or field surface on landing. After some experience with this system, which had its shortcomings, Junkers went to electrically conducting rubber tires (which were identified by a large white *L* in a red circle on the wheel), and was able to discontinue use of the grounding wire coil.

———————————————•———————————————

As the airplanes began to roll from the production line, the "standard models" quickly began to outnumber the special variants. The first wide-scale-use airliner was the Ju-52/3mce, with three Pratt & Whitney Hornet engines of 525 horsepower; these were in service before the end of 1932 in Germany, Finland, and Sweden. Most of these machines stayed in operation with the American-made engines until the supply from the United States was cut off and BMW radials were installed in their place. They were a solid and reliable

airliner, turning in a steady cruising speed of approximately 135 miles per hour.

One of the special-order airliners deserves special mention; the Ju-52/3mba, which carried *Werke* Number 4016, was registered as CV-FAI and named *România*. It was produced as a *private* aircraft for Prince Bibesco and was dripping with luxury accommodations in the cabin. It had several unusual features, including twelve-cylinder water-cooled Hispano-Suiza engines, the 750-horsepower 12Nb in the nose, driving a three-bladed propeller, and wing engines of 575 horsepower (model 12Mb) driving two-bladed propellers. All engines had oversized spinners and were fitted with oversized cooling radiators, one beneath the nose engine and the others installed beneath the wings. It had a tail gear of *two* tail wheels and was intended to be used for hunting trips in Africa, where it would be landed on any convenient open field. To help in cutting down noise levels in the cabin that might annoy the prince, the exhaust stacks from the nose engine ran all the way beneath the fuselage until they were clear of the passenger cabin. This airplane is also a prime example of the futility of chasing after designations that adhere rigidly to

The extremely rare Ju-52/3m/ba—*Werke* Number 4016—built under Romanian order. The airplane had Hispano-Suiza engines, a four-bladed nose prop and two-bladed wing-engine props, and a double tail wheel. It was used for open-field landings on African hunting trips. LUFTHANSA

Lufthansa Ju-52 at London's Croydon Airport. Behind the two men at right is the tail of a Douglas transport. LUFTHANSA

Few Ju-52/3ms carried the full identification of this Lufthansa model, registration D-2468. The tail markings identify the aircraft as a Ju-52/3mce with *Werke* Number 4019. The airplane has a tail skid, at this point lacks radio antennas, and has a unique overlapping no-skid wing strip alongside and aft of the engine nacelles. LUFTHANSA

accounting ledgers, for in 1937 it was transferred from private use to the Romanian airline LARES and was given the new designation of Ju-52/3mbe and the new registration of YR-ABF.

The Ju-52/3mde is already familiar to us, with its 550-horsepower Hornet engines, tail skids, and all three engines fitted with Townend speed rings. There were only two of these aircraft, the *Juan del Valle* and the *Huanuni,* sent to Bolivia and rushed into the Gran Chaco War.

The "second batch" of commercial airliners in the production line was the series Ju-52/3mfe; fifteen were built in 1933. They featured the Townend speed ring for the nose engine and drag-reducing NACA cowls for the wing engines, which were either 525- or 600-horsepower Hornet A-2 engines made in the United States. All were built with tail skids instead of the tail wheel, and, for the first time, the fuselage was built as a single, integral unit instead of manufactured in sections that were later fitted together. The main gear sported the new speed-increasing spats, the cockpit window arrangement was improved, and passenger accommodation was standardized at seventeen. Minor cabin improvements were common, and there was some strengthening of the main gear and the fuselage.

Adolf Hitler chose the Ju-52/3m as the best available transport for political stumping of Germany in his bid to be the nation's leader. He used the Ju-52/3m for whirlwind speaking and appearance tours. CAIDIN ARCHIVES

The *Franz Büchner,* of Lufthansa, shows the excellent finishing detail of the commercial transports. The nose exhausts were routed below the fuselage, and the wing engines were exhausted outboard of the cowls for minimum noise. Note the engine frontal gills in the closed position for cold-weather operations. LUFTHANSA

Included in this group of Ju-52/3mfe airliners was one rather special machine, with *Werke* Number 4021, Registration Number D-2600, and named *Immelmann.* This was the airliner assigned personally to none other than Adolf Hitler, and it is interesting to muse over the odd fact that Adolf Hitler in his travels through Germany and Europe cruised through the skies on those old reliable Pratt & Whitney Hornets.

Later, when Hitler transferred to the four-engined Focke-Wulf Condor, he took with him his special designation of D-2600 and the name *Immelmann* for the bigger airplane. The Ju-52/3mfe known as D-2600 *Immelmann* vanished into the maw of phantom identifications but could be found —if you knew where to look—beneath the new registration of D-AHUT and the name *H. J. Buddecke.*

In 1934 there appeared the new Ju-52/3mge series, again with an improved fuselage, and a dealer's choice, depending upon availability, of P&W or BMW Hornet engines. New Ju-Pak propellers were standardized for this series. American influence in the *ge* series airliner was far more pronounced than is generally realized. The Hornet engines of the T2D2 and T4D2 engines were merely the most obvious, but many propellers were either purchased directly from the United States or manufactured under license in Germany. The systems list included propeller governors and a wide variety of instruments, including Sperry attitude gyros (artificial horizons) and directional gyros (gyroscopic compasses), Kollsman precision altimeters, and other gauges. The Ju-52s now had an automatic pilot for rudder control (directional), and this also was bought directly from the Sperry Company.

Once again we have an interesting aside. In my hangar at Gainesville International Aerodrome is a completely refurbished, perfect-conditioned rudder autopilot built by Sperry that was once installed in my corrugated bird. Since I enjoy physically manhandling *Iron Annie*, the autopilot remained in the hangar rather than the airplane's innards but has now been sent as a gift for the Deutsches Museum, in Germany—which did not have a single one of these priceless pieces of equipment.

The first of the *g*-series airliners featured an increased gross weight, to 20,943 pounds, and this was only the start of a steadily increasing maximum weight, especially for the export versions. Germany's airline bought a fair number of the 3mge airplane, and they were also delivered to many other European countries, as well as being

shipped off to Australia, China, and South America, and a special batch was modified to specific requirements of South Africa. The export models featured a bewildering variety of engines, according to customer needs. Gross weight went up in the Ju-52/3mge aircraft to 22,046 pounds, and later would go much higher (as in the Ju-52/3mZ luxury passenger model, which went to DLH (Lufthansa) and export customers with a gross weight of 27,557 pounds. For the sake of clarification, these could be classed as the Ju-52/3mZge model.

The 3mge-series planes that went to foreign customers were fitted out with Piaggio Stella X, Bristol Pegasus VI, Pratt & Whitney Wasp S3H1-G, and Pratt & Whitney Hornet T2D1 engines. The airliners that went into Scandinavian service also featured three-bladed Hamilton Standard constant-speed propellers, which permitted full-throttle power at ten thousand feet and a cruising speed of one hundred fifty miles per hour with excellent cabin noise levels.

A number of these airplanes (and later from other lines as well) were returned to Junkers for an unexpected modification: The wing-mounted engines, angled outward at 6 degrees from the fuselage datum line, were removed and then reinstalled with the engines pointing directly forward, as in any other standard aircraft. It was felt that this would improve the operating lifetime of the constant-speed propellers. The modification gave up the improved airflow over the tail with one engine out and gained a few miles per hour because of the better-aligned thrust. It seemed pretty much of a wasteful effort. Those who felt the angled engine installation *could* interfere with propeller operation must have been baffled many years later when the Lockheed Electra appeared with four turboprop engines and massive propeller blades angled downward 5 degrees from the longitudinal axis line of the aircraft.

A rainy day for a Ju-52/3m at Croydon Airport, London. Note the tail skid. British Imperial Airways personnel are servicing the airliner. LUFTHANSA

The most powerful version of the commercial airliner was the Ju-52/3mreo, with 880-horsepower BMW 132Da/DC engines. Lufthansa considers the Ju-52/3mte airliner to have been its most highly developed and its best series equipped with German engines. These were all faired in the drag-reducing NACA cowls and had German-made Hamilton Standard constant-speed propellers and the most advanced equipment available.

A rare photograph, taken in 1936 at Tempelhof Airdrome, in Berlin, showing Charles Lindbergh about to board a Ju-52/3m. QUICK

Berlin's Tempelhof Airdrome was the main operational center for commercial airliner operations in Germany. A Ju-52/3m taxis out for takeoff. LUFTHANSA

This recitation of models has been for the essential purpose of identifying the aircraft through progressive versions, but in no way does it really represent the constant use and overwhelming popularity of the machine—in which its crews and passengers alike had such extraordinary confidence. The fact that the maximum weight could be just about what the customer desired, without messing up the balance of the aircraft, and that it could be maintained and repaired with incredible ease, made it one of the all-time economic winners in the airlines circle.

Before the beginning of the Second World War, commercial Ju-52/3m models were flying in passenger service on wheels, floats, and skis, carrying from thirteen to seventeen passengers, for such countries as Germany, Finland, Estonia, Austria, Belgium, Denmark, Russia, Greece, Hungary, Italy, Norway, Poland, Romania, Spain, Portugal, Sweden, England, Argentina, Brazil, Bolivia, Ecuador, China, Mozambique, Peru, South Africa, New Guinea, Uruguay, Australia, Colombia, Libya—well, the list goes on and on, because many customers sold their airplanes to buyers in the market for used aircraft. After the war, the list of users continued to increase and included France, Switzerland, and many other lands throughout the world. In fact, no one is sure just how many countries, companies, and private individuals in various lands flew the Ju-52/3m in many of its variants, but the number is certainly well over fifty.

The conditions under which the Ju-52s operated

extend from the most modern of their times to the most primitive and ghastly. Often they flew schedules on which they operated from roads or open fields or dry river beds. They flew from airstrips from below sea level to more than thirteen thousand feet above sea level. They were legendary for their reliability in scorching desert, they kept flying in jungles and marshland when other aircraft rotted away, and they flew in savage cold where other airplanes froze solid. They operated from mountain ranges and hilly land, and they flew where winds were known killers and fog and mist could whip into existence without notice. At a time when navigation facilities were at their most primitive, the Ju-52s flew long night routes—which was one way, in fact, that the Luftwaffe secretly trained its pilots destined for long-range combat operations at night. Some models were fitted with long-range tanks in the wings, belly, and fuselage and tripled the normal range of the airplane, others were modified to operate almost continuously at high altitudes, and still others were stripped of all but essentials so that they might carry the greatest cargo loads possible.

The civilian airliners were modified catch as catch can for a hundred banana wars, revolutions, and skirmishes throughout the world, and it is a pity that the wild and woolly adventures of these machines and their crews have been buried from public view and likely will remain so, the machines having been long since destroyed or buried by jun-

gle and forest and the crews gone to their permanent rest.

But whenever and wherever there were witnesses, the Ju-52 grew into a legend. How many Ju-52 aircraft were built? Since most reference books demand a reference, writers and editors scurry to what appears to be the safest number, and by some unspoken consensus of opinion there slowly ensues a number satisfactory to one and all. With the Ju-52, that magic number is 4,845 airplanes, but this does not include the single-engine models, the preproduction three-engine models, or even a part of the first production series. Neither does it include the Ju-52s assembled in Hungary, those built by Pestlorinc Industries (PIRT), of Budapest. One source claims that Construcciones Aeronáuticas S.A. (CASA), of Spain, which built their copy of the Ju-52/3m as the 352-L, powered by Elizalde-built BMW 132 engines, turned out just one hundred of the airplanes, while an allegedly equally reputable source claims the number was one hundred seventy airplanes. And what of France's Société Amiot? During World War II, the Germans moved entire factories with all their production machinery into French buildings and started churning out airplanes at a fearsome rate. Thus a whole swarm of Ju-52/3m military aircraft, even though built with German machine tools and equipment, were manufactured *in France*. And when the war ended, the French went right on building the airplane as the A.A.C. 1 Toucan,

The immortal Junkers Ju-52/3m in its early days of commercial service; note the three speed-ring cowlings on the engines and the massive duralumin floats as it starts its water takeoff. JUNKERS ARCHIVES

Lufthansa fleet of Ju-52/3m commercial airliners awaiting flights from Tempelhof Airfield, Berlin. In right background are two Douglas DC-2 airliners. LUFTHANSA

Pope Pius XII deplaning from a float-equipped Ju-52/3m. The aircraft later departed for Brazil for operations as part of Condor Airlines. LUFTHANSA

A rare modification of the Lufthansa Ju-52/3m showing the return to the tail wheel instead of the skid, wider tires than were commonly used, and new propeller spinners.
U. S. AIR FORCE

which was used by the French military as well as commercial airlines and special cargo lines.

So we return to the question: how many? Unquestionably at least between five and seven thousand, but this is a number that Professor Kurt Weil insists is drastically below the actual production run. We put the question to the grand old man of Dessau.

"In addition to the home factory at Dessau," Weil replied, "many Junkers branch factories, and numerous other German aircraft factories, built the Ju-52 during the war, and so did French and Spanish plants. Altogether, eighteen thousand were built between 1929 and 1945."

But the numbers aren't what we remember about the grand old lady of the commercial airways, and even the elements of reliability and dependability and innovation pale with the years. Out of all that has happened to and with the airplane, the word *greatness* emerges, glowing with its own rainbow hues of strength and ruggedness and individuality. The proving flight of the Ju-52/3m that won the Circuit of the Alps contest demonstrated its incredible strength when it was rammed by the Flamingo biplane, shredded the hapless smaller machine all over the sky, and went on to a successful cornfield landing—from which crew and passengers walked away under their own power.

It would seem one head-on ramming was enough in the early life of a new machine to establish its legendary strength, but the commercial Ju-52/3m had a strange rendezvous with destiny that kept testing the airplane. Not too much later, Ju-52/3m D-ANAZ, *Willi Charlet*, was on a scheduled flight with a full load of passengers. Closing in against the airliner on a collision course, its pilot completely unaware of the bigger airplane, was an Arado Ar-66. There was a rushing together of two winged shapes and the Arado smashed into the right wing of the Ju-52. An explosion hammered the airliner, hurling it violently out of control. The passengers had only a glimpse of the Arado literally shredding apart in the air as it whipped by the Ju-52—taking with it fully a fourth of the entire right wing and tearing away the aileron. *The airliner continued on its scheduled run and made an on-time, uneventful landing at Hamburg.*

Operating huge seaplanes—which are quite distinct and much more difficult in water operations than flying boats, which enjoy the solidity and stability of boat hulls—from water is always the kind of exciting event that keeps pucker factors high. As a seaplane pilot myself, I can appreciate flying a huge Ju-52/3m with twin floats—but my enjoyment would be restricted to the kind of operations that take place on nice balmy days with plenty of room in which to make a neat, flat approach straight into the wind. Operations in rotten weather or high winds are a bitch. Period. Which is why I hold so highly—even with a sense of awe—the skill of a Ju-52/3m on floats that was making its approach for landing in Bahia Harbor, in Brazil. Because the weather was rotten, and that's spelled *fog*. The pilot simply couldn't see well enough to

62

Three Ju-52/3ms sold to South African Airways on their delivery flight to Capetown, in August of 1938. Note the outsized radio-compass antenna directly behind each cockpit. MESSERSCHMITT-BOLKOW-BLOHM

make his approach and flare in open water, and he had to keep edging his way down, *hoping* he wouldn't run into something large, very physical, and essentially unmovable.

He was out of luck. As he eased down through the fog, the right float, its supporting struts, the propeller, and parts of the underhanging oil coolers smashed into a harbor pier. The impact was devastating, throwing the airplane violently off to one side and tearing off the float, all its supporting struts, and part of the engine, and chewing up the leading edge of the wing—and, of course, killing the right engine. The pilot pulled up, now knew where he was, circled back, *and made a perfect, one-float, two-engine landing without injury to his passengers!*

Many of the German pilots who flew commercial airliners in the mid and late thirties were "drafted" into service with the Luftwaffe. At that time, the distinction between commercial and government operations was so thin as to be non-existent, and whatever the Luftwaffe needed for extra transports was obtained by the expedient of scratching a signature on a paper ordering the transfer. To many "Yes, sir" and "Yes, ma'am" and a total lack of concern with burp bags and passenger convenience. One pilot who had overnight changed from Lufthansa airliner *Kapitan* to Luftwaffe transport *Kapitan* decided to celebrate his transfer by proving to his friends what he had always claimed about his remarkable airliner: that you just couldn't hurt a Ju-52.

To prove his point, he flew to a decent altitude above the ground, cleared the airspace beneath him, and pushed forward on the yoke until the airplane roared and bellowed. He watched the air speed come up until he had a true air speed of two hundred miles per hour and then came back on the yoke, as hard as he could, bringing the nose higher and higher. As the Ju-52 started over on her back through a giant loop, he went to full power, using overboost for the engines. At the top of the top, completely upside down, he was a bit under the speed he *should* have had and the airplane was falling down through the loop with the wingtips suddenly shaking violently. Other crew members said that the only way they could describe the wingtips was that they were shaking the same way a dog—a very happy dog—shakes his tail. The Ju-52 fell through as it came around the top and eased back into normal flight with its pilot grinning from ear to ear.

They said he was still grinning when they dragged him off to the stockade.

And then there was Luther, who was a test pilot for the Flugzeug-Industriewerk Heiligenbeil in East Prussia. Among other aircraft that he flight-tested was the Junkers Ju-87 Stuka, an inverted-gullwing dive bomber. There's only one way to test this powerful single-engine airplane, and that's to just roll her over on her back and go straight down full bore. That's what the thing was designed to do, including pulling out of those dives on cue.

Luther pondered the enormously squared shape of the Ju-52/3m. He studied the double wing and

63

A picture worth more than a thousand words. This Ju-52/3m had crashed on a mountainside in China. Thousands of workers gouged out an emergency strip in the mountainside, carried a new right wing up the mountain, reassembled the Ju-52 . . . and it was flown out of this short, rough, wind-blown airstrip! KURT STREIT ARCHIVES

mused over the fact that the Stuka had the same wing. He looked inside the wing and nodded at the powerful double-strutted rows of spars and the bridge-like structure. And then he took off in a Ju-52 with a mechanic and an observer and climbed to over ten thousand feet and looked at the ground far below, and then grinned at his crew, and they turned pale, because they recognized the look in his eye, and the next thing they knew, a wing was pointed at the sky and the Ju-52 was rolling over on her back, the nose going steeper and steeper until the great airliner was in a screaming dive, the wind a cyclonic roar, the whole airframe shuddering from the terrific forces of the dive, and the air-speed indicator went around the gauge and the needle just stuck, pegged all the way, as far as it would go.

Still grinning, the world about him gone mad, Luther began a steady and strong back pressure on the yoke to pull out of the dive. The Ju-52 wouldn't have any part of it and screamed its way earthward like a great winged bomb. The mechanic grabbed the other yoke and began pulling and still the ma-

chine wouldn't budge. Finally the observer crawled desperately into the cockpit and added all his strength to the right yoke, and the three men strained and hauled and tugged with all their might. Slowly, the Iron Annie began to lift up her nose, and when she came out of the dive the g-loads were so great they heard violent thrashing and banging sounds all through the airplane, and their vision blurred and began to gray and then darkness from the tremendous pressure hit them as the blood drained from their heads. When they could see again, the Ju-52 was climbing gently— still in one piece.

Luther brought her down, a bit gingerly because of the stunned look on the faces of the other men in the airplane. When they were on the ground and parked, a great crowd assembled; they had all heard the screaming sound for miles around as the Ju-52 howled earthward, and no one quite believed the sight as the airplane emerged from its vertical dive and curved back into normal flight.

Now they looked up at a Ju-52 that seemed to have been run over by a whole convoy of bull-

Right wing down for a stiff crosswind, a
Lufthansa Ju-52/3m "jumps" into the air
for a mountain takeoff in Peru. LUFTHANSA

dozers. The wings were bent up in an impossible
angle, and the upper wing attachments for each
wing had been bent, literally wrenched violently,
out of shape.

The airplane was declared unflyable without extensive repairs and rebuilding.

Yet it *had* flown home, and Luther was still grinning, for it's always a neat feeling to do what everyone knows is impossible.

And everyone *knows* you can't dive a three-engine airliner like a dive bomber. Everyone, it
seemed, except Luther and the Iron Annie.

An Ecuadorian Ju-52 on a high mountain
flight in 1937. LUFTHANSA

"They used to drive us crazy. I mean that. If it was a contest, those bastards were winning it hands down. It was the damnedest game of chicken you ever saw in your life. Obviously they were acting under orders. We were flying DC-2s at the time, working the South American routes, and the Germans had a bunch of their Ju-52s there. The three-engine jobs. They flew for different South American airlines, but the pilots were German. I don't know if they were airline types from Lufthansa, or their subsidiary, Condor, but we tended to believe they were really German Air Force types, you know, the Luftwaffe, assigned to the Junkers that flew the really important routes in South America."

We were seated around a great oaken table in Jacksonville, Florida, a collection of pilots who went back to the earlier days of flying. Within this select group were some of the greatest names in aviation. There were chief pilots of airlines, men with twenty and thirty thousand hours who had flown everything and done just about everything. There were cargo haulers and fighter pilots and two men who had been awarded the Medal of Honor. Quite a group, and a rare privilege for the crew of *Iron Annie*. With me were my wife, Dee Dee, Larry Urback, and Ted Votoe, who was riding this trip as flight engineer. The man who held our attention was in his sixties, a heavy-set pilot still in excellent physical shape, still with all his ratings.

"I'm convinced they were under orders," the speaker continued. "You know, they were out to impress the South Americans that the Germans were real men and the Americans would give way under any real pressure, and so they poured the stuff at us. We'd be coming in for a landing in the DC-2, lined up on final approach, everything squared away—it didn't matter if there was a tower or not, it seemed—and as we came down the last segment of the approach and began to flare for landing, why, there would be this big, three-engine

thing coming straight at us, and one of those airplanes *had* to give. Like I say, it was the craziest game of chicken I'd ever known."

I asked the inevitable question. "Who won?"

He looked at me with open, blue eyes. "Who do you think? *They* did. We didn't doubt for a moment that those bastards were going to keep right on coming even if it meant a head-on collision. I mean that. They just kept boring right in, and a few times we'd hold our course until there was only a second or two left in which to break away, and then we *knew* they wouldn't yield. Well, in that kind of game there aren't any winners, so we would break off and they'd take their bloody time about landing. Then we would land. The South Americans thought it was a great joke, and those Krauts did some pretty fancy strutting about it. Not to us. They sort of looked shame-faced about it, like they didn't want to do what they were doing, but orders were orders. I mean, we were all pilots, we all flew on those pretty rotten routes, mountains and stinking weather and all that, and we respected one another." He sighed. "But it was their ball game, all the way."

———◆———

This sort of athletic flying activity did not go unnoticed in Washington, D.C. Intelligence was one of the great sidelines of foreign pressure in the South American potboiler just prior to World War II, and there was some wild-eyed jockeying going on behind the scenes to get on the side of the power boys who ran governments in the big continent below the Panama Canal. Germany, through Lufthansa and Condor and other heavy interests, was doing an excellent job of muscling in and getting power behind the scenes. In fact, the Germans were so popular that it was the belief of most experienced people on the scene that if there had *not* been a war, within a few years we would have been pushed out of the picture strictly on the basis of German success in the flying, industrial, financial, and political scenes.

But you had to be blind not to recognize what was in the offing. By late 1941, of course, war was raging across Europe. Germany's panzers had swept through almost every country on the continent, and at that moment they were making hash out of the best Russia could do to defend herself against the devastating blitzkrieg of the Wehrmacht and the Luftwaffe.

Meanwhile, in Central America, three Ju-52/3m airliners had been the subject of very special attention on the part of American intelligence. The aircraft were flown for an airlines company whose ownership was unquestionably that of a local government. But the crews were very much German. In fact, Intelligence determined the crews were Luftwaffe—full-fledged members of the German Air Force who had been assigned to the three airplanes for a military mission the exact timing of which was yet to be provided the pilots. But there was some other interesting information: The airliners were more than they seemed, and several agents confirmed that the strange equipment beneath the Ju-52s was for carrying bombs. Then it was confirmed. . . .

As soon as the Germans received word that the Japanese had struck Pearl Harbor, the three Ju-52s would be bombed up and would set out immediately to drop their bombs against the key locks and other installations of the Panama Canal, in one stroke paralyzing the vital waterway between the Atlantic and Pacific oceans. When news of the massive air strike was flashed around the world, American teams that had been keeping the trio of Ju-52s under surveillance moved immediately.

So did the Germans—who were already loading bombs aboard the planes. There was a rush of vehicles onto the field, a flurry of gunfire, and in a desperately short time two of the Ju-52 airliners that were about to become bombers were destroyed.

The third Ju-52 was captured. And it is strange to tell, but had not this third airplane survived, this story likely would never have seen print. I have researched it in hundreds of histories and found only the vaguest references to the use of German aircraft in Central and South America to attack the Panama Canal. Most of these called for the crews to make their bombing runs and then head out to

sea, where they would abandon their planes by parachute, to be picked up by waiting German submarines.

But there is not a single word about the operation involving the three Ju-52s in the untold incident of the Panama Canal. It is the last surviving transport that kept alive the story and of which pictures were finally made available in an obscure publication. For this particular Ju-52 was taken over by the American Government, and it was modified with American instruments and radios, and, among other things, fitted out with new engines, fully enclosed cowlings, and three-bladed constant-speed propellers. And then it was put to work, and it flew the rest of the war under the control of the Department of Public Roads, and *that's* how we know the story, through tracking down the record of this one surviving machine. Its job during the war? To assist in building what is now the Pan-American Highway—by carrying dynamite and various types of explosives and blasting equipment to advanced-field airstrips.

And as we shall see later, this is not the only incident of "ghost Ju-52s" that never quite made it into the history books.

————◆————

About the only role the Ju-52/3m did not play in the Luftwaffe before and during the Second World War was that of fighter aircraft, because it certainly seems to have fulfilled every other possible task that could fall to an airplane. We've seen that the great strength and ruggedness of the Ju-52, as well as its ability to operate in the field with the most primitive of maintenance, forced its use in banana wars and revolutions and the big wars as well. From the Gran Chaco on, wherever a "do anything" airplane was needed and nothing else was available—enter the Ju-52 on stage center.

It was used in the capacity we already know as a transport, and this includes carrying passengers or cargo and often both. It was modified into a bomber. It was an assault transport and often dropped paratroopers on strike missions. It was fitted with an enormous hoop slung beneath the airplane, driven by a gasoline engine inside the fuselage that created various types of magnetic fields to blow up mines floating in the sea. Its first missions as a bomber were simple enough: bombs were rolled out the door or hand-dropped through belly hatches, until the airplane was modified in all its proper regalia as a full-fledged bomber (to the horror of Hugo Junkers, it should be added, who saw in this move a desecration of his design). It was an airplane, a ski-plane, and a seaplane. At times it was a flying arsenal: in its early days of revolutions and private wars it was used as a platform from which men fired pistols and rifles and finally machine guns. But there were also military versions built with a gun position just above the cockpit (the gunner, in fact, stood on the control quadrant *in* the cockpit, between the two pilots) and a gun position in a manual turret far back along the fuselage. Some models even had power turrets amidships in the cabin, so that one might see a Ju-52 with one, two, or three dorsal gun positions. Some models placed the cockpit gun within a bubble, a sort of great plexiglas bowl, because it got pretty nasty standing up in the blast of the nose engine and the air stream, and it even got damned near impossible to breathe in that sort of screaming gale. There were other weapons, such as a machine gun in a dustbin that hinged down into position between the gear. Some models had six machine guns—as well as all the upper guns—in side-firing positions. And some Ju-52s were built with bomb bays and bomb racks beneath the fuselage and the wings. No one ever knew what to expect from the lumbering Ju-52, for at times the plodding old lady seemed to sprout machine guns like a porcupine growing new needles in every direction. German troops, facing enemy fighters or bombers boring in at them, would smash out the windows of the cabin, leveling their personal machine guns in defense to augment the regular gun positions.

The Ju-52, like the C-47 (the DC-3 in military colors), was a do-everything airplane (yes, there were C-47s with gun turrets and that also carried bombs), and most of its missions were those that wore the crews weary, that had them flying in miserable weather, that had them trying every trick in the book to keep from being shot down when fighters came howling in after them—roles for which neither airplane was ever intended, in which they were never well represented, and from which they survived only by dint of their great strength.

◆

The first attempt to develop a bomber from the basic design of the Ju-52/3m died in conference. Hugo Junkers and Kurt Weil, at that time develop-ing the design philosophy of the machine, were approached secretly by members of the German Government and asked to prepare a complete bomber modification. Junkers responded with that sense of horror reported before: not at the idea that a Junkers airplane would be used for combat (for Junkers produced some of the greatest combat planes ever made, such as the Ju-87 dive bomber and that all-too-splendid machine the twin-engine Ju-88) but because he simply thought it was a lousy idea. He felt the Ju-52, in essence, would be a lousy bomber. To Junkers, you designed an airplane from the outset for its job and made whatever design inputs were necessary for the machine to perform its job. Last-minute design changes were to Junkers a disease to be avoided at all costs.

His aesthetic sentiments notwithstanding, Junkers was finally forced simply to follow orders. In 1934 the new German Air Force—the Luftwaffe —was still officially a secret organization, but it tested one of the airplanes and then ordered two versions: the straight transport model and a bomber modification. During the 1934–35 period, the Luftwaffe received *more than four hundred and fifty* of the new Ju-52/3mg3e aircraft fitted out to serve either as a transport or a bomber, but most of the machines went into a program of training pilots and air crews, building up a powerful logistics fleet, and starting the development or airborne assault forces and gliders for both invasion and cargo-supply missions. It was an enormous effort and one that seemed well concealed from most of the world.

What is just as surprising about the development of the bomber version of the airplane is that even the German Air Force, in its initial study of the design, *turned it down* because of very obvious shortcomings. They had discovered on their own precisely what Hugo Junkers had told other officers long before. Luftwaffe designs and production called for the use of bombers in which the bomb bays would hold their cargoes in a horizontal position. And this couldn't be done with the Ju-52, because directly beneath the cargo compartment was the wing section, with its four sets of double-strutted main wing spars. The spacing between the spars was so narrow (which gave the wing its great strength) that it was impossible to place a bomb in a horizontal position, even if the bomb size was only one hundred ten pounds. But there was another way, and the Luftwaffe took it, be-

The bomber variant of the Ju-52/3m that first armed the Luftwaffe in the mid-thirties and then went into combat in Spain. Armed with top and bottom turrets, it carried 3,360 pounds of bombs and was known to the Spanish as Pavo—Tough Turkey. CAIDIN ARCHIVES

cause at that time they *needed* the Ju-52 as a bomber. The airplanes being developed from the outset as bombers had run into a disastrous string of development problems, and the Air Force wanted the Ju-52/3mg3e to fill the gap.

What they couldn't do with horizontal racks could be done by storing the bombs in a vertical position. Engineers produced what was known as the "vertical bomb magazine," typed as the DCAS/250, and installed three of these magazines in the freight cabin of the airplane. These held up to thirty-three hundred pounds of bombs, in combinations of either twenty-four 110-pound missiles, six 550-pound bombs, or mixtures of these.

The Ju-52/3mg3e was given the rather inelegant name of *Behelfsbomber* (auxiliary bomber) and further modified for its new role. The bomb magazines were installed without doors or covers beneath the racks, simplifying dropping the weapons.

Just cut 'em loose and away they went with nothing to impede their drop. A Lotfe bomb-aim mechanism was mounted in a fairing beneath the fuselage, controls for setting fuses were placed in the cabin, and the bombardier was provided with a mechanical lever to trip the bombs free. If conditions permitted, the bombardier had a control stick he used to complete final course corrections as he sighted through the Lotfe device.

For the first time, gun positions were built into the aircraft. There was the dorsal position, well aft of the cabin, with its windscreen and a D30 or D52 circular mount for a single machine gun, which mounted the equivalent of either a .30- or a .50-caliber machine gun, the final decision often being left to the crew, which usually grabbed the heaviest firepower available. For protection against belly attacks, there was the hinged dustbin. For takeoff and landing, the lower portion of this rather precarious and drafty gunner's position, which hinged like a folding basket, was winched into its up position and, when airborne, was winched down so the gunner could clamber into his odd-shaped eggshell.

The expected military modifications went into the airplane. Radio and navigation systems met Luftwaffe specifications, the gravity-feed fuel tank in the cockpit was removed because of its obvious fire danger, two additional tanks were installed in the wings, and provision was made to jettison wing fuel in flight (the last item was soon deleted in following models as a complete waste). The crew was usually four men, sometimes five, depending upon the mission. The engines were standardized as the BMW 132A variants each of 660 horsepower, giving the airplane an honest cruise of about 125 miles per hour.

When the Spanish Civil War erupted, in 1936, twenty Ju-52/3mg3e bombers, along with six Heinkel He-51 biplane fighters, were rushed to Spain to fight under the colors of General Francisco Franco Bahamonde, who led the revolutionaries. At first the bomber role was ignored, and the bomb magazines, in fact, were removed from the aircraft so they could carry out the bulk of a vast troop movement: flying nearly ten thousand Moorish soldiers from Morocco to Spain. As many as fifty soldiers were carried aboard each aircraft on a nearly constant troop transfer. With this initial mission out of the way, German pilots began training Spanish crews at Seville, even as the Germans were in combat while wearing Spanish uniforms.

But by November of 1936 there was little pretense left as Germany formed its Condor Legion of "volunteers" who manned bombers, transports, fighters, seaplanes, and special support groups. The Germans wore Spanish Nationalist uniforms and flew in Spanish-marked aircraft, the same sort of role American pilots filled when flying as volunteers for the AVG (American Volunteer Group) in China in 1941, using Curtiss P-40B Tomahawks as their fighters.

The Ju-52s operated through all of Spain and through almost all the fighting, and were soon favorites among Spanish crews because of their ability to stand up under primitive field conditions and their reliability in remaining operational. They were known to the Spanish crews as Pavo, which can be roughly translated as "tough turkey." In that little-known air war of the Ju-52s in their first military role in appreciable numbers, the Pavos flew thirteen thousand operational hours on fifty-four hundred combat sorties, dropping six thousand tons of bombs. They were considered a major factor in Franco's success, and Hitler went so far as to trumpet that without these airplanes the issue would have been seriously in doubt.

Only five Ju-52s went down in battle (three more were wiped out on the ground from air strikes by enemy planes), and among old-time pilots there is the legendary struggle still talked about in awed tones of a single Ju-52 caught by twenty-four Russian I-15 fighter planes. For twenty minutes the Russians swarmed all over that lone Ju-52, firing almost steadily, hacking and chewing the hapless transport into flying junk. Pieces of metal were shot away, oil streaked both wings, the cockpit was a shambles, and the cabin was shattered from front to back. Again and again the Russians tore at the Ju-52 until, finally, like a huge whale whose great energy has been sapped by an endless stream of sharks, the big airplane began to slide off on one wing, its crew dead or dying, and fell to earth.

But in legend it would fly forever. . . .

If it had to be moved to the front, then almost certainly, if it could be fitted into an airplane, it went by Ju-52. There were other transports, but they were scarce in numbers in comparison to the fleets of Ju-52s that crossed Europe and droned through the Mediterranean and North Africa. The Ju-52's role of bomber was gone by the late thirties, for by then the Luftwaffe had the bomber fleets it needed and the Ju-52's most critical assignment was logistical support for the ground and air forces. Thus the greater majority of combat action for the Ju-52 crews was this plodding, incessant, repetitive hauling of every kind of cargo and freight one might imagine, as well as always returning fully loaded from the front with wounded or returning veterans.

A large number of Ju-52s were pulled from combat units and assigned to research, development, and special missions. To the Luftwaffe and the various technical people there could hardly have been a better machine for research and testing than the stable, reliable Ju-52. Early in the war, special pilots were flying into airfields under zero-zero conditions, using the latest navigation aids to prove that with proper training and ground crews equally as skilled as those in the cockpits, the airplanes could be flown under conditions otherwise assumed impossible. One of the men who flew these initial tests of landing in thick fog was Kurt Streit. He was also part of that special force of test pilots who towed gliders with rigid towbars or hauled as many as three large, troop-carrying gliders on a single tow behind one Ju-52. Testing new de-icing equipment, carrying other aircraft atop the Ju-52 (the early Mistel piggyback composite flights), engine tests—name it and the Ju-52 was doing it.

At one point the airplane was even studied, and very seriously indeed, as a special flying platform to be used against tanks and armored vehicles. The Germans modified the fuselage and mounted an 88-millimeter, high-velocity, anti-tank cannon beneath the aircraft. In combat trials the flying artillery piece proved unusually successful because of its extraordinary stability, but the project was passed by for several reasons, paramount among them the fact that Ju-52s were needed desperately for their cargo role, and if they were flying in areas where enemy air defenses were strong, they would absolutely need heavy fighter escort to guarantee their survival.

There's no question that the overwhelming evaluation of the Ju-52 was that it fully earned its name of Iron Annie, or, with somewhat more affection, as Tante Ju (Auntie Junkers). It was without doubt the most successful transport aircraft of its type ever built.

All this becomes even more remarkable when one remembers that this airplane was a *1929* design, and that its secret of success was not adaptation or major improvements in the basic structure of the aircraft but its absolutes of simplicity, ruggedness, and reliability. Consider the great number of Ju-52s built, its use as the main *fleet* of aircraft, and in that context what becomes meaningful is the strong fixed landing gear, the fixed-pitch propellers, the manual systems throughout. Except for the compressed-air system to operate the brakes and the vacuum systems (pumps and external venturi tubes) for instruments and windshield wipers, everything was operated by muscle power. There was never a problem with the control surfaces or the trim or the great flaps. The "Mighty Wheel" attended to the latter items. Even electrical power, if the engine-driven generators went out, could be maintained by an external generator mounted on the upper fuselage to provide power for radios and lights. There wasn't a hydraulic line in the airplane, and all the problems associated with constant-

A rare picture showing a Lufthansa airliner that, by a stroke of the pen, was pulled from the Lufthansa register and transferred to the Luftwaffe. This is a 1939 aircraft in the process of being repainted for military assignment. The top turret has not yet been installed, but what is remarkable is the dustbin belly-gun position already on the airplane, shown just behind the landing gear. MESSERSCHMITT-BOLKOW-BLOHM

speed propellers, governors, hydraulic motors and systems, electric motors and systems, ad infinitum, were *absent* from the Ju-52. It is not difficult to understand why its reliability index was so incredibly high, and why the crews and passengers had such overwhelming faith in the corrugated-iron bird.

Now, there are some minus factors as well as all the plus elements, and it behooves us to examine these weaknesses and judge them for what they were. For the weaknesses inherent in the design of the military transport *did not exist in the airplane designed for its commercial role.* And what faults were present in the civil Ju-52 were within easy correction without seriously complicating the basic design.

That the Luftwaffe hierarchy did not recognize the weaknesses that would spring instantly into reality when they impressed the Ju-52 into service as a military aircraft is not a fault of the aircraft but, rather, an expression of utter stupidity on the part of German thinking and practice. Perhaps the industry is equally guilty of not pursuing the matter, but in any event, weaknesses in the military version were so glaring *they could easily have been avoided from the outset of military operations.*

For example, we noted earlier that the fuel tanks within the wings were in the form of drums, bolted into place and secured with metal and leather straps. These were not of self-sealing materials and were therefore extraordinarily vulnerable to enemy gunfire, especially if tracer ammunition was used, and even more so if the tanks were partially empty so that they were subject to inner explosions from their vapors. Sending an airplane with this fuel tankage system into a combat environment was both murderous and stupid, and yet this is precisely what the German authorities did. Someone up high in the decision-making process decided that the fire-extinguishing system for the engines, which pumped a fire depressant through five nozzles into each engine, would suffice against any fire. But it didn't, not in the slightest, simply because a fire in the wing tanks would never be affected by what was going on within the engine. Self-sealing tanks, which the Germans had developed to a very high degree, would have cut the loss rate of Ju-52s from fuel tanks set aflame by perhaps 80–90 per cent—and this is based on estimates made by fighter pilots who fought *against* the Ju-52. Their reports remain remarkably consistent: you could shoot the hell out of the airplane and it would weather its blows, so you went for the two really vulnerable areas: the fuel tanks in the wings, and the flight crew, which flew into raging air battles, as well as massive ground fire, *without* any armor plate for protection!

The durability of the Ju-52 in the Gran Chaco War, and its incredible record in Spain, misled many of the authorities as to its survivability under heavy firepower. It was a lesson to be learned by all combatants, of course, for certain aircraft were more likely to burn than others, depending upon the vulnerability of fuel cells, hydraulic lines, electrical systems, and other areas.

In any event, the conclusion is inescapable: the Ju-52 was vulnerable to tracer ammunition and fire in its wing tanks, and it lacked sorely for crew armor plating.

Other than these two items, it was about impossible to fault the Ju-52. It was such a hell-for-leather, stout airplane, so intrinsically strong and durable, an airplane of which every part played a role, that its usefulness finally was categorized as extraordinary.

By now we're sufficiently well acquainted with the Ju-52 to identify the progressively different and improved aircraft built specifically to the needs of the German Air Force. The basic Ju-52/3mg3e, which was produced in such large numbers in 1934-35, is one clue to the sudden rapid production of the aircraft and reflects on the growing expansion of Junkers plants throughout Germany. Another indication of much greater production than is indicated in the factory tally sheets is that before the year 1935 was over, the g3e production line had already been changed to accommodate the newer Ju-52/3mg4e. This was the first military transport in the Ju-52/3m series produced from the outset for this role, yet provisions were also made for carrying bombs. There is some confusion as to just when this model first rolled off the production lines and when it first flew. German records show that the airplane *officially* replaced the g3e model in 1935, but other records also indicate that the first test flight of the airplane came about in 1937. I am inclined not to believe that the entire year of 1936 and part of 1937 went by without a single Ju-52 under manufacture for the Luftwaffe.

In any event, the g4e reflected the future role of the Ju-52/3m series. It was built in so many variations that it was impossible to know what specific subtype was involved unless you referred to a specific aircraft. All the g4e models came off the production line with the same BMW 132A engines of the g3e, but the floor of the main cabin, the freight compartment, was strengthened, extra-large cargo loading doors were installed in the roof and the right side of the fuselage, load-securing rigs were installed along the cabin interior, and the landing gear was beefed up to meet the needs of a basic gross weight of 23,150 pounds. In its military role it was essentially a transport—but that meant carrying troops or paratroopers, serving as a flying classroom, a squadron staff aircraft, or an ambulance, or even being outfitted with luxury accommodations as a commercial airliner, for a number of the g4es were put into service with Lufthansa.

As an armed transport, once again the variations in equipment were unpredictable. Some machines retained the oversized dustbin—the gunner-carrying metal bucket—beneath the belly, but these were soon discarded as cumbersome and excessive in drag and weight. There were g4e models with one turret and others with two turret positions, and the types of weapons varied from .30 to .60 caliber. All models except those assigned to flight-training crews were able to use window mounts for additional machine guns—including the civil versions, which could be pressed into military service at any time.

The g5e model came along with BMW 132T engines, which also showed up in models from 660 to 830 horsepower, and again the variations in type were many. This was the first military Ju-52 to recognize one of the aircraft's few dangerous characteristics: The Ju-52 was not an airplane made for flying in icing conditions, because an accumulation of ice buildup between the trailing edge of the main wing and the leading edge of the second wing often locked the ailerons in place, or even reversed their effect in control. So the rule of thumb was that if ice was encountered in flight—*get the hell out, and NOW.* The g5e was the first move to eliminate this problem. A space was provided just aft of the leading edge of the wings, from the engines outboard to the wingtips, through which very hot air from the wing-engine exhausts was ducted to keep the wing leading edges too hot for ice to form in flight. The tailplane was kept ice-free by rubberized moldings that changed shape, popping in and out along the leading edges, to break up any accumulating ice (some g5e models used the rubber moldings for the main wing as well). The molded systems were powered with a pneumatic generator operated by the nose engine. Sufficient experience had been obtained by then with severe weather to call for improved carburetor (preheat or ice-removal heat) heat systems for

Adolf Hitler—having departed the Ju-52 (in Lufthansa *and* Luftwaffe markings)—preparing for a formal military review. QUICK

all three engines. The g5e was also set up for quick changes from wheels to skis or floats, and operated in all German theaters. It was one of the most heavily armed transports, with two top turrets and at least five machine guns in side-window mounts as well. The empty weight had gone up to 24,200 pounds in the float version. The g5e was in full production early in 1941.

The only real changes in the g6e model were in radio equipment and assignment to units where floats would not be needed. By the Ju-52/3mg7e version, the type was rather well standardized, and in effect the g7e was a g5e capable of wheel or float operations but with a larger loading door, some cabin changes, and a fully automatic pilot. It was used for every job that came along but was intended as a "pure transport aircraft" with the as-

signment of carrying eighteen fully equipped troops or twelve stretcher cases. Armament was standardized at one turret weapon in the after fuselage and two side-firing machine guns, but this arrangement remained standard no longer than the time it took the airplane to get into the hands of operational units.

Along came the g8e, with all the refinements of its predecessor but also an improved cockpit-window arrangement for greater visibility, heavy defensive machine guns, and engines that varied from the BMW 132T to the 132Z models. The g9e featured a strengthened gear to handle a new gross weight of 25,350 pounds. Many of these types were modified for operations in tropical areas and were also known as the Ju-52/3mg4e Trop. Its successor, the g10e, was intended mainly for cargo work and featured much larger loading doors. It was needed in a great hurry for combat work and was rushed to the field without de-icing equipment. This was felt to be a great error, and the g11e showed up at once, being the same as the g10e except for full de-icing gear. The g12E, g13e, and g14e were essentially of the basic Ju-52 design, by now so far beyond special-purpose intentions that the aircraft were officially considered "multipurpose transports." After they rolled from the factories, they were fitted out for special missions as needed, and one reflection of closing the barn door after the horse was long gone was retrofitting armor plating to the cockpit area.

———◆———

In describing the historical development of the Ju-52/3m as a military aircraft, I did not mention the Junkers K45, which played a critical role in the development of the Ju-52, nor did I mention, of course, where the K45 was developed and then put into manufacture.

This is because the K-45 is the Ju-52/3m. At that time, when the German Government was planning for the re-creation of the German Air Force, it was necessary to move *out* of Germany in order that long-term preparations might be started for the forthcoming Luftwaffe. The Versaille Treaty limited the size of the German military forces and restricted development of weapons. The Junkers Company, like many others, followed the dictates of Berlin and established a major industrial facility in Sweden (as it did in several other countries), and it was in Sweden that the first military aircraft were developed in secret. Note that the original order, for four hundred and fifty g3e machines, was placed in 1934 but that the Luftwaffe was not officially organized until 1935, at which time the Germans felt it vital to have an *immediate* bomber presence, and thus the impetus for the auxiliary bomber category, until Heinkel, Dornier, and other manufacturers could get into the act with machines rid of their teething troubles.

But it is for these reasons, as well as many others, that I have refused to accept hard specifics as germane to the *accurate* history of the Ju-52. Iron Annie deserves better than this, and accuracy is best served by acceptance of the fact that secrecy, destroyed records, deliberately misleading designations, factories scattered through various countries . . . well, if generalization is our lot, better to accept that reality than to insist on securing rigid numbers that are meaningless.

It is another element of strange when we consider that the Ju-52 was the backbone, the great airborne logistics strength, of the Luftwaffe, that the machine fought in several wars before it ever entered a combat situation under the German flag—and then only as a show of strength. The first major use of the Ju-52 by the Luftwaffe, openly, before the eyes of the world, came about in March of 1938, when hundreds of Ju-52s in impressive formation, carrying airborne troops and paratroopers, made up much of the German show of strength in the Austrian *Anschluss.* The anvil was the hapless people staring in numbered awe and fear at the clanking thunder of German armor and troops on the ground and the darkened skies with hundreds of Ju-52s as well as Luftwaffe fighters and bombers. Thus the first combat mission of the Ju-52 as a German weapon under German colors was so eminently, even brilliantly, a success.

It never fired a shot.

The crews assembled mainly at Tempelhof, in Berlin, and other selected fields, under high security, in Silesia. Hundreds of Ju-52s fueled up, weapons at the ready, crews standing by their aircraft, waiting to take on paratroopers and heavy forces of ground troops to be moved to the forwardmost wedge of the blitzkrieg forces. On the first of September of 1939, the Wehrmacht struck, the powerful armored forces thundering ahead behind wave after wave of bombers, devastating the stunned and overwhelmed Poles.

The paratroopers and special forces deployed throughout Lower Silesia, members of the 7th Air Division, waited in vain for their signal to move out, to attack bridges ahead of armored columns, to isolate Polish combat forces in the field, and to leap into any situation in which need for airborne forces would emerge. But the paratroopers never jumped, they never received their signals to commit. The panzers and motorized infantry columns, spearheaded always by the shattering attacks of fighters and bombers, tore apart effective resistance. The war ended before a single need for an airborne drop could be demonstrated, and the hundreds of Ju-52 transports flew what can only be described as a leisurely war, bringing in fresh troops, supplies, and curious observers from Berlin. What was to the Poles a terrible defeat, to the German Army and Air Force a stunning victory, was to the flight crews of the Ju-52s an easy and rarely dangerous support of victorious armies on the ground.

Not so the invasions of Denmark and Norway, launched by Berlin simultaneously on April 9, 1940. Paratroopers were critical to this double operation, and the men were committed in heavy numbers to special targets in what would be the first operational airborne invasion in history: Exercise Weser (*Weserübung*). The occupation of Denmark—accomplished in a matter of hours—was really no test

of airborne forces, because the Danish Army was so small and weak, the country itself invaded by powerful armor and infantry, again behind overwhelming fighter and bomber cover, that resistance to the invasion was already history within twenty-four hours of the first move.

The Norwegians were another matter. The distances were so great that the key to a swift invasion and equally swift success depended to an enormous degree on air cover by the Luftwaffe

Ju-52/3m assault transports with paratroops, shock troops, and war supplies were assembled by the hundreds in special combat-ready zones for major assaults and invasions. MESSERSCHMITT-BOLKOW-BLOHM

over the German ground and sea forces committed to the attack. This meant that Norwegian airfields had to be captured almost at once and placed at the disposal of German fighters, which would then operate directly in the battle area.

The key to the invasion of Norway became the available forces of Ju-52 transports. Paratroopers would attack and seize airfields in northern Jutland (Denmark), while others flew on to fields in southern Norway, to be reinforced by Ju-52-transported infantry the moment the airfields were secured. It was a tight and intricate operation, and the German planners had little help from Hitler, who refused to release to the invasion his 7th Air Division, of several hundred transport planes and more than twelve thousand crack troops—*they* were already involved in plans for the invasion of Russia in the near future (a date ultimately moved back to 22 June 1941).

One is never quite sure how history will record events on which the fate of nations hinged, but whatever is said or written of *Weserübung* will unquestionably miss its mark. The entire invasion of Norway was a complete reversal of what had happened in Poland. There the Germans struck with shattering firepower and overwhelming weight of their forces. It didn't matter if the strikes were on time or delayed or even took place too early. Whatever happened, the German sledgehammer rose and fell again and again with ultimate impact. It was a monstrous bulldozer clanking inexorably across the land and utterly mauling all in its path, its catalyst the German troops, who showed no quarter in their slaughter of their outnumbered enemy.

The airborne assault against the critical airfields of Jutland and southern Norway called for the use of but *one battalion*. The commanding general of the operation, General Nikolaus von Falkenhorst, was told he could have the 1st Battalion, 1st Parachute Regiment—with four companies of airborne troops. One company would hit in Jutland and the other three in Norway. And even more tempting of utter disbelief was the fact that one platoon—*one platoon only!*—was to drop against and seize immediate control of two separate (and vital) airfields at Aalborg, in northern Jutland.

One platoon!

Despite all the seaborne forces (which had to go in on warships because there were no landing craft) and other support, the invasion of Norway must go down in history as one of the most audacious and outrageous military strikes of all time. There was no bludgeon here, no great lines of motorized vehicles holding fresh troops, no panzers wheeling across the countryside, no swarm of fighters and bombers from the skies to crush all before them—here there were superb timing, a small but outstanding force of paratroopers, and a brilliant psychological appraisal of the enemy facing the Germans. For the German planners were well aware that while the Danish Army would crumble like ashes squeezed in the hand, the Norwegians were liable to fight violently at key spots, and the presence of the British, especially at sea, provided the greatest risk to the invasion plan.

Everything hung on the success of the paratroopers and whatever fighters could hover above them for air support, and the only fighters with sufficient range to do that job were Messerschmitt Me-110 twin-engine jobs. And everything that moved needed, of course, at least a hint of some decent weather.

John Weeks, of *War Monthly*, summed it up well: "It was a tremendously risky plan of great daring. If the landings were not exactly simultaneous, all the Norwegian coast would be altered. Late landings would thus end in disaster, for . . . the only way to put troops ashore was to come alongside a jetty and put down gangplanks. As soon as the landings had been made, it was vital that the Luftwaffe give them continuous reconnaissance and support. For this the airfields had to be taken, hence the urgency of the parachute operation. The sea landings were to go in three hours later, after the Luftwaffe had strafed the airfields and cleared off any fighter opposition."

I wonder what Von Falkenhorst must have thought of all this, as well as a chill warning from Berlin. The general would have at his disposal more than five hundred troop-carrying planes for the invasion. Ten groups of Ju-52s would carry paratroopers and assault infantry, and behind them would come another group of four-engine Junkers Ju-90 and Focke-Wulf FW-200 transports for final operations to wrap up the operation. But, cautioned Berlin, Von Falkenhorst must exercise special care with his transports. He was warned by headquarters that under no conditions was he to use the transport planes unless conditions were favorable to them and there would be no undue risk to their survival!

The invasion of Norway, despite whatever serious, grim, and even tragic overtones were involved, every minute became more and more a gap-toothed parody of a military operation. And had the British any concept of just how flimsy was the time scale and the paratroop forces, they could, with a single sweep of fighter planes, have utterly and unquestionably wrecked the entire invasion.

But the Germans were correct in their assessment. Strike with daring, use savagery wherever necessary, and at once, to leave no questions for the Norwegians that resistance would be crushed, and proceed as if all the hordes of Germany were supporting the initial aerial assault.

And everything depended on the Ju-52s. . . .

How fate doth flip its coins! The German forces prepared themselves the long night of April 8–9, a great springboard to be unleashed with first light of the ninth. Five hundred Ju-52s and the small force of four-engine planes, *and* the reconnaissance planes, *and* the fighters, stood silent and unmoving as dawn brought with it heavy rain, clouds scudding low over the ground, and winds that often howled from forty to sixty miles per hour. The weather was atrocious. Even at sea the outlook was bleak, and if one could listen to the German troops moving through a thundering storm, the anvil chorus of *Weserübung* would have been to the tune of thousands of men retching violently from seasickness.

Then came the electrifying word that the cloud deck at Aalborg, Denmark, had lifted enough for a jump from low altitude—and *that* meant going out at approximately three hundred and fifty feet above the ground. Two Ju-52s were off the ground at once and sped to their targets, flying on the deck and then lifting enough to send the troops out. Thirty men—the entire force of thirty men in one platoon—dropped from the two Junkers with perfect precision, directly into their intended target zone. German parachutes left much to be desired; compared to American and British parachutes, they were clumsy, even archaic in their handling, and the German paratroopers couldn't even carry rifles with them. All weapons except pistols were dropped in separate containers.

Against all these odds, the thirty men of the *Fallschirmjäger* (paratroop) platoon ran at full speed for two airfields, rushed to their targets—*and*

occupied the fields without a single shot being fired at them. There was simply no opposition, and within thirty minutes of leaping from the open doors of the Ju-52s, the paratroopers had the field in a defensive crossfire (but with no one against whom they could shoot) and flashed the word back to the German airfields. The Ju-52s began roaring in, one after another, accompanied by the long-range Me-110 fighters, and before the morning was over, Aalborg was an operational German airfield.

Other jumps with small forces went with the same spectacular success, even with defending troops facing the Germans. To take a critical two-mile-long bridge, the paratroopers went out of two formations of Ju-52s, each formation a tight vee. They hit the ground and without waiting even to pick up their rifles and heavier weapons, slipped from their harness gear, firing their pistols into the air and shouting and yelling battle cries at the stunned Danes defending the bridge posts. So terrified were the Danes at the sight of men pouring from the skies and opening fire at them immediately that they surrendered at once. Sixty paratroopers took over the most vital bridge in all Denmark and *then* went back to get their rifles, machine guns, mortars, and ammunition.

Daring, courage, and split-second timing had paid off with incredible success, for not a single German life had yet been lost. But it would be tougher going, up at the Sola Airfield, in Norway, near Stavanger. The weather could be described only as horrible, and General Nikolaus von Falkenhorst had some bad, nail-biting moments when he was told his Ju-52 pilots were ignoring their orders not to take unnecessary risks. The Me-110 fighter pilots shook their heads in disbelief as the transports, holding tight formation, *bored down to thirty feet above the rugged terrain* to find their way to the drop zones. Most of the fighters pulled up into the thick murk and started back for their home fields, but as great good fortune would have it for the Ju-52s, just one hour before they groped their way to Sola, six Me-110s had reached the field and torn it apart with devastating strafing runs. Stable and armed with two cannon and four machine guns in the nose, as well as a gun firing from a rear position, the Me-110s were exceptionally destructive as they went around and around the field on the deck, tearing up defensive machine-gun positions. This cut down the firepower available to the Norwegians, but there were still some Norse troops full of fight as the Ju-52s burst out of the low cloud. There were breaks in the clouds and fog, and the Norwegians stared in disbelief as the formation of Ju-52s, still flying at treetop level, hauled up in steep climbs, leveled off in formation at four hundred feet, and disgorged their paratroopers.

Two concrete pillboxes with heavy machine guns dominated the airfield, and the descending paratroopers took heavy casualties. With another of those extraordinary strokes of fortune, two Me-110s descended from the clouds and ripped up the pillboxes just long enough for the battered troopers to collect their heavy weapons and storm the bastions. Grenades sailed into the bunkers and it was all over, and within a few hours the Ju-52s had landed two complete infantry battalions, the regimental headquarters, and heavy weapons to secure the area.

Another force of paratroopers received sudden orders to drop on Fornebu Airfield, outside Oslo, the Norwegian capital. Easier said than done in weather so bad the attacking force of twenty-nine Ju-52s couldn't even find the coastline, let alone the airfield. The weather closed to a visibility of barely fifty feet, and two transports collided with a blinding flash, tumbling the wreckage into the sea with the complete loss of all aboard. The leader ordered the others to return to Aalborg, and the planes turned back—discovering, by radio, that the follow-up force of Ju-52s carrying troops to be landed at Fornebu were already on their way to the target, expecting paratroopers to be in control on the ground.

By another quirk of the Norwegian weather, the lead plane of the occupying formation hit Fornebu just as a great patch of clear sky opened over the field. The commander couldn't understand why all his planes were receiving a recall message, and he was further confused when he caught sight of Me-110s tearing up the airfield. One Wagner, leading the Ju-52s, bored in for his landing, although, all about him, other pilots were following the radio orders and were turning back to Aalborg. Another wild scenario was in the making, prompted in part by the fact that the radio frequencies of the Me-110 fighters and Ju-52 transports were not the same and the pilots couldn't talk to one another! Wagner used the smoke from burning Norwegian planes to judge the wind, lowered his flaps, and eased down to a landing—at which point the Ju-52

was ripped from nose to tail by a long burst of machine-gun fire. Blood, bone, and skin sprayed through the airplane as the bullets shattered the troops, and Wagner himself died from a hail of gunfire. The copilot went to full power and hauled wildly on the controls to climb away from the machine-gun fire.

The scenario went beyond the point of sanity. By now, the Me-110 fighters were almost out of fuel, and below them was an enemy airfield controlled by enemy troops with heavy firepower. When there's nothing better to do (and your fuel tanks are almost down to fumes), then you may as well attack. The Me-110s came around in another devastating strafing run with cannon and machine guns and then landed on the main runway, the pilots turning their fighters so that the rear crewmen, each with a single machine gun, could open fire on the entrenched defenders—*who were so confused and stunned by this move that they surrendered on the spot, without the Me-110s firing so much as a single shot after touching down.*

Behind them came the blood-soaked Ju-52 with most of its occupants already dead or wounded, but the German troops who were able to drag themselves from the transport joined the fighter crews and took over Fornebu. For the next three hours, this was the entire force that held captive the major airfield of all Norway, on the edge of the nation's capital. By midday, the Ju-52s were landing one after another to bring in paratroopers, six companies of infantry, and the regimental band. The companies formed up, saw German bombers flying over Oslo in precision formation to impress and demoralize the population, and behind the oom-pah-pah of the regimental band, they marched off into Oslo. While the band entrance confused Norwegians in a town square, the German troops raced to key points in the city.

And that afternoon—to all intents and purposes —the invasion was complete.

No one would ever have dared put to fiction the reality of the first paratrooper invasion in history.

————◆————

It didn't *all* go this way, of course. The transports had other duties to perform: essentially, these were to accomplish in the treacherous terrain and weather a powerful striking and occupying force into key points throughout Norway. The Ju-52s flew in every manner of supplies from food to fuel, to heavy weapons and motorcycles, and even landed troops in float-equipped Ju-52s deep within fjords where no other aircraft could possibly have operated. This was, of course, the less glamorous role of the airplane, but it certainly represented the greater majority of its flying throughout the war. The number of paratroop operations was only a tiny fraction of the total flying effort of the Ju-52s in all theaters, but they occupy attention far out of proportion to their *time* in the air, because without airborne assault with the Ju-52, several operations would have been impossible and others far more costly than they finally were to the Germans.

During the entire Norwegian campaign, which involved heavy fighting in isolated areas before the country was considered firmly under German rule, the Ju-52s, with a smattering of other types of

A force of float-equipped Ju-52 combat transports was vital for the invasions of the Scandinavian countries, taking troops into otherwise inaccessible areas. MESSERSCHMITT-BOLKOW-BLOHM

transports (less than 3 per cent of the Ju-52 force), flew 3,018 sorties and split up this effort with 1,830 carrying paratroopers or infantry forces and 1,188 with the wide variety of supplies needed by the invaders. The totals for the time were rather impressive, since the Ju-52s hauled over 29,000 men and 2,376 tons of supplies into Norway, and also droned back and forth between Germany and the invaded land to fly in nearly 260,000 gallons of aviation fuel (the equivalent of almost 300,000 U.S. gallons).

The Germans lost 150 planes, of all types, in the entire invasion.

⎯⎯◆⎯⎯

One month later, the scenario had changed and the stakes had risen dramatically. Hitler ordered the invasion of France and the Low Countries for the tenth of May, 1940. With Denmark and Norway completely under German control, it was time to move in new directions, and a massive, finely honed strike force was assembled for the multiple invasions. Not only would there be massed waves of paratroopers, as well as follow-up landings with Ju-52s carrying shock troops into the heart of the battle, but DFS-230 gliders able to carry troops and heavy weapons were to be thrown against enemy positions in a series of lightning strikes. Even the 22nd Infantry Division, which initially was to be "saved" for the Russian invasion, was committed to the attacks on Belgium and Holland. Four thousand five hundred paratroopers stood by to be air-dropped and then backed up by the twelve thousand men of the 22nd Infantry Division, to be flown by the Ju-52s into fields secured by the paratroopers. The basic operation called for small forces to be thrown against Belgium, where many hundreds of dummies would be dropped amid paratroopers to confuse the enemy as to the size of the attack, while the great majority of the forces would slam into Holland.

The gliders were released from thirteen thousand feet over the German border to begin a silent flight of thirty-five minutes into the Belgian garrison at Eban-Emael. Two gliders crashed, two landed on the wrong targets, and seven brought crack troops into the powerful fortress who swiftly overcame the defenses, blew up the heavy weapons, and in a dazzling stroke opened the way for fast-moving ground forces.

Altogether, five hundred eighty Ju-52s were used in the paratroop, glider, and airborne-infantry attacks. It was a successful operation in terms of the mission finally being accomplished and avoiding slow, heavy fighting by the main elements of the German Army pouring across the borders, but it was not carried out without a heavy cost in casualties of crack assault forces and aircraft.

"This was the first airborne operation in history and . . . was under the over-all direction of Second Air Force," explained Field Marshal Albert Kesselring in an interview. "The operation was divided into two basic parts, led by General Kurt Student. (1) An operation with gliders alone against Fort Eban Emael and the Maas Bridge. With the capture of Fort Eban Emael, the enemy flanking actions against the Maas crossings were eliminated. The capture of the most important bridge guaranteed that the Maas River would be crossed according to plan and thus established the necessary conditions for the co-ordination of ground and air operations in Holland. The dawn mission succeeded surprisingly well. (2) A major airborne operation by two divisions to capture the Moordijk bridges, the Rotterdam airport, the city of Rotterdam, and the Dutch capital of The Hague and its airfields. Since the second part of the mission (22nd Infantry Division—The Hague) was not successful, the subsequent operations in the Dutch coastal area failed to take place.

"The attempt at surprise was successful. Today one cannot even imagine the panic which was caused by rumors of the appearance of parachutists, supported by the dropping of dummies, etc. Nevertheless, the surrender of Rotterdam was the result of the bold actions of the parachutists and the air attack against the defended positions in Rotterdam. The operation had been organized by General Student with the thoroughness characteristic of him. In fact, it had been a small military masterpiece."

The paratroop attacks in the area of The Hague ran into fierce Dutch resistance, and out of three groups of Ju-52s flying into the battle zone in tight formation, fierce ground fire shot down or destroyed on the ground no fewer than forty-one planes. Violent resistance by Dutch troops blocked off use of the airfield at Ypenburg, but two hundred fifty Ju-52s managed to get down onto the field at Waalhaven. Floatplanes—Heinkel He-59s and Ju-52s—put one hundred fifty shock troops into waterways. The Ypenburg fighting grew ever more intense, and the position of the troops waiting to be landed at the preselected airfields was now getting desperate.

In one of the most incredible tributes to the Ju-52, the transport commander judged the field as suicidal for landings, studied the area beneath him, and made an on-the-spot decision that may have turned the tide of action for the day. With a great fleet of Ju-52s circling, he ordered one plane to land on the main Rotterdam-The Hague highway, near Delft.

Easier said than done, because the highway was lined on both sides with trees. The commander repeated the order to land—and in this airplane, flying copilot for this mission, was the same Karl Frensch who today flies in *Iron Annie* with me. He set up the approach with his pilot, watching wide-eyed as the road came closer and closer—and the trees grew larger and larger—and then the Ju-52 was down in a small clear stretch. Immediately, Frensch hauled full back on the control yoke to keep the tail down, as the pilot slammed the throttles full forward. Accelerating swiftly on the ground, the wings of the Ju-52 smashed into the trees on both sides of the road—and the airplane proceeded in this fashion, smashing down or slicing in two with its wings the trees that had blocked the highway for the use of any large number of aircraft. When the Ju-52 finally came to a stop, more than two miles from where it had touched down, the roadway was cleared of trees, and other Ju-52s were coming down in a steady file, releasing their troops as soon as they had stopped. That lead Ju-52? The leading edges of the wings were smashed flat, *but the main wing structure was still undamaged!*

The parachute assault against The Hague handed the Germans staggering losses. One unit lost eighteen transports, and another had forty out of fifty Ju-52s destroyed, and the organization (KGrzbV 12) was so shattered in morale that the group was broken up and the survivors reassigned. Another group took a blow just as severe, with thirty-nine of its Ju-52s destroyed. Many of the Ju-52s landed on assigned airfields, immediately to come under heavy artillery fire that took a savage toll of their numbers.

The main air attacks lasted four days, during which five hundred and eighty Ju-52s crossed the Dutch borders. One hundred and sixty-seven of these airplanes were destroyed, the majority to anti-aircraft fire, almost all the remainder to artillery fire on the ground. Nearly 30 per cent of the entire assault force of transports were lost forever, and many more were severely damaged and put out of action for weeks.

The remainder of Ju-52 operations in the steady march to the English Channel was the familiar one of supporting ground units, of rushing supplies to areas where they were needed in a hurry. It was logistics instead of combat, and life returned in the transport groups to the daily grind of milk runs.

Ju-52s, in an advanced loading area, taking on drums of fuel and oil, bombs, and critical supplies for combat forces in the field. MESSERSCHMITT-BOLKOW-BLOHM

Hundreds of Ju-52s were kept in readiness for the planned invasion of England but were soon released when Hitler abandoned Operation Sea Lion and turned his attention to the Balkans. Once again, the Luftwaffe became a critical element of the campaign, and while there was little argument that the greatest battles were still decided by victory or defeat of ground forces, there was also little argument that what happened with airborne units (or, conversely, failed to happen) could decide the outcome of far greater organizations that operated on the land. Nowhere would this be truer than in the Greece-Crete operations.

Yugoslavia and Greece were struck with a devastating punch by the German military, the leading wedge made up of air-transported combat units. It took every available Ju-52 to move masses of troops into desired positions for the onslaught, and the faithful Junkerses droned along day and night to ready the life-and-death chess pieces. On April 6, 1941, the blitzkrieg opened with massive air and armored attacks. German bombers hammered Belgrade day and night for eleven days, at which point the Yugoslavs found further resistance futile and capitulated to the invader. Greece did not last much longer; twenty-two days after the invasion cracked defensive lines, the country was abandoned to the Germans.

The island of Crete was the last remaining thorn, for this was the last bastion frustrating complete German domination of all the Balkans. It was not a simple goal, for in the evacuation of Greece by the British Navy, twenty-seven thousand experienced troops had been landed on Crete, where they added to the defensive garrisons already tightening up the positions.

Hitler was engrossed in his forthcoming invasion of Russia (which was finally nearing its day of reckoning after many postponements), and he had no desire to see any of his panzers or artillery or even infantry units pulled from that preparation. He gave his consent for the airborne assault of Crete, named Operation Mercury, on the condition that it be entirely a Luftwaffe operation. Since the German Air Force controlled its paratroopers as much as it did its aircraft, this was a perfect opportunity to demonstrate airpower as never before. The Luftwaffe was still smarting from its whipping over the British Isles, and the forced postponement (and admitted dumping) of the invasion of England made it all the more urgent for the Luftwaffe to show its stuff at Crete.

The "all air-force show" had one hundred fifty Stuka dive bombers, plus three groups of Dornier Do-17 and Junkers Ju-88 twin-engine bombers, and six fighter groups with single-engine Messerschmitt Me-109s and twin-engine Messerschmitt Me-110s. But these were assault and cover weapons, and the real cutting sword was in the form of ten air transport groups of Ju-52s along with three groups of gliders.

It was not going to be an easy task. The size of

Crete is deceptive, forty miles wide by one hundred sixty miles long; it is not a small island, and its terrain is rocky and mountainous. The Luftwaffe planned on demoralizing bombing assaults followed by paratroop drops, after which the Ju-52s would return to the mainland to pick up troops to be flown back to be landed on the captured airfields. Facing the Germans would be a total strength of some 42,500 British and Greek soldiers.

The strike opened on May 20 at seven in the morning, the Germans trying their best to stick to meticulous planning that would put 15,750 men on Crete by air alone; seaborne landings to follow would strengthen the aerial invasion. Seven hundred and fifty men were to land first by 80 DFS-230 gliders. The Ju-52s droned in, the gliders were cut loose, and waves of paratroopers spilled into the sky.

Normally the Ju-52 operated with a crew of four as a combat transport: the pilot (first officer or captain), the copilot (often a mechanic, rather than a pilot), the radio operator, and the rear gunner. MESSERSCHMITT-BOLKOW-BLOHM

Directly into a hellish machine-gun fire from British, New Zealand, Australian, and Greek troops. Before the first day was out, none of the principal objectives had been taken, although the Germans had managed to dig in tightly to await reinforcements and a new day of fighting. Nightfall to the German assault forces was a blessed relief. Several battalions (notably 3rd Battalion, Assault Regiment) were virtually annihilated by the fierce crossfire of defending machine guns *before they*

even reached the ground. The air was filled with gliders tumbling out of control and paratroopers hanging lifeless in their harness. Several other major forces were slashed to ribbons in the air as they descended and, once on the ground, were so weakened and confused that the defenders ripped them apart in continuous crossfires that left only a few survivors. It was a bloodbath the like of which the German airborne forces had never anticipated in their worst nightmares.

The Luftwaffe had prepared 493 of the Ju-52s for the Crete invasion. A greater number of transports might have seemed called for, but the main airfields on Greece proper were but an hour's flying time from the combat zone, and it was planned to have the Ju-52s on a steady back-and-forth shuttle. Altogether, they would drop ten thousand men by parachute, land another five thousand on strips cleared by the paratroopers, and then pour in supplies for the airborne forces and the seven thousand more men to be landed by sea.

But it didn't work out that way, and the slaughter of men was frightful, and the toll of Ju-52 transports devastating. No one had bothered to check a recent history of the weather (there had been a bad drought) but had simply selected areas where the paratroopers would prepare the temporary runways for the Ju-52s to land. The Germans were blissfully unaware that the surface was almost powdery dust.

Thus the hellish chaos that resulted. As the first planes landed, their wheels threw up enormous plumes of choking dust, and the propellers turned the fields into huge storms that towered high into the air and spread out laterally as well. These were also second and third drop zones for paratroopers, but the Ju-52 pilots flying into the boiling dust found visibility so destroyed they could not hold tight formation, they couldn't see—literally—the drop zones, and they couldn't even co-ordinate their approaches to the zones. Consequently the air was filled with milling planes and confused pilots and paratroopers being scattered everywhere—resulting in their slaughter by the entrenched defenders. In many cases most of the men were killed before they reached the ground, and the survivors, trying to regroup and get their heavy weapons, were simply picked off and kept isolated, which eliminated them completely as an effective fighting force.

Evaluating Operation Mercury, the official document titled *Airborne Operations: A German Appraisal* notes that the "initial attack contained all the germs of failure. Only the fact that the defenders of the island limited themselves to purely defensive measures and did not immediately and energetically attack the landing troops saved the latter from destruction. Even though the situation was still obscure, the German command decided to commit its reserves (5th Mountain Division) in an all-out attack against the point which seemed to offer the greatest chances of success; the energetic,

the Ju-52s, and those machines were flying directly into Hell itself. Most of the glider drops ended in disaster, because German intelligence proved to be hopelessly inadequate; anticipated open fields were strewn with hills and great boulders, which shattered the gliders, killing most of their occupants.

The Germans desperately needed the major airfield at Maleme, for then the Ju-52s could come in in a steady stream, free of the choking and blinding dust that was wrecking one plane after the other at the temporary airstrips. When German

Losses in the paratroop and air assault of Crete were devastating: more than half the entire attacking forces of Ju-52s were destroyed, the great majority of them on the ground. MESSERSCHMITT-BOLKOW-BLOHM

purposeful, and systematic commitment of these forces in an attack immediately after their landing changed the threatened failure into a success."

It must be emphasized that although the British at the start of the invasion controlled the sea about Crete, the Germans had total, even absolute, air superiority. Nevertheless, the invasion faltered so badly that it was on the verge of being wiped out —especially if the defending forces had counterattacked.

For no matter how strong the German intentions, they were tied completely to the effectiveness of

troops stormed the field and announced the runways were clear, the Ju-52s lined up in a stream of landing aircraft—and at slow speed, flaps down, heavily loaded, they flew straight into a charnel house. For while the Germans had the runways, the areas nearby were still under enemy control, and intense artillery fire began pouring onto the field. Desperate for replacements, the commanders ordered the Ju-52s to land. Down they came, sliding out of the sky into a horrifying scene of transport planes blown apart and burning fiercely, of shells exploding in the air and along the runways, of planes tumbling into sudden craters, of Ju-52s colliding and falling in shredded masses of burning metal and flailing bodies.

Had there been *any* Allied fighter planes, the debacle would instantly have become a slaughter, but the air remained in German control from the outset. It was this mastery of the air that began to negate the effectiveness of the British Navy and, finally, pinned down the ground defenders as the paratroopers and mountain shock troops began to emerge from the stupor of their brutal losses.

Finally, because of the overpowering buildup of German arms, the British Navy (which lost nine warships sunk and seventeen more damaged) began its withdrawal and managed to carry approximately twenty-six thousand of the defending troops off the island to Egypt. This successful evacuation enraged Hitler, coming as it did on the heels of the savaging of the invading German forces.

The German victory was in the form of a vast funeral pyre. Out of sixteen thousand troops in the airborne forces, nearly four thousand were killed in battle (one fourth of the entire air army), as well as many thousands more badly wounded. (Altogether, six thousand men were killed out of twenty-two involved, including air landings and seaborne troops, making the ratio of dead even worse.)

Some of Germany's best leaders were lost, especially the men with the brightest minds and the most experience. As Winston Churchill noted in his evaluation of the struggle, they had lost Crete, but the elite of German airborne leadership and fighting power had been severely mauled, to such an extent that Crete was the last major airborne operation by Germany for the entire war.

There was little to be thankful for among the pilots and air crews of the transport groups. Fewer than five hundred Ju-52s had been committed to Operation Mercury—and more than two hundred fifty of these planes had been destroyed, many with their crews.

What especially stuck in the throats of the pilots was that they had taken their devastating casualties—more than half of all their planes—in skies without any defending fighters, and that most of their losses were suffered on the ground from blazing artillery fire, shell craters, and the screaming chaos of blinding smoke and dust.

It was perhaps the greatest *waste* of skilled men and good airplanes of the entire war.

The dust was still settling over Crete when the Wehrmacht unleashed the full force of its power against the Soviet Union. Operation Barbarossa was many things, among them the death knell of air transport operations. From the twenty-second of June, 1941, until the close of the war, there would never be enough Ju-52 transports to meet the growing clamor for men and supplies in North Africa, Russia, and elsewhere. The attrition rate

respite. The vastness of the Russian front, its incredible lack of decent roads, and the destruction of rail lines under the scorched-earth policy of the retreating Red Army made air transport all the more vital. At times, the Ju-52s had to fly in their own spare parts and mechanics, and the very fuel and oil with which to make return flights to main supply centers. Any decrease in carrying capacity meant additional missions to be flown, and the

A Ju-52 being worked on, in a rear area, for active duty. Note the top-loading cargo hatch as well as the side-fuselage cargo door. MESSER-SCHMITT-BOLKOW-BLOHM

would grow steadily. Trained pilots would become scarce, and youngsters would be pushed hastily through flight-training schools. Along with the marked decline in flight crews, there would appear a shortage of good mechanics. Supplies would fall into short order, and the quality of materials also would begin to suffer. It was a steady downhill slide, none of it made any the better for the spreading use of inferior materials in new airplanes to be rushed from the battered production lines.

The crews became hollow-cheeked and sunken-eyed from flying for months with little or no

presence of two pilots in the cockpit was often the only way the men managed to stay operational. After takeoff and settling down to a long run, one pilot would leave the cockpit to sleep, and a radioman or mechanic would take the copilot seat in the front office. On the ground, especially in the more remote areas, the flight crews found it necessary not only to service their own aircraft but also to unload their cargo and help load stretcher cases or walking wounded.

The distances of Russia were matched by the grueling flights to support the German Army in

Africa. Heavy transport operations had always been an integral part of the German North African campaign, but as Allied airpower gained in strength and allied naval units began to dominate the seas, the Germans were forced to depend almost completely on air transport to remain operational. And air transport meant in the main none other than the Ju-52.

There were other transports, to be sure, but their number was only the smallest fraction of the Ju-52 fleet. There were some Junkers Ju-86s, but their capacity for carrying men and cargo was as limited as their number, which was never more than a few dozen machines in the entire Luftwaffe. The Junkers Ju-90 was a splendid four-engine transport, but only ten of the Ju-90s had been built for Lufthansa, and these were impressed into military service. A limited number of Ju-290 models, military versions of the Ju-90, came out of the factory, but most of those were used for long-range maritime patrol and as bombers. There was the well-known Focke-Wulf FW-200C, another four-engine airliner drafted into military service. Most of these were converted to bombers and operated in this role, especially against Atlantic convoys. At times they were pressed into service as transports but never proved successful in this job. They were maintenance nightmares, suffered from structural problems (such as having the fuselage break in half on hard landings). The Heinkel He-111 was an excellent airplane, a commercial airliner converted to a bomber and often converted on the spot back into transport use, but, again, its numbers were limited.

Much is made by historians of the Heinkel He-177 *Grief* four-engine bomber, also used as a transport, but of all the trouble-plagued He-177s built, no more than two dozen were ever in service at any one time, and operations with these airplanes often saw 20 per cent—one out of every five planes—going down in flames. Not from enemy fighters but from engines tearing apart!

There was even the Ju-252, a three-engine advancement of the Ju-52, along with a Ju-352 model, which could cruise at over two hundred miles per hour and carry double the load of the Ju-52. But, again, only a handful of these airplanes ever went into operational service. There were also a number

A heavily loaded Ju-52 takes off from Orel Airport, in Russia. In the immediate foreground are air-cargo drop canisters, and in the background is a Junkers Ju-87 Stuka and (right) a Dornier Do-217 bomber.
MESSERSCHMITT-BOLKOW-BLOHM

of the huge Messerschmitt Me-323 gliders fitted out with six engines and able to carry loads of enormous size. They were important to German aerial logistics, but their greatest number at any one time was, again, limited to a small fraction of the Ju-52 force.

Study the Luftwaffe operational records and you'll find that the one airplane type, the Ju-52, flew more than 95 per cent of all German air transport operations.

———◆———

This picture was handed to me personally by the man who took it on a mass formation flight to North Africa: Heinz Manthau, who was also a Luftwaffe ace flying Me-109 and Me-163 fighters. Heinz Manthau is one of the former Luftwaffe pilots who has "met with *Iron Annie*" in recent years. HEINZ MANTHAU

What is there to say of air transport operations in the North African campaign except that this was a Ju-52 campaign, with a desperate throwing in of the Me-323 goliaths, the latter plagued with mechanical problems, structural weaknesses, and a dazzling tendency to burn wildly with the first burst of gunfire into the vitals of the outsized whale with wings? In November of 1942, air transport activity in North Africa was almost the sole province of the Ju-52, with some support from Italian planes, again a minuscule fraction of the total operations. Then, as Allied fighters appeared in sufficient numbers to concern the Germans (this was the time when the first P-38s went into combat in Africa) and the vast Allied invasion of North Africa became a reality, the Luftwaffe rushed ten complete groups of Ju-52s to Africa to supplement the five groups already operational.

Ju-52 operations were long and tiring flights across the Mediterranean and within the dusty, sandy, and primitive conditions of the African desert. It might have been easier with permanent installations for maintenance and support, but these were luxuries banished forever by changing battle lines and the ever-growing number of American and British bombers tearing up German airfields. Only the fact that the Ju-52s operated from roads and isolated fields kept them from being decimated.

Ju-52 transports and a mixed bag of Messerschmitt Me-110 twin-engine fighters in a North African staging area. CAIDIN ARCHIVES

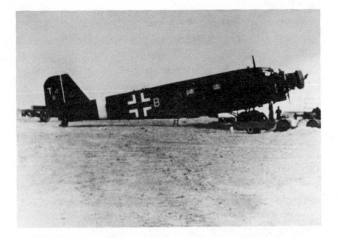

Ju-52 undergoing field maintenance in forward combat staging area. CAIDIN ARCHIVES

The *Libyan Clipper*, a Ju-52 captured in North Africa fighting and commandeered by the British as a personal carry-everything freighter. CAIDIN ARCHIVES

But nothing could stem the growing numbers of Allied fighters and bombers that, in the air, began to tear apart any German transport that came within their sights. German hopes for North Africa were no more than a shadow of what they had once been when aerial intercepts of the German transport groups by fighters *and* bombers sealed off any light at the end of the tunnel. Not even escorting German fighters could save the day as Lightnings ripped through their formations. The effect of a P-38's four heavy machine guns and one cannon clustered in the nose is almost unbelievable. It would, and did, blow apart any fighter or bomber, and when this overwhelming blast of heavy metal and exploding shells ripped into the Ju-52, the end was inevitable. At times, Spitfires and Kittyhawks found great formations of transports hugging the water, and the Spitfires stayed upstairs to handle the German fighters while the Kittyhawks, each with six .50-calibers, went in low and slow. In one 2-day period, twenty-four Ju-52s and fourteen of their escorting fighters went down in two sharp battles. On the eighteenth of April of 1943, one of the worst catastrophes caught up with the Germans: an enormous fleet, of more than a hundred Ju-52s, was caught near Cape Bon, and the fighters screamed in for the massacre. And a massacre it was: *fifty-two out of the hundred transports were destroyed.*

There were terrible air battles when swarms of American fighters escorting B-25 bombers encountered fleets of German transports and, brushing aside German fighters, tore into the slower Jun-

kerses. The fighters were brutal, but no less so the B-25s, which flew alongside the Ju-52s, the gunners pouring hellish fire into the cockpits and cabins from .50-caliber-armed turrets.

Four days after the horror of Cape Bon, the Luftwaffe sent twenty-five huge Me-323 transports to Africa. They were carrying fuel needed desperately by German armored forces in the desert—and they had the misfortune to run into a loose swarm of American fighters. The call to battle was shouted with glee over radios and the hunt was on. The great, lumbering Me-323s went down one after another in huge gouts of fire streaming through the skies.

Two survived. . . .

Between April 5 and April 22, 1943, the Allies lost thirty-five fighter planes in these attacks against the German transports. Four hundred and thirty-two Luftwaffe transports were shot down.

The North African campaign was ended.

———◆———

There is only one way to understand the role of the Ju-52 in Russia. The entire stage is too vast, too overwhelming, too numbing from sheer size and numbers to encompass in one short section of a book. The same can be said of the tremendous distances involved, the savage cold and wind in winter, the roads and airfields that became seas of mud in the spring, the shortages of men, matériel, supplies, parts, food, medicine—of everything, including time. Incredible battles were fought simultaneously along the great front, and *any one* of

A plush Ju-52 used for transporting Hitler
and his top staff for visits to forward areas
of operations by the German Army. QUICK

these monstrous conflicts exceeded in size, fury,
and manpower the Italian or the Western front. In
one battle alone, the struggle for Kursk, the Germans threw in more armor than they could total
for every other front in Russia and Africa and
Italy and in every occupied land. The numbers
simply cannot be comprehended.

So we focus into one struggle, and even this is titanic in scope. Late in 1942, the Wehrmacht
smashed its way to the gates of Stalingrad, fought
grimly to penetrate the city, and then came to a
bloody and furious grinding halt. Here was the
Sixth Army of the Wehrmacht, one of its finest

fighting forces, and it was at a dead standstill. And
then the worst happened: On November 19, 1942,
the Russians launched a massive offensive across
the River Don, and within four days the three hundred thousand men of the German Sixth Army
were completely surrounded. As the German general staff understood the situation, the Sixth Army
had only to stand fast until the powerful Fourth
Panzer Army could cut through the Russian lines
and open the way to an organized withdrawal.

Easier said than done, for if the Sixth Army was
to survive until the panzers could break through
the unexpected Russian strength, the force of three

hundred thousand men must be supplied from the air. The Fourth Air Force of the Luftwaffe, commanded by Colonel-General von Richthofen, did not for a moment believe it was possible for his air units to fulfill such a task. Strangely enough, Colonel-General von Paulus, commander of the Sixth Army, who looked out on a world where in every direction there were only Russians to be seen, radioed Berlin that *he* thought the operation feasible.

No one in the higher echelons of Hitler's headquarters chose to disagree with Paulus, and finally Hitler approved the airlift operation. Had he not been led to believe the air supply effort could be successful, he would have ordered Paulus to fight his way out of the trap no matter what the losses, and similar experiences indicate some measure of high success would likely have resulted. But the dice were thrown, Paulus' views held sway, and the Germans thrust themselves into one of the most barbaric and costly periods of all their history.

Paulus had his command draw up their requirements, which worked out to three hundred tons of fuel and thirty tons of all types of ammunitions *per day*. Shortly afterward, they increased this demand by one hundred and fifty tons of food to be flown in for a daily total of nearly five hundred tons every single day they would wait for the panzers to break through the Russian forces.

Now the problem had to be resolved in aircraft logistics. Winter had struck, and that meant devastating problems with cold, poor serviceability of aircraft, limited airfields, long distances to fly, lack of crew replacements—in short, taking everything into account, the air bridge into Stalingrad, carrying supplies in and flying out wounded and German Army women, demanded no fewer than eight hundred operational Ju-52 transports.

At this time, in all the Luftwaffe there were only seven hundred and fifty Ju-52s in actual operation, and several hundred of these were already hard-pressed to keep the Wehrmacht in North Africa supplied with their critical necessities. Each month, German industry rolled sixty new planes into the transport squadrons, and this was recognized immediately as woefully inadequate. Attrition, combat, accidents would all take their toll, and many more planes would be needed. The high command of the Luftwaffe could hardly believe the demands and the means of supplying them, and immediately they ordered the conversion of every available

Ju-52 transport group that operated in the Italian-Balkans area. CAIDIN ARCHIVES

Heinkel He-111 bomber into a transport. They ripped out the guns, armor plate, bomb bays—everything that could be stripped away to make room for cargo. Word had already been sent to every Luftwaffe unit that anything on wings that could be used for transport purposes was to be sent immediately to Russia, and that included even the personal transport plane of Goering. By the twenty-fourth of November, the great wheels of air supply began to grind; even the highly prized Ju-90 four-engine transports from Lufthansa were being pressed into service, and Goering reassured Hitler that the five hundred tons *would* be delivered every day to Paulus' encircled forces.

It did not go well, and the future, to those Germans who viewed the world through experienced and realistic eyes, was grim and foreboding. The logistics reports alone were frightening.

A major Ju-52 force had been moved into Tatsinskaya, one hundred and sixty miles from the German-held fields at Stalingrad, and each airplane could carry two tons of supplies to the Sixth Army. The Tatsinskaya airfield, however, was rather much of a primitive and rotten affair, with virtually no maintenance and support facilities, and it held little hope for *sustaining* a major operation in the teeth of a screaming Russian winter. Another inadequate field was set up at Morozovsk, about one

Hauling it on the deck, a Ju-52 air-drops supplies to advanced units in Russia. The soldier in foreground is holding a flag to indicate the surface wind. MESSERSCHMITT-BOLKOW-BLOHM

hundred and thirty miles from Stalingrad; from there, the He-111 could carry perhaps one and a half tons. But the load was misleading, for the supplies were to be contained in "supply bombs," and no one seemed to have figured out that the payload, of three thousand pounds, also included the weight of the containers.

If Goering's lush promises to Hitler were to hold any validity, then he must—every day—land at least three hundred planes within Stalingrad. He must land a transport every two and a half minutes, which meant a skilled ground force always ready to unload supplies and reload with wounded and army women. He must do this under the pressure of accidents, combat losses, and terrible weather, as well as of the Russians closing the ring on Stalingrad on one front and pushing *back* the Fourth Panzer so that the air distance from the German airfields to Stalingrad, instead of at least remaining static, began to increase. Payloads must go down and flying time must go up, along with attrition from all causes.

By the first week of December, every available Ju-52, including a force from Africa, and (at long last) another six hundred Ju-52s from various flight-training schools, were flying the airlift. There were also some Ju-86s, the few Ju-90s, the Heinkel He-111s, and even some Ju-290 *prototypes*, which had yet to have their development problems resolved. Little matter; a Ju-290 could carry a load of ten tons into Stalingrad and could leave with at least seventy wounded in place of the inflown cargo.

Within a week of starting the airlift, everyone on the Russian front knew that Goering was an unmitigated liar whose only purpose in promising Hitler grandiose accomplishments was to please the German leader and ward off the violent temper that could sack even the highest figure in the Luftwaffe. Losses in aircraft were from the very outset crippling, and here the human element begins to emerge from the unemotional pages of logistics.

A crew that crashed its transport in Stalingrad was as good as dead. No one believed Stalingrad could be kept supplied by air, no one believed they could hold off the Russians indefinitely, and everyone could read his own war maps and watch other Russian forces pushing inexorably westward, further isolating Stalingrad from all help that might come their way by panzers.

Debacles come in well-announced phases. By Christmas of 1942, the vital airfield at Tatsinskaya felt the grinding rumble of Russian tanks on its runways, and the last remaining Ju-52s barely got off the ground as shells exploded about them. Now logistics took on grimmer meaning. The Ju-52s were flying from fields more than two hundred miles from Stalingrad. The payloads were down and the number of flights were down with them, and in Stalingrad, hammered and ripped relentlessly by the Russians, Germany's finest soldiers were beginning to starve. To these men, their Air Force was the epitome of the worst; their failure was spelled betrayal.

And there were new problems. It was one of the worst winters the men could ever recall, the flying conditions were ghastly, and airplanes simply did not maintain schedules, with screaming winds, blinding snow, thick drifts on runways—and an ever-decreasing space in which to land within Stalingrad.

By mid-January, the total supplies flown into the beleaguered city were averaging one hundred tons

Staging area within the surrounded pocket of the German Sixth Army at Stalingrad. Airplanes ready for takeoff just pointed into the wind and went. MESSERSCHMITT-BOLKOW-BLOHM

per day, and just to hold off starvation the Sixth Army *must* have three hundred tons daily. But it was even worse than these figures indicate, for, every day, the Russian winter took its toll of the available planes.

Enter here the name of Kurt W. Streit, one of the great veterans of the Luftwaffe. A master pilot. An instrument instructor for the German Air Force who had been sent to the Junkers Company as a test pilot, a man who could fly a Ju-52, equipped with new instruments, to the ground in zero-zero weather, and was doing it day after day.

"It was well I did," explained this quiet man who accumulated more than four thousand hours' flying time in the Ju-52 alone, much of it in Africa and Russia, "because the experience I gathered in all that instrument flying, even landing without autopilots in zero-zero, helped me to survive the hell of Stalingrad."

I brought question after question to Kurt Streit. We had flown together in N52JU, and our bond was meaningful and ran very deep. Flying in the last Ju-52 of its kind in the world slices open the barriers of time. . . .

———◆———

"The numbers are always misleading," Kurt told me. "Before we were through with Stalingrad, the airlift had more than a thousand Ju-52s committed to the air bridge, and more than eight hundred of these were lost, many to Russian fighters and flak, but just as many to accidents and, above all, to the terrible weather conditions in which our pilots had

to fly. As we were forced back to fields more distant from Stalingrad, our chances worsened. The longer we spent in the air the more time the Russian fighters had to come after us, and we were their choice targets, of course. What we would have given for self-sealing fuel tanks! But we didn't have them, and one good burst into those unprotected fuel cells and any airplane became a torch. We had no more fighter escort. Most of it was destroyed, and what was sent to the front to protect the transports didn't have the range to go all the way with us. So it was a matter of flying on our own. The fighters simply weren't there.

"Let us face the truth: There were more brave and courageous crews in those Ju-52s than I could possibly remember. But there were also many men who did not want to fly these missions. None of us really believed, no matter what was the propaganda from Berlin, that the Sixth Army would survive. We just had to keep grinding away to do our best. But it is no secret that some crews made sure their airplanes had problems on the ground, and often could not take off. They were in the minority, but we needed every plane so badly that even the loss of a single transport meant more men would starve, more men would die, more wounded, more women, would never emerge from the holocaust at Stalingrad.

"Consider what happened when we landed. Those troops were exhausted, starving, frozen, and they had almost no provisions or facilities to unload our planes. Several times, our transports would land at fields, such as Gumrak, and there

93

One of the most dramatic pictures of the Stalingrad operation: a flight of Ju-52s has just landed with supplies, shown being hauled away by German soldiers. The transport engines are kept running so they will not freeze in the savage cold. BENNO WUNDSHAMMER ARCHIVES

would be no one on the ground to unload the cargo. The flight crews couldn't believe it. They had flown through fighters and over terrible Russian anti-aircraft zones to bring in the cargo and there was no one to do a thing about it. After a few doses like this, they just dumped the cargo onto the frozen ground, took aboard whatever wounded could crawl or be dragged to the airplanes, and left. Many of those crews in future flights felt it was stupid to land, and so they flew as low and slow as they could over the dropping zones, and dumped out their cargoes. Unfortunately, much of this material landed in deep snow, and the troops on the ground either couldn't find the cargo, or had no way—without transport—to drag it from the drifts. It kept going from bad to worse.

"Many of our planes tried to make drops at night, for few Russian fighters would go up in the dark, and their flak guns would be much less dangerous. But you need something on the ground to guide you for these kinds of operations, and our flight crews were nearly mad with frustration, for there were no flares, no fires, no lights; only darkness. So all they could do was aim for what they *thought* was the airstrip and dump their loads out of their planes.

"I had been to the field at Zverevo. The conditions there were absolutely ghastly. There was no place on the ground for the men to work on the Ju-52s. Not a single hut. And the conditions were almost beyond all believing. The wind was screaming at fifty miles per hour and the temperature was way below zero, and every man was exposed nakedly to the cold. They couldn't even dig a trench in that frozen ground. How do you work on

Loading stretcher cases of wounded into a Ju-52 in the shrinking airfield area at Stalingrad. U. S. NAVY

airplanes under conditions like *that?* There are ways, but you need men who know everything about their planes. You must improvise. If you use normal procedures, you are dead. Mechanics would try to work on an airplane in a wind of fifty miles per hour with the temperature down to minus twenty-five degrees, and in no time at all their hands froze to their tools. I remember that at one time there were more than a hundred Ju-52s at Zverevo. The commanders had grounded more than forty of these because they needed some repairs. But they could have flown without the repairs. You can fly a Ju-52 if it has been battered and beaten, and these were not that bad. The men and their brains were numb, frozen. Of the other sixty planes, only about a half dozen had made it into the air on their way to Stalingrad. Only three got through; the others turned back because of having to fly blind and losing their way.

"Some of the crews had come from Africa, and they were helpless. Their airplanes were in great snowdrifts, and everything was frozen solid, including the engines. But those radial engines—ah, you could do anything with them if only you knew *what* to do and *how* to do it. There is a cold-start procedure for the Ju-52 that will start up that machine in any kind of weather, and that includes the worst of the Russian front. There was even a special fuel we had for starting engines in the coldest

weather, and it always worked, but, as I said, you must know what to do. The African crews had never even heard of it, so we sent in special teams. And it was as we expected: without heating trucks, you could start the engines.

"Now, let me make it clear there were also many crews who were experienced, who had initiative, and who would stop at absolutely nothing to help their men trapped on the ground at Stalingrad. At times we couldn't start the engines of my own Ju-52, because the cold-start fuel simply wasn't available. There are other ways: We would erect shelters to ward off the wind. Canvas, tents; anything would do. Then we would collect wood beneath each engine and start a fire. That's right: a bonfire. A big blaze, a fire to give off enough heat to loosen the oil, to unfreeze the lines, to let the propellers turn. And we would start our engines this way, and there was nothing in the instruction book about such a thing, because it was mad to start an airplane like this, *but it worked, and we flew our missions.*

"I told you before that there were some crews who took every excuse not to fly, and I cannot blame them, for they knew the situation was hopeless. But there were so many other crews who flew not one but two and three missions on a single day into and out of Stalingrad! Those were magnificent pilots, and so were their mechanics and cargo handlers and gunners. They all knew that every mission was about as suicidal as one could manage, and yet they kept going in again and again, some of them crying with the sights they saw. They saw —and I did too—horses dying on their feet and starving men who would bash in their skulls with rifle butts and eat the brains raw, because they had not eaten in days. We were under orders not to bring out any men who were able to fight. Only the women and the worst of the wounded.

"And that was about the worst of it all, because the soldiers were crazed, they were mad by then, they would do anything to get out of Stalingrad before the Russians squeezed them all tight. They knew they had been abandoned by their leaders to die, and they were wild with rage and desperation. After we landed, and were trying to take on the wounded, some of the soldiers would smash in the heads of the wounded to kill them, or would throw them into the snow, or even shoot them, run over them, anything, simply to get into our planes. Some of the men who were trapped could fly, and then they tried to capture transports, they tried to kill the crews and take over the planes themselves, and our machine gunners had to mow them down as they ran at us firing, and while we were defending ourselves and our planes, protecting the wounded and the women, the officers on the ground were shooting their own men who had gone mad and would do anything to escape. I don't know how many hundreds of German soldiers died like this, but it must have been . . . I don't know, I would have to say, from what I myself experienced, and what others told me, that it must have been in the thousands. The slaughter was terrible.

"So much depended on luck! You would be taking off and a blizzard would sweep the field and the winds would become violent, and suddenly you couldn't see, and one plane would crash into another, so that both of them were thrown out of control into the ground with a violent impact, many times exploding, and burning the wounded and the crews to death, and the others could only listen to them scream as they burned; if they could, they would shoot the men burning alive as an act of mercy. Pilots would land, or take off, and there was no way to see the craters in the blinding snow, and men who had done everything perfectly would suddenly find the field beneath them gone, they did not yet have flying speed, and the nose of the air-

plane would smash into the frozen ground, and there was no escaping such things.

"You couldn't fly into or out of Stalingrad without running the gauntlet of their damned flak guns. There was one anti-aircraft battery in particular that was manned by Russian women, and they were the best gun crews I have ever known. They shot down dozens of planes, and many times they hit my own Ju-52, blowing holes in it and killing crewmen and the wounded we were flying out.

"The Russian fighters wanted to catch our transports more than any other kind of airplane, because they knew we were carrying either supplies into Stalingrad or wounded and the army girls out. They would come after us at point-blank range, shooting with everything they had. There wasn't any way to fight them off, really. You shot back with everything you had, but you had no protection from beneath. More than once, I was hit by the Russian fighters, and there was only one thing to do: Full load or not, I would go to full power, the throttles all the way forward, and roll the Ju-52 over on her back and dive straight down, as fast as we could go, so we could get down to the deck and hedgehop, restricting the passes of the fighters or losing them in a snowstorm. How that airplane ever stayed together is a mystery or a miracle, or maybe it was both, but we actually threw those Ju-52s around in the air, punishing them terribly, and they always came through for us.

"We survived one Russian fighter attack by a strange sort of miracle: The fighter was on our tail and closing in, and the gunner was out of ammunition, or his gun had jammed, whatever. So all he could do was to throw things at the Russian fighter, and without thinking, he even threw out a roll of toilet paper. Instantly it was unwrapped by the wind, and this long, serpentine object floated back, and the Russian pilot must have thought it was some kind of aerial mine, because he immediately broke off his attack and we escaped into cloud. We were astonished that it worked, and we were even more astonished that it worked again and again. The Russian didn't figure it out for more than a year after Stalingrad, because I used this trick all that time. Finally, they must have passed the word around and it didn't do any good any more.

"We managed—all the planes, and most of them Ju-52s—to fly about twenty-nine thousand soldiers and army girls out of Stalingrad, during which time

The crew is aboard, flaps down, engines running hard—hoping the troops will be able to "unstick" the Ju-52 frozen to the ground.
MESSERSCHMITT-BOLKOW-BLOHM

we also flew in many thousands of tons of supplies. But, to me, the numbers mean nothing. It was what the Ju-52s could do that we will remember forever.

"I was starting a takeoff once when a Russian shell exploded by one wing. It shook us very badly, and when the smoke cleared away, we saw that nine feet of the wing was completely shot away from the airplane. No matter. It was throttles to the wall, push the engines to overboost to get maybe 120 per cent of power, and off we went with a full load. We had planes with tires frozen so badly that a single bullet would shatter the rubber. In this kind of case, you couldn't move. Not with one tire in pieces on one wheel and the other with a full tire. The best thing to do was to shoot away the good tire or cut it away with axes, and we would take off—and I have done this myself—without tires, rolling the airplane on the rims of its wheels.

"There was no way to expect this airplane to do such impossible things, and yet it would always bring you through. We had crews of four or five, depending on the gunners, and we were supposed to bring back from twelve to twenty wounded on a flight. One time, we took off from Stalingrad with fifty-nine people on board, and that was in addition to the crew. We tore out all the seats and the floorboards to the belly hatches and anything else that was removable, and with all those people we took off and we climbed to five thousand feet and went to a German airfield.

"Many times, with a full load aboard, we would find only two engines operating. The third would be shot out. So you still would go. You would start up from a standing position and increase your flaps as you went. The heavy, cold air and the wind helped, and there were hundreds of takeoffs made on only two engines. It was not supposed to be possible to do this, with a full load I mean, but it was done time and again. And I will never forget one very young man, a soldier frightened out of his wits, who jumped onto my airplane as I was starting a takeoff. The doors were closed and he couldn't get inside the airplane, so he slid back on the after fuselage, behind the gunner's position, hanging on for dear life to the vertical fin. He remained there the entire flight, dying slowly, and when we landed, he was frozen as solid as a cake of ice. He was very dead."

By February 2, 1943, it was all over. The transports had flown out nearly thirty thousand men and army girls. More than one hundred sixty thousand Germans were already dead as the Russians finally squeezed the trap tight. They took one hundred eight thousand prisoners.

Of these men, only six thousand ever returned to Germany.

PART THREE

Iron Annie

Only the fanatics were still fighting. Germany lay in ruins, her cities mostly gutted, the Russian front a vast graveyard with German names, and the Allied armies moving relentlessly from the west and the south. Precious little German land was left for the Germans, and even less airspace through which a Luftwaffe machine might fly without being cut at once from the skies. Where once this had been the high domain of the Messerschmitts and the Focke-Wulfs, it was now the hunting grounds for Mustang and Lightning and Spitfire, of Thunderbolt and Typhoon, and all the others whose pilots searched constantly for the ever-vanishing targets with the black cross and the swastika.

Those who could choose turned from the east, away from the hordes of the Red Army. If they must be prisoners, then better the Americans than the Russians. And so, on the last day, the official last day of the war, with the fanatics dead or numbed from the concussion of countless bombs and shells, a lone Ju-52 droned its way toward the American lines. None of the men in the cockpit or the cabin was a transport pilot or crewman. They were fighter pilots whose machines were starved for fuel and helpless derelicts on the ground, and they had discovered the well-worn but still working Ju-52 in a hangar. With the Russians advancing on their field with the inexorable motion of the ice age, they worked on the engines of the Ju-52, got them running, and grabbed their parachutes and flew to the west.

Now they worked their way through cumulus cloud, slipping from one great mass to another, comfortable in the rocking motions of wing-slapping turbulence, even grateful for the shocks, because the clouds were their only defense against the killers prowling German skies. They checked their position. "We have made it," the man in the left seat told the others. "Down there . . . see? It is occupied by the Americans." Through a cloud break, they saw a large airfield. Their destination.

"Look. I don't know. . . ." The copilot shifted uncomfortably in his seat and looked at his friends. "It just seems a lousy way to end it all. I mean, just giving up."

Another pilot laughed. "Shall we challenge the Mustangs to a dogfight with Tante Ju?"

"Maybe the old girl will pick up her skirts and frighten them away." The fourth pilot grinned.

The man in the right seat didn't laugh. "I don't mean that. I just don't want to land like a sheep and surrender."

The laughter died and the others nodded. "What do you suggest?"

"We land in our parachutes."

"Just . . . bail out? Just like that?"

The copilot shook his head. "No. We fly this machine right to the end that befits her. A loop."

"Aha! Very good. She can't take it. She'll break up in the air."

"*Then* we bail out."

"Good! Let's do it." The pilot gestured. "Tighten your chutes. Get the doors. Jettison both cabin doors, left and right, and let's get this cockpit hatch all the way back. When she breaks up, we may have to get the hell out of here in a hurry."

The others nodded, jettisoned the doors. Two men in the cockpit and two in front seats of the cabin, strapped in tightly, wind loud through the open spaces. The pilot moved the three throttles forward and the engine thunder increased; at the same time, he pushed forward on the yoke. The Ju-52 nose went down, the horizon seeming to swoop upward as the angle of the dive increased. Their speed rose dramatically for an old transport, and the wind was now a thunder of its own. The big airplane vibrated through her wings and fuselage as they dived faster and faster.

What they didn't see was a loose gaggle of Mustang fighters, about a dozen in all, coming around the flank of a cloud. The fighter leader caught sight of the Ju-52 and called out the target to the others. Immediately, the Americans went to full throttle and raced after their quarry. They were eager for the kill; this could be their last chance. Then the Mustang pilots stared in disbelief as the Ju-52 continued its screaming dive. The flight leader ordered the others to hold their fire, and the fighters eased into a wide turn to watch the impossible happening.

Inside the cockpit, the pilot was pushing hard on his left rudder to hold the dive on a steady course. The air-speed indicator read three hundred twenty kilometers per hour—two hundred miles per hour—when he started coming back on the yoke, the copilot pulling with him. The nose came up with the hard pull and the corrugated machine came level with the horizon, holding her speed, and then the nose went higher and higher, until they were vertical, and they pulled as hard as they could on the yoke, because they were over on their back now, the speed down to ninety miles per hour, but the nose was coming down through the vertical, and they yanked back on the throttles as they dived straight down, easing off some of the back pressure—and they stared wonderingly at one another as the Ju-52 came out of the dive, shaking herself like a wet dog as she eased back into a climb and, without even thinking, the pilot went to cruise power.

They said nothing, but their looks told the story to them. If the airplane could survive an inside loop, well . . . an *outside* loop is another matter; many fighters would break apart under such a maneuver. The airplane is started into a dive until it becomes vertical. At this point, instead of coming back on the yoke to bring up the nose into a pullup and continuing entry into a loop, in which the airplane traces a circle, inverted at the top, in the outside loop you continue pushing forward on the yoke until you send the airplane onto her back while diving. The bottom of the loop occurs when the airplane is inverted and in level flight and then starts coming up the climbing part of the loop, the pressure on the wings reversed from normal, and the g loads transmitted upward to the pilots' heads. This is the "redout" situation, in which blood floods the brain and eyes. It's a bitch in any airplane except one designed for it, and the best and easiest outside loop ever flown is still something of a horror. The pressures, especially in a large aircraft,

defy imagination.

Nevertheless, the four Luftwaffe fighter pilots had started out to break the airplane apart in the air and then bail out, as their final act in a drama that had destroyed their country. Down went the nose, faster and faster, and the Mustang pilots watched in wonder as the nose went vertical and the Ju-52 began to tuck under and thundered, shaking and vibrating madly, into the killer maneuver. Inside the airplane, radios tore loose from their brackets, and equipment crashed wildly through the airplane and turned it into a mass of tumbling, tossing debris.

And she came around the bottom, upside down, and with the engines screaming under overboost, she climbed and clawed her way up the outside of that ripping maneuver and settled back into level flight, still in one piece, the main structure undamaged, while four men looked at each other in stunned disbelief.

Then they saw the Mustangs, and they cursed, because those American fighters were swift and deadly and their .50-calibers could tear them apart in the Ju-52 even before they had a chance to bail out. They started for the doors to jump when the pilot shouted at them. "Wait!" he cried out. "Look. . . ."

One each side of the Ju-52 was a Mustang, the gear coming down and the flaps full down so the sleek fighters could stay with the Ju-52, and they looked left and to their right, and the American pilots were grinning, and one saluted, and pointed down toward that airfield they had seen.

The German pilots shouted and laughed and slapped one another on the backs, because this sort of thing just didn't happen any more: *those Mustangs were escorting them in.* They were saluting them, recognizing them as pilots above and beyond national flags, and they went downstairs, power back, and lowered the flaps and let the Ju-52 settle onto the runway, and taxied off to the ramp and shut her down, Mustangs landing all around them, several already at the ramp, their big propellers stopped and the pilots waiting to greet them.

It could have been a page out of World War One. The German pilots were prisoners of war, but this same night they were not turned in to the military police or the ground combat troops. Not yet. That would wait until the morrow.

On this night it was a time to share drinks and get very, very drunk. These same men who had fought as killers against one another raised their glasses high.

To one another. . . .

———◆———

It was all over. The spring of 1945 ended, and there were no more fighters or bombers or transports flying with the sign of the crooked cross. They were all down now, the Junkerses and Dorniers and Heinkels and Messerschmitts and Focke-Wulfs and the rest of them. All across Europe, from Norway to the southern recesses of Russia, from France to Germany and in Italy and the Balkans and in Africa were strewn the wrecks and carcasses of the Ju-52s that had flown so long and so hard. No one knows how many were left, but the majority were in terrible shape and little time was wasted in scrapping the machines and melting down the metal. Those Ju-52s still able to fly were gone over by skilled mechanics and brought back to excellent condition. The best of engines were installed and new tires moved onto the gear and the instruments replaced. The iron crosses and the swastikas were painted over, and the airplanes flew transport duties wherever they were needed. But there were so many new machines, much faster and available in great numbers, that the Ju-52s fell steadily by the wayside, their number diminishing.

Strangely, only for a while. Most of the German airplanes went to airlines and companies and governments of the same countries they had helped defeat. The French kept the airplane in production, calling it the A.A.C. 1 Toucan, and built hundreds of them for various airlines and for the French Air Force, where it went into full use as a personnel and cargo transport—*and was returned to service as a bomber!* The Ju-52, alias A.A.C. 1 Toucan, soldiered on in Africa with French roundels on the wings and the fuselage, and they went to a place called French Indo-China, that is now Vietnam, where bombs were hung beneath the wings and the fuselage and they unloaded their explosives against native targets until finally the French were driven from the land, which was yet to know still another war and another period of its own particular hell.

There were Ju-52s flying in Finland and Hungary and China and all through Africa and Turkey and Portugal and England and Scotland and France and more places and lands than we will ever know. The Spanish built one hundred seventy airplanes known as the CASA-352L, which was the Ju-52/3m manufactured under license and powered by engines built in Spain that were copies of BMW radials that were copies of P&W radials.

The Ju-52 that had flown with the dynamite and construction equipment for the Pan American Highway, throughout the war, was finally written off the active register of aircraft and disappeared in limbo. No trace of this machine has ever been found. There was another Ju-52 in the United States, and this one bore the markings of the Army Air Forces and was brought to this country as a test article at Wright-Patterson Field, up in Ohio. If you want to win some more of those free-beer bets, just ask your flying friends to identify the C-79, and it's unlikely that they'll know this is the AAF designation given the war-prize Ju-52 while it was under testing by our Air Force. And even *that* Ju-52 vanished somewhere, because in a rash of disposing of tens of thousands of warbirds, that airplane went onto the scrap heap also, so that the Ju-52 that resides today in the Air Force Museum in Ohio isn't really a Ju-52 at all but one of those Spanish 352L copies.

The British flew their commercial versions for a little more than a year, and the world suddenly had its hands on all sorts of newer, more powerful, faster, longer-ranging transports. There were literally *thousands* of DC-3/C-47 airplanes available for a fraction of their original cost. Four-engine Douglas C-54 Skymasters were painted over in civilian colors and went into wide service under their original designation of DC-4. Curtiss C-46 Commandos were available by the hundreds, and Lodestars and Venturas and Harpoons and Catalinas and so many more began to push the Ju-52s from the scene. In the Scandinavian countries, the Ju-52 remained strong in its service, flying for Norway and Sweden and Finland, because it still operated for commercial airlines in the far-north country, still on wheels or floats as the weather dictated, and for ten years after the war ended, these aircraft were still flying passengers and cargo on scheduled routes.

———◆———

Long after the end of that war in Europe, there were Ju-52s that kept on flying their mountain and jungle operations in South America. Some of the familiar corrugated shapes did not even reach their new airfields and strips until 1956, for they had flown in Europe until they were no longer wanted and were scheduled to be melted down into scrap, as if they had never existed. But because they had been replaced, because their value in fiscal terms was low, they could be bought—and there were men who understand a Ju-52 and know that its age is immaterial, and because there were still so many spare engines and tires and parts to be found, the machines could still fly, and work, and do the job expected of them.

And fly they did. The years rolled on and the Ju-52s became weary, metal bent and torn. They could be called scarred and battered, for in every true sense of the word they were. And finally the spare parts were no longer plentiful, and then they were gone completely, and the only way to keep the old aircraft still flying was to scavenge and cannibalize, or make new parts by hand. But this took time, it demanded effort, and most of all it asked a great love of the old winged beasts. Finally there was only one left. Only one of the original airplanes that had emerged from a factory in Germany itself. The last of the *deutsches* breed.

On her wings, in broad, sweeping brush marks, was her registration: HC-ABS. She flew on when no more of the original line of Iron Annie still flew. There were Toucans and Pavos still flying in Switzerland and in Spain, but these were the copies, the offspring, as it were, of the original. There were Ju-52s still in existence, but they were either preserved in museums or they were deteriorating skeletons abandoned in rocky fields or desert sands or jungle growth.

And finally none of the original line was left to take to the air.

In Ecuador, nearly two miles above sea level off the edge of the main airport of Quito, there could barely be seen the corroding remains of a once magnificent airplane. The registration HC-ABS was barely visible in flaking, curling paint. On the flank of her squared-off nose, behind a rotting BMW engine, was a metal plate, painted over a dozen times, concealed from the eye. If one could have looked beneath all that scabrous covering, it would have been possible to read the *Werke* Number: 130714.

One of the original—the German—Ju-52s. Unflyable now, a dying and nearly dead creature of bent and battered metal that had already flown able, now, a dying and nearly dead creature of even the fable of the phoenix, let alone any possible resurrection. It would take a miracle, a series of miracles—some of which had already taken place with this machine to have kept it in the air as long as it had flown—ever to hope for renewed flight.

But it happened. And because of it, we are able to bridge from the past, some forty-five years ago, to this moment. We become part of living aviation history.

Wolfgang Wenck (left) with the author during an air show in Florida in 1976; Wenck was a master Luftwaffe pilot and personally flew Hitler several times to the area of the Russian front. He spent twelve years in a Siberian prison camp with other pilots before emigrating to Canada. NICK SILVERIO

Werke Number 5489 rolled out of the Dessau plant, gleaming in new paint, enjoying in her structure the benefit of experience gained from several years of operational service of her predecessors. The Ju-52/3m went through routine ground checks and was then taken up for flight testing by a Junkers pilot. She was signed off, and a final inspection was made of her seventeen passenger seats, the instruments in the cockpit, her fittings inside and out. A crew came to take her away, and the Junkers production manager marked off on his ledgers that *Werke* Number 5489 had been delivered to the shipping and airlines firm of Det Norske Luftfartselskap (DNL).

Her new owners assigned her the registration of LN-DAH, painted the Norwegian flag on the rudder, and christened her *Falken*. She flew with wheels and she flew with floats, and for five years *Falken* turned in memorable service on her grueling routes over mountains and within fjords. And then, in 1940, the German fighters struck and the sister ships of 5489 showed in the sky with black crosses and paratroopers spilling from the open doorways, and very quickly it was all over—and *Falken* was now among the spoils of war.

Built in Germany, sold to Norway, she was now back under German control, impressed into the Luftwaffe and painted with iron crosses and swastikas. The name *Falken* was dismissed, and the Luftwaffe had another combat transport. Originally she flew the routes between Norway and Hamburg, then moved on to other duties, and her wartime records vanished, as did so many other documents that will never be seen again. To guess as to what were the duties, the routes, the theaters in which this airplane flew would be only that: guesses. We are certain only that 5489 served as a combat transport in the German Air Force during World War Two.

The war ended for Germany in May of 1945, al-

most five years to the very day Norway was invaded, and when the conquerors capitulated, there were 512 German aircraft of all types in the country. By a great stroke of good fortune, among this number was 5489, come full circle. The Allies sorted through whatever records they could find, but little matter in the case of this particular airplane, for her *Werke* Number was well known within DNL, and the aircraft was returned to her former owners.

This is where it all began: *The Saga of Iron Annie.* The airplane being flown today in the United States in its original form as a Norwegian commercial airliner on floats in 1935. TOM WEIHE

It took time to sort out the pieces and restructure the country, and 5489, minus her original registration of LN-DAH, flew as an interim transport until all the dust settled. During the winter of 1947, DNL judged that the airplane had been hard used during the war and that it would be best for the machine to be rebuilt as completely as possible.

There were other Ju-52s in Norway, and one of these aircraft carried *Werke* Number 130714. This was a Ju-52/3mg8e model, representing the best and strongest of the production line. The original wings, tail, engines, and many other elements of the old airplane, LN-DAH, were mated to the new fuselage, and the airplane was re-equipped as a "new" airliner. The passenger seats were the highest-grade leather, the interior was made as comfortable as possible, and Norwegian identity plates and signs replaced the German markings.

Thus there was created the "new" LN-KAF and, in her new, gleaming paint, LN-KAF was christened *Askeladden*. Gone forever was the airplane once known as *Werke* Number 5489, although her wings and tail assembly and other parts had been mated with and were still flying as LN-KAF.

For the next nine years, *Askeladden* flew with

Enter onto the scene one *Kapitan* Christian Drexel, a man whom Kurt Streit describes as "one of the greatest pilots ever to fly, a true master as a military pilot and probably the best who ever flew with Lufthansa." Drexel bought the airplane and immediately registered it under the new ownership of Transportes Aéreos Orientales, S.A., of Quito, Ecuador. Arrangements were completed for the airliner to be taken by merchant ship to South America, and the Ju-52, on floats, was being towed from her mooring dock in harbor to the ship when —and nobody knows precisely what happened— her floats split wide open *and the airplane sank to the bottom of the harbor.*

She was raised immediately and, streaming

Twelve years and a major war later, the original LN-DAH has become LN-KAF, and with the serial number of its 1941 fuselage: 130714. It would fly another nine years on Scandinavian routes. CAIDIN ARCHIVES

DNL and with Scandinavian Airline Systems (SAS), until late 1956, when, as the last Ju-52/3m still flying in commercial operations in the Far North, her retirement was ordered. The airlines offered the machine as a gift to the Norwegian Technical Museum, in Oslo, but to the outrage of aviation enthusiasts and most officials of the country, the offer was rejected on the grounds that the museum lacked sufficient space to display the airplane. There was no small uproar over the decision of the museum to refuse to accept the machine, but it did little good and the airplane was offered up for sale.

water from every opening, moved to land. There an agonizing decision was made: *Clean her out thoroughly and rebuild wherever was necessary.*

Another of the small miracles in this life's game we call longevity was under way. Completely overhauled and put back on wheels, the airplane was loaded aboard the merchant vessel SS *Margrethe Bakke*, which departed Oslo in late 1957 bound for Ecuador with the former *Askeladden* lashed to her deck. She was unloaded from the merchant ship and transported to the nearest strip for reassembly back into a complete airplane. Ready for flight, she was tested thoroughly and then flown to her new

Iron Annie—the same aircraft that was built in 1935 with Serial Number 5489, rebuilt as SN 130714, and finally registered as HC-ABS and named *Amazonas*. The picture was taken in 1958 on a dirt road being used as an airfield high in the Ecuadorian mountains. R. S. APPLETON

base, at Quito—*more than nine thousand feet above sea level.* There she was given her new registration, HC-ABS, and put into service.

———◆———

No one is ever going to be able to tell us just what this airplane did operating out of Quito for the next five years. First, there isn't one man who knows it all. Second, of those who knew, many are dead. Third, many others who have some knowledge won't talk about it. I did a lot of research on this aspect of this seemingly immortal aircraft's time flying in South America. And what had been hard flying up to that point—twenty-two years by then, in fact—was replaced with relentless, hard, driving service all through South and Central America.

It might be best to wonder just what this airplane did *not* do. Just operating out of Quito was a miracle unto itself, because her pilots drove the Ju-52 with almost "cruel and unusual punishment." It was tough enough for an old bird with original German engines and fixed-pitch propellers to operate from low altitude with a full load, or to operate under very light weight from an airfield at ninety-three hundred feet, but to combine the worst of both—maximum loads and overloads at maximum

altitude for takeoffs and landings—is mind-boggling. And Quito was only her home base; we discovered that HC-ABS was operated from terrible airstrips in the middle of jungles and high atop mountains, that she was flown with loads so heavy the gear seemed to groan from the weight, and that she hauled just about anything and everything one could stuff into the fuselage.

We've confirmed that she flew machinery and tools and heavy equipment into remote jungle strips. At times her fuselage was jammed with slabs of beef. She carried construction crews and their families. They shoved goats and mules and chickens and wild animals in cages into her fuselage. If some of the tales about her are true, and there seems no reason to doubt them because of the sources I know but will never identify, she hauled gold many times—and almost as many times on some of these flights was the target of furious gunfire. Illicit operations? Not for us to say, because we weren't there, but there *were* bullet holes in this airplane that did not come from any war in Europe.

They didn't just fly this airplane, they pushed and shoved and drove and pounded and slammed and jerked and hauled and banged her about so roughly that any continued flight seemed a miracle.

107

But fly she did, and the maintenance performed on the airplane at first was barely acceptable, but it managed to worsen as the years went by, and then it became a sick joke. There was an abundance of happenstance patchwork. If there was a hole, forget it. If the hole was too big to forget, cover it with tape. If insects ate the tape or rain blew it away, just patch it up with metal from the airplane graveyards. Oil? Well, all oil looks the same, so just pour it into the tanks. Any grade would do, because any grade *did* do.

Aha, there is corrosion. Bad corrosion. Paint it over. How shall we paint it? It's a big airplane and there's no use wasting time, so the ground crews—if we can be forgiven this semantic blasphemy—walked along the wings and fuselage, dipping mops in buckets and swabbing the paint onto the airplane. Those multiple coats of housepaint covered corrosion, bends, tears, rips, gouges, gashes, holes, and only God knows what other ills that afflicted this stepchild of flight.

By now, the old BMW 132E engines were starting to come unglued, and when the throttles went forward, she shuddered through her thickly corrugated wings and body. *How* those engines ever managed to keep operating and kept hauling that overloaded, scab-strewn machine at high altitudes is a mystery that defies any hope of explanation by science. But operate they did, in a glory of praise to Pratt & Whitney and to the Bavarian Motor Works—and they continued to operate for many years yet to come.

But the airplane was literally starting to come apart. The corrosion was chewing at her. Instruments didn't work. Control systems were clogging. Valves stuck, lines froze, brakes faded, makeshift modifications fell apart and no one knew how to repair them, because nobody remembered how they'd been done in the first place.

The day came when they gave her up for lost. Ancient and bruised and ugly, she was dragged off to the side of the airfield, on a remote patch of ground at the edge of high jungle, and simply left there. That was about the worst of all. When you just walk away from an airplane, what you do in that abandonment is to condemn the machine. Rot and decay and mildew collect there, and she lies fallow to continuing corrosion and drying seals, and the sum of it all is guaranteed death, like a carcass left in the jungle for thousands of tiny creatures to scavenge to their fill.

About the only insult the Ju-52 didn't receive was open assault by vandals. Especially kids. They can do more to an airplane than a brace of 20-millimeter cannon. But at Quito, especially at this particular field, the mob with steel vises and crushers for hands weren't there. They really weren't needed.

The tires rotted, the hydraulic lines fell apart, the electrical systems were eaten by all manner of crawling, chewing things. A condor built a nest through a gaping tear in her huge tail. Snakes and rodents and insects took up domain in her wings, and most of her deep belly hatches and all manner of secret compartments became jungle-creature habitat.

The end of the road. The closing of the last flight plan. Shut her down, guys. She'll never fly again. *Finis.*

HC-ABS high in the Ecuadorian Andes. The nose fairing directly behind the speed ring, to deflect engine grease, was removed before the airplane was flown to the United States. R. S. APPLETON

Several years went by, and HC-ABS rotted away, a metallic abscess in Ecuadorian jungle. There was no more use for her, which in its own way was strange, because Drexel had a hangar filled with spare parts: engines, wheels, tires and instruments, pitot tubes, and screws and nuts and bolts and cables and wiring and structural parts and magneto housing for the quadrant and—well, he had a small mountain of parts. But, whatever reasons he had, Drexel knows better than anyone else why he no longer bothered with restoration or even upkeep.

The big iron bird lay forgotten and ignored until

1968, when a German woman landed at Quito. With some time to spare, she wandered about the airport, caught a glimpse of metal within thick foliage, and went to look—and gaped. Her name was Barbara, and many long years before, she had been a stewardess on a Ju-52, and she was also a pilot and had even flown Tante Ju and God, but she wanted to *buy* this airplane and bring it up to the United States, where she was now a citizen. Whatever happened, she wasn't forceful enough or Drexel didn't believe her. What does matter was that she left Quito and promised to return to purchase the airplane. Drexel must have wondered what the hell was going on, because within a few months he had another visitor who wanted to buy HC-ABS, and he was willing to close the deal right then and there.

Lester F. Weaver, at the time of his trip to Quito, was with his wife and family visiting at the American embassy. Weaver's life was assuredly a quiet one; he lived in Polo, Illinois, and made his living as a barber. To him, the Ju-52 was the perfect buy. Weaver had been in B-17s during the Second World War, and he was well aware of the explosive growth of interest in the surviving warbirds of that era that had been sparked by such outfits as the Confederate Air Force, which operated out of its headquarters of Rebel Field, at Harlingen, Texas. If Weaver played his cards right, then he could put the only known German Ju-52 in the world up for sale and make a killing. You can't blame a man for taking his shot at some of the long green. No one to this day except Drexel and Weaver knows just what were the negotiations to transfer ownership of HC-ABS from Drexel to Weaver, but with whatever dexterity and manipulation required, they did it. Now, according to one of the leading aviation magazines in this country, which did a bit of research shortly after the deal was wrapped up, the airplane was supposed to be in good shape. In fact, the magazine quoted Weaver as saying the airplane was "ready for the long trip to the United States."

The remark was good public relations on Lester Weaver's part, but the airplane not only wasn't ready for the trip, it was a dog. There were also some strange shenanigans between Weaver, the Ecuadorian Government, and the U. S. State Department. As soon as he had signed the papers with Drexel, Weaver made contact with the Federal Aviation Administration (FAA) Records Center, in

Oklahoma. By paying a small fee for the privilege, he had a new registration number assigned to the airplane. N130LW obviously has as the letters for its call sign the initials LW, which work out to Lester Weaver.

Apparently, the Ecuadorian Government and Weaver were now involved in a hassle about ownership and getting former HC-ABS, now registered as N130LW, out of the country. That magazine I referred to, *Air Classics*, stated that Weaver "managed to outlast the Ecuadorian Government in a long struggle to get it out of South America. And even then, only U. S. State Department pressure turned the trick." The magazine further explained that getting the registration number also got Weaver "a ferry permit to bring it into the country. Ultimately, it saved the plane for him."

There was still the matter of flying the airplane out of Ecuador to the United States. Part of Weaver's deal with Drexel was that the former Lufthansa captain would attend to those arrangements. But Drexel was busy, and he was *tired* (he said so himself), and he didn't want the hassle of getting the airplane back into shape. No matter that Weaver was quoted as saying the Ju-52 was "ready for the long trip to the United States," it not only wasn't in good shape, it couldn't even turn over its engines or hold fuel in its wings or do anything except lie in the jungle like a great heap of winged sludge.

Drexel didn't want to fly 130LW out of the country, but he knew an American pilot who could fly *anything*. This was George Hamilton, the director of operations for Argosy Air Lines, Inc., who flew at times to Ecuador and had built his own brand of fame as a pilot of extraordinary skills. George is a very large and beefy man, with his weight slung from a big frame with broad shoulders, and he's got a sort of crooked smile and crow's feet at the corners of his eyes, and when he looks at you there's a smile in that look, and he's quiet, but you know that, by damn, *this is a pilot*. He contracted with Drexel to fly the airplane out of Ecuador—all *very* legal—into the United States. To do so, he needed more than permission from Ecuador. He had to get a ferry permit from the FAA through the GADO-5 office at Opa-locka, in Florida; this is the General Aviation Development Office, which at the time was being run under the helm of Jaime Serra. The man who signed the papers for the ferry permit was Red Gargaly, and Gargaly, a whipsawed cutting blade if ever there was one, studied all the data and approved the deal, with the proviso that George Hamilton receive a *very* thorough checkout from Drexel.

Here is where some of the previous comments just don't fit in with the dates. The aircraft log for N130LW isn't exactly the acme of accuracy in all respects, since among other things it mixes up Bavarian Motor Works as the manufacturer for the Ju-52 (instead of Junkers) and identifies the engine type as manufactured by BMW and the engine models as Ju-52 instead of BMW 132E. Little things like that. But it *does* show that Bud Weaver entered into the aircraft log for the Ju-52, Serial Number 130714, that he was the owner of the airplane (for which he had closed the deal in 1969) as of the date of May 25, 1970.

And the airplane was not ready to fly—despite its being in good shape and ready for the long trip to the United States—*for another six months of rebuilding and repairing.* And that George Hamilton made his first flight, a local training flight at Quito, on November 10, 1970, for a total of three hours and ten minutes.

Now, George was in Quito for some time getting that thorough checkout from Drexel. At first this wasn't nearly as easy as it sounds, because the airplane simply wasn't able to fly. Among other things, they had to set off smoke bombs under the airplane and inside the airplane to drive out the incredible number and staggering variety of creatures that had taken up permanent residence in the Ju-52. The engines hadn't turned over for some *eight years,* and there were accumulations of rust, dust, fungus, mildew, corrosion, and anything else rotten you may choose. The lines had rotted away just about everywhere, the brakes were a mess, and what George and his copilot *didn't know* was that even the main carry-through spar in the fuselage center section had succumbed to corrosion.

As one shining example, after weeks and then months of repair work had gone on, the plane once again came within a cat's whisker of being destroyed. The job of honcho on the operation of getting the bird ready for flight fell to a local mechanic, who might have been an Ecuadorian colonel for all George Hamilton knew, whom they all called Colonel Okey Dokey. Not as strange as it seems, for every time Hamilton asked this chief of rebuilding operations how a certain task was going, he would receive a broad smile and an exuberant

"Okey dokey!" It just didn't matter what was the question, the answer was always the same. George paid very special attention to the fuel tanks. Among other things, his life would depend on the ability of those tanks to retain the fuel he needed to get over a lot of mountains and across a lot more of water. When he questioned the mechanical wonder on the state of the fuel system, he received his anticipated huge toothy grin and the upraised thumb and the shouted "Okey dokey!"

They finally fired up 130LW, and as they did, George Hamilton looked out of the cockpit and stared in disbelief as aviation fuel cascaded back of the wings and splashed on the ground as if every faucet in the airport had been turned full on and was sending its contents through the wings of this particular airplane. And someone was standing idly by with a lit cigarette and just as idly tossed it into the gasoline-soaked high grass, *and there was a huge ball of fire that boomed along the ground and boiled up to encompass the Ju-52.* Hamilton and Drexel were both hammering the throttles full forward and the Ju-52 lurched like a wounded elephant stung in its backside with a sharp spear. The propeller flattened out flames, pushed them away, and the airplane rocked and swung away under its own power from the now roaring blaze.

Colonel Okey Dokey hadn't lied to George Hamilton about the fuel tanks being in good shape. They were. But what he hadn't told anyone, and maybe it was because they never asked him, was that the lines between the individual tanks inside the wings weren't connected, and when they were filled and the airplane began drawing fuel through those lines . . . it gushed onto the ground.

There were more errors and comedies of errors but very little comedy. But what really matters to us is that eventful date of November 10, 1970, when 130LW, with Drexel and Hamilton at the controls, showed that a phoenix truly could be rebuilt, that the battered old BMW engines were close to eternal, and that even from an altitude of 9,300 feet to start her flight, the old corrugated maiden still had her stuff—and they were off the ground and into a training and checkout flight that lasted for three hours and ten minutes. They flew the next day for five hours and on the twelfth of November for two hours and ten minutes, and Drexel signed off George Hamilton as the new chief pilot of the now-ancient aircraft.

It wasn't all *that* easy. Starting up the Ju-52 is an

arm-bending and neck-twisting act of dexterity all its own, and it had to be learned on a one-on-one basis with Drexel, because among the other minor problems associated with this procedure, there wasn't any aircraft manual. None. *Nothing.* It was all verbal and George taking notes and using his vast experience—and his immediate familiarity with the airplane—to assure his full control. After the third flight, on the twelfth, Colonel Okey Dokey and his cohorts began stuffing spare parts into the Ju-52. Their procedure was simple. Drexel told Hamilton what he felt was most important from the hangar full of old parts and subassemblies, and Hamilton pointed to these, and Colonel Okey Dokey grinned anew and shouted his happy words, and then abused the men working for him into hustling along with the job. Take everything at which the *Americano* pointed and stuff it into the airplane. Into the belly hatches below the floorboards. Into the cargo compartment in the rear. Into the water closet. Into the fuselage; anywhere and everywhere it would fit. When they were done, the airplane was as stuffed as a porker being carried to a Hawaiian luau, overweight by some monstrous figure no one dared to compute (and lacked the means to do so), and faced takeoff from that field nearly two miles above sea level.

A hell of a way to start for home!

Every time I think of George Hamilton with his crow's-feet-creased eyes and that warm, crooked smile and his huge gentleness, big hands wrapped about the wooden yoke of that lumbering monster, I'm not sure whether to think of George as my friend or as someone who set a new benchmark in aviation history by his piloting of that heavily overloaded Ju-52. Of course, George was legal, for there's a little FAR (Federal Aviation Regulation) that allows a pilot to overload his airplane for a ferry flight and when he's carrying crew only. In the latter case there were only George and his tight-jawed copilot, Gregory C. Tompkins, and all that stuff crammed into the airplane and the fuel tanks filled to the brim.

How many of us would have been willing to make that takeoff, with the ancient engines, the fixed-pitch propellers, and all that soggy weight . . . from the ninety-three-hundred-foot altitude of Quito? It was but all in a day's work to George as his skilled touch gave *Iron Annie* her new breath of life as she took to the sky. On November 14, 1970, he and Tompkins flew from Quito to Cali, in Columbia. It was not an uneventful flight. There were high mountains and there were bigger clouds, and there were storms, and the radios often made no more noise than a gnat whistling in the wind. But they pushed through the bad weather, that included some tropical rain that made them think of flying through Niagara Falls, and finally landed at Cali. They stayed there long enough to collect a group of a thousand or so visitors who cheered the takeoff of the lumbering tri-motor for its leg of three hours and thirty-three minutes to Medellín, Colombia.

By now, many of the idiosyncrasies of those BMW radials were coming home to George, for sometimes it took a while for the engines to warm up and do a strange dance of spitting out grease. The BMW 132E models had external rocker-arm

boxes that demanded greasing—filling them chockfull of grease—every ten hours of operation. This is one reason you see so many photographs of wartime Ju-52s with what appears to be a fully cowled nose engine. It's not. It's the Townend speed ring that encircles the engine, but the rocker-arm boxes of that engine brought many German pilots, in desperate frustration, to put up a grease deflecting shield between themselves and the rocker-arm box system.

They threw grease. That is a gentle way of saying that often they emitted a furious storm of grease. Not tiny globules, but drops and spatters and great big globs, all of which came back from the nose engine and smeared the cockpit windshield. Add to the grease some oil from the engine, and then stir up this appetizing brew with dragonflies and mosquitoes and butterflies and bumblebees and moths and every other kind of dusty and furry winged creature that have spattered against the windshield, and the net result is flying blind. Instead of being in *Iron Annie*, you're in Captain Nemo's *Nautilus*, with the sole exception of having some visibility to the sides, and there's a slim upper window in the cockpit that you can use to look through by standing up until the last moment when you need to apply rudder. I know; I did it often enough, and when I think of where George Hamilton was flying, and through what conditions, I think the man must have had some sort of bionic vision with the ability to see through thick grease splattered with all those friendly dead creatures on his windshield.

On November 15, it took three hours and forty-six minutes from Medellín to Tocumen, in Panama, and then, after refueling, another hop, of two hours and thirty-nine minutes, to bring them into Puerto Limón, Costa Rica. Their overnight stay was another opportunity for mobs of people to gawk at the airplane. The next morning, the sixteenth, they kept the flight short: one hour and ten minutes from Puerto Limón to El Coco, still within Costa Rica. More fuel, setting up the flight plan, and they were off for a flight of three hours and fifty-seven minutes from El Coco to Tegucigalpa, Honduras, where they quit for the day.

They were learning many things about the airplane: its marvelous docility in cruise, its rock-steady approach to a landing, and the fact that those weary old engines and their heavy weight meant they should consider themselves fortunate to average about 105 miles per hour true air speed in cruising flight. On the seventeenth, onward from Tegucigalpa to Belize for three hours and fifty-eight minutes, and enough for the day. The next morning, they flew for two hours and twenty minutes to Cozumel, Mexico, landed, and did a lot of hard thinking.

There were two ways of going on up to the States: They could take that long route up along Mexico and into the southwestern United States, because it would always keep them with land in sight beneath their wings. Or they could fuel up to the last gallon of gasoline, express great faith in the ancient BMW radials, and cut across the Gulf of Mexico. George opted for faith (and perhaps a rabbit's foot and a few dozen assorted good-luck charms), which was not without reason, since by now he had collected enough information to *know* precisely what were the fuel consumption and the oil consumption of the engines. Since the Ju-52 has a mechanical standpipe leading into a mechanical fuel gauge housed in a shark fin on the wing nacelles, you can look outside the airplane for a reading of your fuel level. This is fine, except that often grease and oil splattering back from the wing engines obscure all sight of the gauges. There is only one way to fly the Ju-52 in terms of fuel, and

On the flight line at Savannah, Georgia, in 1970 while en route from Quito to Illinois, HC-ABS has a new registration, N130LW. The big iron bird shows off her multiple layers of white housepaint—which didn't stay white very long. SILBERMAN COLLECTION

Iron Annie looked far better in her housecoat than she did internally. The Savannah stop took most of its time to pour in almost ten gallons of oil per engine. SILBERMAN COLLECTION

that is to learn what your fuel consumption is at selected power settings and leaned mixture and altitude, and then, after using a dipstick to make certain the tanks are really full, constantly check the clock in flight. There is no other way, period.

Dipstick study completed, the airplane checked out, George and Tompkins climbed back into 130LW at Cozumel, fired up, and pushed their way into the Big Blue. They climbed slowly and steadily, monitoring the gauges, willing to accept their laborious speed, and five hours and thirty-four minutes later, eased the smooth tires to the runway of Fort Lauderdale Executive Airport, just north of Miami. Red Gargaly and Jaime Serra and assorted other disbelievers stared at the white-grayish form of the airplane, not really believing what they were seeing.

"You're lucky to be here," Red told George.

"I know," he said, and although his tone was laconic and he was relaxed, if not worn in body from all that flying, he was still unwinding.

There weren't any mechanical problems to upset George on the way across the Gulf of Mexico, but there had been a screw-up in certain paper work. And so *Iron Annie* droned across the warm waters, closing the distance slowly but steadily to Florida, without any flight plan ever having been received by the Air Force. In those days, you did not just go bumbling across international waters and wander into American territory without observing all requirements of the ADIZ—the Air Defense Identification Zone. Believing that they were cleared through the ADIZ, George and Tompkins were understandably perturbed when radar picked them up, no record of a flight plan showed, and two jet fighters scrambled with hot guns to intercept the "unknown." The jet pilots' first reports of what was lumbering through the sky brought disbelief, anger, frustration, and the temptation to order the unknown shot down. Cooler heads prevailed, the fighters kept a hot-guns watch on the airplane, frantic telephone calls were made, and permission was finally granted (again) for the Ju-52 to land.

Hamilton and Tompkins rested for several days and went through the reams of paper work that inevitably accompanies an experience of this nature. On the twenty-first of November, they took off from Executive Airport and put in four and a half hours in the airplane until they touched down at Savannah, Georgia. One of the people who gawked in disbelief at the corrugated thing on the ramp was an ex-military pilot by name of John Silberman, who was so intrigued by the Ju-52 that he couldn't wait to volunteer to help service the machine—which in this situation meant refilling the oil tanks one quart at a time.

Such enthusiasm invariably carries its own rewards: years later, John Silberman flew into Lake-land, Florida, for a big whoop-de-doo with the Experimental Airplane Association and a great bash of warbirds. The airplane John was flying, along with Jay Hinyub, was a DC-3 that was owned by a former president of Mexico and that John had repainted in the colors of the original DC-3 that for a while had been the personal plane of one Donald Douglas. Be all that as it may, John and Jay ended up in the cockpit of the Ju-52 and fulfilled a long-delayed frantic urge to "cut loose" with the old girl.

Watching George Hamilton taking off from Savannah that same day must have given Silberman some mixed emotions. After the long haul up from Quito, the left engine (number one) on takeoff or

Standing under the left engine is George Hamilton, of Argosy Airlines, who flew N130LW into the United States. Atop the wing (top photo) is John Silberman, just discharged from the U. S. Army, who poured "limit-less" oil into the tanks. Hamilton and Silberman (bottom photo) are together on the wing, commenting on oil consumption. Seven years after this picture was taken, John Silberman joined Martin Caidin in the cockpit of N52JU (ex-N130LW) for an air-show flight at Lakeland, Florida.
SILBERMAN COLLECTION

at any time of full power was emitting a long plume of uncomfortably thick white smoke. The consumption of oil had, in fact, gone almost out of sight. It was a problem soon to be faced by Bud Weaver.

George took three hours even for the leg from Savannah on up to Knoxville, Tennessee, where he quit for the night. The next morning, they put in a leg of two hours flat from Knoxville to Junction City, Kentucky, landed for fuel and a break, and

went back to the airplane for the last leg: four hours and twenty minutes from Junction City to Dixon, Illinois. It was early evening of the twenty-second of November, 1970, and the long ferry flight from Quito, Ecuador, was ended.

Bud Weaver had his airplane, and he was about to learn a whole series of lessons in the unexpected, when it came to the care, feeding and flying of a machine that for so long had been a derelict. It's a hell of a classroom.

Straining mightily, N130LW roars down the Savannah runway in 1970—and the housepaint does little to hide the smoke streaming from the number-one (left) engine, which already was coming unglued. She's in the air (bottom photo) and on her way to delivery in Illinois.
SILBERMAN COLLECTION

116

The Fairchild was five miles out of the municipal airport at Sterling, Illinois, dropping from the sky on an invisible rail at 140 knots. Inside the cockpit, Scott Johnson, in the left seat, and his copilot were going through the everyday checklist of power settings and gear and flaps and trim. "It was like always," Scott said, "the ground rushing up to meet us, our shadow preceding the machine as it grew larger on the concrete like a praying mantis descending upon its victim. Then holding the flare, and we're on; the prop buzzer, like the staccato report of a tommy gun, interrupts the hypnotic whine of the turbines. Okay; ground fine pitch and put it all to rest. Done. Five lights, the man at my right tells me. Now the gust lock and turn off at the end. Rollout speed dying away nicely with the air brakes hissing each time they're released and—

"My copilot, Lenny Smith, stares out his window. All the officialese of Ozark Airlines Flight 871 is forgotten. 'What in the hell *is* that thing?' is the query, followed by a low mutter. 'It looks like the Luftwaffe has arrived here, and all this time I thought the war ended way back when.'

"We turned and I looked where he pointed and I couldn't believe it. Fantastic! I was excited by what I saw. Grotesque, monstrous, a great hunk of corrugated metal with the iron cross plastered all over it and paint peeling and curling away from one end to the other. I didn't believe it. I'd never seen one of these things, but I recognized the Junkers Ju-52 at once. Thoughts went through my head like dust before a windstorm, about getting up in that cockpit and looking through the greenhouse and holding the yoke with one hand and my right hand on a fistful of throttles and— Hold it, I told myself. Let's shut this down. We're driving an airliner with a lot of people. I glanced at my watch. We'd been running late and we wouldn't have much time during this turnover before firing up and taking off. We were shutting down and we got the signal the

chocks were in and I didn't waste a moment getting out of my airliner and running across the tarmac, Lenny right with me, and we were like two kids, gaping. It *was* fantastic. A page out of history. God, look at those tires. Smooth as a baby's ass and without any tread and I started around the left wing toward the tail and touched metal and I just couldn't believe it, and then I looked back at Ozark 871 and the last passenger was climbing aboard, and the ramp agent was hollering at us about schedules. We sprinted back to the Fairchild and I went up and got into the seat. We punched the right buttons and moved the right switches and we were powered up and taxiing away from the ramp, and it was only a few minutes more when I snapped up the gear handle on our twin-engine Dog Whistle, the jet engines spinning madly and the big props a blur as we climbed toward Moline, Illinois, to the southwest. Beyond Moline would be our next stop, in Kansas City; I'd flown this trip

N130LW at Rockford Airport—her engine cowls already painted black where the housepaint had curled and peeled away. The antenna array was for show only; none of the radios worked. SCOTT JOHNSON

maybe a thousand times and I'd flown it in the DC-3 and the Martin 404 and now in the Fairchild 27 and I think I really knew the whole thing blindfolded, the same towns, same altitudes, same rivers, same frequencies, and the only things that changed were the weather and the radio frequencies. And all the way to Kansas City all we could talk about was that incredible machine out of time. Where the devil had it come from? What the hell was it doing in Sterling, Illinois? Who owned it? We'd have to wait for the answers."

— ◆ —

That was Scott Johnson's first look at and introduction to *Iron Annie.* N130LW sat on the flight line at Sterling like a phantom out of the past, and something about her tugged deeply within Scott and he felt a calling and a yearning such as he'd never known before.

Scott is an old flying friend of mine. He's a big, beefy guy with corded wood for arms and a heavy gut that's as soft as a keg that holds nails, and he smokes the worst damned cigars in the world and he flies like an angel. It's important to understand, to *know* this about a man so wildly enthusiastic and turned on with no more than this first and brief introduction to *Iron Annie.* He's like a kid hanging onto an airport fence with unquenchable longing in his eyes. He's the airport bum who'd empty garbage cans and wash airplanes and mop the john and do *anything* to fly.

He's also been an airline captain for more than seventeen years and holds his Air Transport Rating in the DC-3, DC-6, DC-7, DC-9, F-27/227, the Martin 202 and 404, the Convair 240, 340, and 440, and the A340 and A440, and a bunch of others, plus commercial-type ratings in the B-17 and the B-25 and the B-26 and, oh, another whole bunch of heavy military iron with wings.

That first meeting with the Ju-52 would result in major activity with the airplane for two years, but first there's a bit of a preface. . . .

The logbooks tell the story. On November 22, 1970, George Hamilton flew N130LW into Dixon, Illinois.

The next flight for this airplane didn't take place until—according to the aircraft log that was kept by Bud Weaver—the twenty-first of May, 1972. *That's a year and a half later,* and the reason the airplane didn't fly before then is that it was a long, long way from being in the great condition described by Weaver when he was quoted in *Air Classics.* The engines needed work, the instruments were within the capabilities of George Hamilton and no one else at the time, and there was a disastrous problem with the old Ju-52 itself. A ferry permit brought the airplane from Quito to Dixon, but when it arrived in Illinois it was no longer a legally airworthy machine. It had new and far more stringent standards to meet than had been imposed on it *for decades.* To compress a long and somewhat sorrowful story, an inspection of the aircraft revealed severe corrosion in the center section. I quote from the aircraft log:

— ◆ —

8/18/71. The following work completed this date. Replaced corroded carry-thru spar in fuselage center section (See FAA Form 337 this date for details). Installed battery box in number two baggage compartment in right side of compartment. Greased wheel bearings, repaired hydraulic leak in right wheel cylinder. Installed ten sets of Rupert seat belts. Replaced rudder trim bungee cords. Inspected controls, control linkage, cables, drained sumps. AD [Airworthiness Directive] compliance checked through 71-16. AD Note 61-8-2 on Rupert seat belts does not apply. I certify that this aircraft has been inspected in accordance with a 100-hour inspection and was determined to be in airworthy condition.

— ◆ —

The logbook entry was signed off by Gordon W. Rutt, who carries aircraft inspector identification of IA 303528.

Three months later, the FAA, out of its Chicago office, signed off a Special Airworthiness Certificate under the category of Experimental-Exhibition. This was signed in the logs by E. Winter, of GADO-3.

The next entry in the log shows the first flight in Illinois as May 21, 1972—eighteen months after it arrived in Dixon. It made a number of local flights and some abbreviated cross-country trips and went through interminable periods on the ground when it never moved—and was assailed by weather from steaming summers to winters of screaming cold, ice, and snow. Through all of 1972, it flew on only thirteen days.

In all of 1973, it flew only five times.

Between September 1973 and May 1974, it sat on

the ground. Then, on August 25, 1974, it was flown from Rockford, Illinois, to Cape Girardo, in Missouri, and then flown on to Charlotte, North Carolina—no longer the property of Bud Weaver. By now it was just a battered, beaten-up, rundown flying wreck that had been sold at auction to the highest bidder. The dreams of making a financial killing with the airplane had vanished like wispy smoke in a gale.

Don Anklin, of Cannon Aircraft, had bought N130LW and had it up for sale—and it spent month after month continuing to rot, to corrode, to deteriorate. They ran up the engines now and then, and Anklin told anyone who asked that the airplane was in really good condition and was flown at regular intervals to keep it in great flying shape, but it was so much snake-oil sales pitch.

But let's go back to Illinois and N130LW and her infrequent flights, which likely would never have taken place had not Scott Johnson showed on the scene.

First, however, let me make some things very clear about our aging and battered airplane. Outside of what was obvious to some very capable mechanics, *no one knew what the hell he was doing with this airplane.* There wasn't any German manual. There wasn't any manual of any kind for a long time. Finally, Bud Weaver got the Air Force to make a copy of the Spanish manual they had on their CASA 352L, and this was the only reference on the German airplane, and there were so many things that were different the matter was laughable to the point of being nearly lethal. Weaver finally got some engine manuals on the BMW radials, *but they were in French.* Everything that was happening to N130LW was an incredible by-gosh-and-by-guess routine that makes the airplane's survival more of a miracle than anything that had yet happened with it through all its years of grueling service and abuse.

On the official documents identifying the aircraft and listing its operating characteristics and limitations, I discovered just how much blind groping was going on in place of hard and realistic knowledge. The airplane was listed officially as a Ju-52/M3 (instead of a Ju-52/3m), and the records were still burdened with the fuzzy engine identification of 13ZE, which never existed. The empty weight was shown as 15,950 pounds, and that was surprisingly accurate. The gross weight of 23,100 pounds was right on the money, since this was the allowable gross weight as taken from the Spanish manual (which I later confirmed to be a copy of the figures from the German manual). But those weights had a gap in them as wide as three front teeth in the smile of your best girl. The airplane hadn't had a weight-and-balance for untold years, and the CG (center of gravity) was a mystery. Fortunately for all told, Hamilton's checkout met all legal and safety needs, and the Ju-52 has a remarkable CG that is one of the most forgiving of any airplane ever built.

I didn't believe the performance limitations. The never-exceed speed was listed as 125 miles per hour, and that meant that this was purely a guessing game, because even the Spanish copy flew a hell of a lot faster than that when the nose was pushed down, and it had a never-exceed speed of 170 miles per hour. I guess that at this point they still didn't have even that Spanish manual. The guessing continued with the listed cruise speed of 110 miles per hour, and then came the stall-speed listing, 80 miles per hour. And I *knew* this was pure guesswork, because the Ju-52 *fully loaded* can be held off until you're down to about 62 miles per hour, and without a heavy load you can drop flaps and grind in the power and bumble about the sky at about 55 to 58 miles per hour. That's from a series of stall tests we made with the airplane when it still had the BMW 132E engines.

Oh, well. Scott Johnson confirmed, from conversations he'd had with Bud Weaver, that Weaver really did stand a great chance to make some very big bucks with N130LW. The warbird heat was on in the country, and the Confederate Air Force was doing a smash job of fanning that heat, and there wasn't a German-built Ju-52 in the country. Weaver, according to what he told Johnson, bought the airplane for fifty-two hundred dollars from Drexel. That's as slick a deal as you can make, and it's all huzzahs for one Bud Weaver and my compliments. He then had to bear the costs of paying for the ferry flight plus the fuel and the paperwork and such nasty goodies that always accompany such transactions, and when he got that airplane that was in such great shape into Illinois, he faced the replacement of the carry-thru spar in the center section, and *that* cost somewhere between twelve and fifteen thousand pieces of green. So the price was rocketing upward.

He also had a problem in that the airplane, since it had never been legally certificated in the United

States, was kept in the Experimental-Exhibition category, and that meant you could not carry passengers in the big iron bird. So the market for a buyer narrowed immediately, because future flights meant tooling around with a great, empty cabin. And you couldn't fly over densely populated areas or fly on any congested airways, except for takeoff and landing, and, because no one was really sure of the stopping distance on landing, the pilot was required to notify any operating control tower that 130LW was experimental and then receive permission to land and/or take off.

Item Number Four of the "Operating Limitations" had a Catch-22 phrase in it that would haunt the pilots who flew the airplane, and one with which I would wrestle: "Passenger carrying not permitted unless the pilot has an appropriate type rating or letter of authorization." We'll return to *this* one later.

———◆———

Bud Weaver was going to sell N130LW for $125,000. Pretty good, except that the odds were far greater than he knew, and mainly because the airplane was in desperate need of work, and Weaver wasn't about to spend any more of the long green than he could get away with. That's a self-defeating premise, because it's difficult to sell an airplane that's covered inside and out with scabs and sores and is old and worn and is going to get worse, because airplanes, especially old airplanes, need the kind of tender loving care that costs a lot of bread, and there is just no way out of that box.

Bud Weaver owned the airplane, and since he was a commercial pilot and had his multiengine rating, he was legally the pilot-in-command, but the fact of the matter is that except for just under one hour with Weaver at the controls, most of the flying performed when Weaver owned the iron bird was done with Scott Johnson in the pilot's seat. And this was a critical saving grace for this Ju-52, for it's doubtful the airplane would have survived its several years in the central northlands of our fair country. It took a hell of a lot of flying to handle 130LW in her shape in those days, and fortunately, Scott Johnson is a hell of a lot of pilot.

Now a word about the FAA up in the northland. The more I try to picture just what was taking place with this airplane the more I can empathize with the FAA officials involved in the licensing of the airplane. There was no question but that it was

airworthy, for George Hamilton had flown it to Dixon from Quito, and it had been inspected (and found wanting, with those wants attended to), and the proper restrictions in the interests of safety attached to the operation of 130LW. The GADO office went strictly by the book, which in all but a few rare cases is why the book was written in the first place, and they granted the necessary paperwork within the pertinent Federal Aviation Regulations for the machine to fly.

But an Airworthiness Certificate that attests to the airworthiness of an airplane is good only so long as that airplane is maintained in that flyable condition. That's a damned important thing to remember. The FAA doesn't play Big Brother by staring over a man's shoulder all the time. It has set up a system of properly designated authority down the line that reaches out to and encompasses the man who owns the airplane, who in the case of 130LW was also legally pilot-in-command. PIC can be exercised from any seat anywhere in the airplane. It is that ultimate authority resting with one person, and there are no ifs, ands, maybes, or buts about it.

The measure of caring for an airplane is an enormous variable, and as every pilot knows, there exists an enormous gulf between maintenance as a minimum legal requirement and throwing all your effort into taking care of an aircraft. Where 130LW was concerned, and this was a fact that emerged only slowly, airworthiness went from an inspected and approved reality to a question mark and finally to outright nonsense.

Because an airplane can fly does not mean it is airworthy. If something fails ten minutes after the FAA inspector has driven off the field, all you have is a ticket and not necessarily an airworthy machine. If you know parts are failing and you're liable to suffer catastrophic failure, you can still take off—but the airplane is not airworthy in the proper sense of the word, because its safety has been compromised before you even turn on the battery switch.

This seems to have been the yoke under which the Ju-52 labored, and most heavily indeed. Systems began to fail, parts came unglued, and there was so much of a demand for maintenance and rebuilding that in order to remain airworthy, 130LW needed not simply mechanical work *but dedication.* She didn't get it. Period.

Every hour in the air required a hundred or two

hundred knuckle-bruising work hours on the ground. On a hot day, even with a light load, 130LW could barely stagger to fifty-five hundred feet. The airplane that could lift from Quito at ninety-three hundred feet with a full load at takeoff now groaned her way to just one mile above sea level. The airplane *wanted* to fly, but the old pizazz simply wasn't there.

———◆———

Lenny Smith, Scott Johnson's copilot on Ozark Airlines, finally managed a direct telephone contact with Lester Weaver. Johnson and Smith had been told Bud Weaver was looking for someone qualified to fly the Ju-52, and Lenny told Weaver they were hot to trot. It was a long conversation. "Lenny's ear was getting sore," Scott Johnson recalls. "That was pretty obvious as the minutes went by. *First, Weaver tried to sell him the airplane.* That was out of the question, and then Bud decided that he was looking for someone to fly it with him and share the expenses."

On the ground in Illinois—where N130LW spent most of her time for the years 1970–74. SCOTT JOHNSON

Lenny didn't go for that, and so he tried to sell Weaver on the idea of getting a sponsor to handle the costs of maintaining and running the Ju-52. "You know," Scott said, "maybe Lufthansa, because they used so many of these birds. It would have been great promotion, but Weaver wouldn't hear of it. This was his machine and nobody else was going to get a piece of the action unless he was in the limelight, stage center, and all that. It finally boiled down that I was willing to share expenses, *anything* to fly that Ju-52, and Lenny made a date with

Weaver sometime in the next couple of days, when the airplane would be flown back to Rockford from Sterling."

Saturday arrived. Lenny Smith didn't show, but Scott was there. He had some doubts about the airworthiness of the airplane and figured the only way to settle the doubts was to see for himself. He finally met Bud Weaver, who could always be recognized by an old and well-worn flight cap, and a grin clamped onto a dead cigar. Their first meeting was strictly on the ground. They climbed up into the cockpit and, as Scott says, "I climbed into the left seat and Bud climbed into the right one. He went through everything in the cockpit with me,

Bud Weaver (left in both photos) and Scott Johnson with N130LW. SCOTT JOHNSON COLLECTION

from the great big trim and flap wheel to the vertical T-shaped handle that protruded straight up from the inside of each rudder travel slot. After thirty minutes or so we climbed down from our rather hard seats." They had a long conversation about sharing the costs of the airplane, and Bud Weaver worked it out to fifty-two clams an hour, and the visit ended with their agreeing to meet the following Saturday to fly the airplane to an air show.

"A week later," Scott recalls with a crooked smile, "I found myself fueling and pouring oil into *Iron Annie*'s innards in preparation for my first flight in the old girl, over to the Aurora air show and back.

———◆———

"My first flight in the old girl was on a hot and windy June afternoon, with ominous thunderheads speckling the southwestern horizon. Well, Aurora wasn't that far away and we'd be back before any of the meteorological fireworks started. Bud took the left seat and I climbed into the copilot seat, on the right, and immediately discovered I didn't have any rudder pedals, only a rudder bar, and that meant no brakes. I'd been in this thing twice and it was the first time I'd noticed that about the right seat. Shame on me. The last time I had been faced with this arrangement was in a Widgeon many years before, and I didn't like it then and I wasn't sold on it now. I sure hoped this guy to my left, my cigar-chewing, red-cap-wearing partner, knew how to fly this thing and, more precisely, how to handle it on the ground. If he didn't, this could prove interesting. Suddenly I felt naked, too naked for comfort. Visions of leaving the side of the runway and removing several lights before cutting across the grass and heading for the boonies crossed my mind. Don't look now, you dummy, I told myself, but you belong in the *other* seat, where all the handles and goodies are. Not over here to the right, cooling your heels, fat, dumb, and happy.

"'You get the wobble pump, Scott, and I'll start the engines. Number three first. Ready? Let's do it.' He went right on like that. 'Master switches on, fuel flow to wobble-pump position, master and individual mags on, number-three-engine energizer, ah, push.' The inertia starter wound up slowly. Ten seconds later, I gave the T handle on the far right of the quadrant a quick pull, up, the starter engaged, the prop turned, and number three was

alive. At least I thought so, but I was wrong. Round and round went the propeller, Bud jockeying the throttle, and suddenly she belched once, twice, I got the fuel to RUN position, the engine struggled to come alive, she belched some more, and finally responded with a roar with Bud trying to retard the throttle to IDLE. The routine went that way until all three were turning and the airplane shook and rattled in protest. Oil temps coming up nicely, oil pressure right up there, unlock the tail wheel, and away she rolled with a big chunk of manifold pressure on each engine helping her along.

"With one hand, I held the control wheel that was attempting to beat me to death, and the other hand was groping for the flap handle. Pushing hard on it, the handle finally gave way under the pressure and I cranked the flaps down halfway. I had my doubts as to whether this old bird needed any flaps to get off the ground, but that's what my fearless *Kapitan* in the left seat said and that's what I gave him. I finally asked Bud why he wanted the flaps down, and what I got for an answer was a dirty look. With that huge wing out there and only Bud and myself in here and us being damned near empty, we'd be off the ground like an elevator. I told him so and got some more displeasure, so I shut up. If the flaps made him feel good, fine.

"We went through the run-up and got tower clearance and we went charging down the runway, and before you got ready for it we were airborne, just *that* quick. No time to worry about the rudders, brakes that I didn't have, or my partner running off the runway. I got the flaps up and I didn't like our air speed, we were too damned slow, and I wanted to shout, for God's sake, don't stall it! Bud must have had a fifteen-degree deck angle on old *Iron Annie*, and the air speed was hovering back and forth around 65 miles per hour and I wasn't used to it and didn't like it, and quickly but diplomatically I put my hand on the yoke and pushed *Annie*'s nose over to a more respectable attitude. All of a sudden I was aware that my partner in the left seat didn't appear to be all that red hot and I wasn't too damned sure at all that he knew what this machine would do or wouldn't do. I was rapidly getting the vivid impression that good old Bud might be depending *on me* to straighten out any mistakes he might make, sort of bail him out of jams, and I'd never even seen the flight manual on this thing to find out for certain what it would and

Scott Johnson in the right seat of N130LW—his first and only flight from that side of the cockpit.
SCOTT JOHNSON COLLECTION

wouldn't do. I called myself a lot of bad names for that lapse on my part. Every five years, I have a habit of doing something real dumb and today was that day. I stared at Bud and it suddenly dawned on me that he had to get this thing back on the ground, and after that takeoff, how in the name of God did he plan to do that? The light penetrated my thick skull: I was here to do that, because I already knew Bud couldn't hack it, and no way, *but no way,* am I going to sit over here and watch him pile up this thing with me in it. Now, how do I tell him all this without insulting him? I had maybe thirty minutes to figure it out before we'd start down.

"During the years that I'd flown DC-3s and C-46s, I'd watched beginning copilots do a better job than Bud had done with *Annie,* and like it or not, those were the facts of life. It had nothing to do with personalities. Only flying.

"While I pondered the diplomatic mess I'd have to face, I scanned the cockpit to find out what worked and didn't work. The instrumentation was a bastard, haphazard, and motley collection of German and American and Norwegian and Spanish stuff, of which some worked and the rest had been pure decoration for some time. There were American and German radio compasses, and none worked. The German directional gyros were inoperative, and only the turn-and-banks and the German rate-of-climb gauges seemed operational, although they were all metric in their readings. Jesus. . . . We had good suction on the gauge, for what it was worth. The air-speed indicators were

American and *seemed* to work okay. The German radio altimeter was a defunct museum piece. The only manifold-pressure gauge that we could read, understand, or whatever, again, promised to be functional. The other manifold-pressure gauges were in a mysterious foreign language with metric readout and all they gave me was a headache. The reliability of all this was a question that belonged on a quiz program. There was going to be a lot of eyeball work on my part, inside and outside the cockpit. Bud didn't seem at all concerned about what functioned or lay there like a dead dog with its legs stiff in the air, which only made *me* all the more concerned.

"But I lived through and loved every minute of it. A strange feeling came over me when I looked out the side window and saw that big iron cross stretched across my right wingtip. But no enemy fighters after us today; only that line of thunderstorms growing ever larger over my right shoulder. With them around, who needs enemy fighters? One thing became clear; Bud damned well knew how to navigate. His selected course hadn't changed a hair and he brought us face to face with Aurora Airport. Look at all those goddamned airplanes down there! They were all over the place and using the east-west runway for landing to the west, and the traffic pattern was *littered* with airplanes. Bud started his descent from thirty-five hundred feet to traffic-pattern altitude and literally took his slot in the procession downwind. He was cutting it too close. I told him to widen it out a bit, and he took up a heading with a 'staggering' ten degrees away from the airport and I told him to add another twenty degrees, but he didn't react fast enough and we were then too far in and he maintained his altitude too long. I hated to keep coaching him, so I tried to keep my mouth shut and wait it out, but that soon got crazy and I couldn't wait any longer. 'Get her down, Bud, get her *down!* You're too high and too close in! We'll never make it, pal!' The wind was out of the south and giving us a twenty-degree crab, not to mention the line of airplanes parked along Runway 27. They stretched all the way to the intersection of the parallel taxiway to 18-36 and they appeared to be no more than fifty feet from the edge of the runway. The whole thing stank, and with that wind it looked for sure we could drift off to the side, and that would be disaster for us and a hell of a lot of them.

"I told myself there wasn't any way out of it. It was time to take over. This was my very first flight with Bud and I already knew what I had to do, or there could be a very large curtain blocking off all view of my future. *And* his, as well. I was as diplomatic as I could be about it and I told Bud, 'I'd just feel better if you'd let me have this one. That's a damn strong wind out there.' I didn't wait for an answer but had my sweaty paws on the yoke, and Bud—give the man credit—got the idea and without any protest relinquished the controls. It was too late to land, our approach was messed up, so I went all the way forward on the throttles for a go-around, and what I wanted to do was to land on the shorter runway, because it was right into the stiff wind, and if this iron monster lived up to her reputation and I could keep the *Kapitan* the hell off what little brakes we had—'Bud, I'm dragging her in and I'm going to three-point her, and whatever you do, *don't touch the brakes.*'

"Around I came, and Bud called out he'd give me full flaps and I barked 'No!' at him. Half flaps would do nicely. Jeez, I could see myself doing another go-around with him trying to CRANK up the flaps that needed a gorilla's arm for any real movement. We crossed the fence around seventy on the needle and touched down nicely and no brakes, and I handed her back to Bud, who parked her and shut her down.

"My only reaction—and Bud's grin at me was infectious—was that this thing was absolutely *fantastic.* I knew I had a love affair going, but there was also reality to face: 'Bud, I've got one request,' I told him, and I was absolutely sincere about this. 'If we're going to fly her together, from here on out I'm going to have the left seat. I feel more at home there.' To my delight, Bud agreed at once, with the added comment that he knew his own limitations and was mighty glad I was along.

"The Aurora air show came and went and we were back in *Annie*, this time for my second flight but very much in the captain's seat, on the left side of the cockpit. It was incredible just how well Bavarian Motor Works had built those engines. More than thirty-five years old and three, two, one, they fired up. The tail-wheel lock moved in a vertical groove, instead of side to side like the DC-3, and I had some careful and slow thinking to do, and we were on grass, using the nose engine to pull us through the soft stuff and the wing engines for differential power for turning. *Bee-yootiful!* Better

than my old DC-3, and God, this bird was as simple as ABC, fixed-pitch props and fixed gear. Like it was all done for you. I checked the mags and control movement, where things belonged, and left the flaps up; temps and pressures were in the green. I lined up, locked the tail wheel, and let her lumber in slow motion down the runway. Tail coming up nicely by itself, keep it straight, and work that rudder, more left aileron, and right through 50, 60, 70, and at 80 miles per hour we were off and I tried a climbout at 90. She was a bit nose-heavy and I used the big wheel to trim off the yoke pressure and it was Fantasy Time all over again, *Luftwaffe Flight Eins departing the Rhineland with Kapitan Johnson in command, and hot damn!*

"I was absolutely thrilled. This was the ultimate, the culmination of a dream for me, and it had been a very long time in coming. *Stop dreaming, Ace,* I told myself, *and fly this thing.* 'Gear up, Bud!' I hollered at the man with me, and his grin was plas-

Cross country on a summer day in the Ju-52—view from the left seat. SCOTT JOHNSON

tered all over his face. The noise from those three BMWs was deafening, but he'd heard me call for gear up and he was laughing at me. I turned crimson. Tough to get a gear up when it's down and welded.

"Thunderheads were too close for comfort, and I began to push the engines. We were nearly empty, and *Annie* started to creep up past 120 miles per hour and then I had 125 miles per hour on her, the engines banging away, and I had to hold her at no more than 125 miles per hour, because in those days we didn't know if she'd start shedding parts or what.

"At Rockford I started down with half flaps and had her at 80 miles per hour and I just could not believe the sensitivity of the elevator. It responded instantly. I porpoised all the way around my sloppy downwind and cut around base to final. The big tires screeched on concrete and the tail was coming down, yoke all the way back. I kept talking to myself . . . *be ready with the power and watch the brakes . . . be easy. Easy, damn it! Too late! There she goes; get on it, get on it!* Annie heeled into the wind from the right and suddenly I had my hands full. *Left brake, power up on the right engine and get that rudder in there! Aileron; more aileron!* The brakes were a gutless waste of time and the edge was coming up fast. *Here it comes!* Agonizingly slow, *Annie* answered my desperate control motions and finally responded to the helm. With inches to spare, she straightened out to parallel the edge of the runway. We taxied off the active and Bud looked at me with a dirty grin on his face, which I had coming. 'She's still got some life in her, right?'

"Jee-sus, *yes*.

"We put her away and discussed our next flight, a few days or a week off, and I started for home in my trusty Buick, and the drive home gave me the chance to do some hard thinking. I began to wonder about the ramifications that could attend the experimental category of the airplane in terms of its restrictions. Bud was the owner, and in a strict, technical sense he could retain that position of pilot in command, but that was always an arguable point. What counted were the papers on the airplane, and I faced the fact that it was really pretty tough to comply with Item 13, which stated: 'This aircraft shall not be operated other than in accordance with appropriate military technical orders or the manufacturer's flight instructions.'

"I'd never laid eyes on the technical orders or a manual of any kind on this Ju-52 and I didn't even know if they still existed or not. I began to study everything in sight. There wasn't any problem in *flying Annie*, but the FAA words their requirements in a very careful way. They didn't say 'flying' in Item 13; they said 'operated,' and therein lies a great gulf of difference. I had a lot of homework to do, because if there is one thing I learned a long time ago in this business, it's doing what you're doing *within* the regs.

"This sort of thinking had me study the three engines with a jaundiced eye the next time we flew. How much longer would those old BMWs stay together? How much time did they *really* have? How much more did they have—ten minutes, ten hours, fifty hours? I swear that airplane burned more oil than it did gasoline. And from then on, every flight was made with a meticulous study of the gauges and some record-keeping on the ground, and the awful truth came home to me. Those engines needed an absolute minimum of an immediate top overhaul and probably a hell of a lot more to boot.

"The fantasy world I was living in concerning the Ju-52 was giving way slowly to the harsh reality of the true condition of the airplane. My better judgment was swimming upward through my intense desire to go charging ahead blindly.

"However, the siren call to fly to the air show at Du Page overwhelmed all, and if nothing else, we were still legal, even if ragged edges were showing. Almost as if attuned to my thoughts, *Annie* was letting me know that TLC was as much a part of her needs as fuel and oil. We fired up engines three and two, but it was no go with number one and it wouldn't even engage. Must be the starter. By now Bud was chewing on a dead and very ripe cigar and was muttering quaint and colorful profanities. We shut down and I went to get a mechanic to see if we could get a quick fix and still make the air show.

"It wasn't an analysis—it was a postmortem: death from loss of parts; all but one of the attaching bolts on the starter were gone, and the only one remaining was so loose it was on the verge *of just plain falling off*.

"We didn't fly, of course. No quick fixit possible. It was hard to believe that the starter gave us no trouble signs on the previous starts, but, believe it or not, that's the way it happened. And the one thing that kept going through my mind all the way home was that here we had a million dollars' worth of antique airplane and a five-and-dime maintenance department. How the hell could we keep this thing running at this rate?

"A week later, the starter fixed, we figured to meet a desire of Bud's and take the airplane to his home town to exhibit his prize, and I agreed with his feelings. We got her fired up and had a bitch of a time just getting out of the parking space. The brakes were rotten and getting worse with every flight, and you had to keep up hydraulic pressure to get anything, so that meant lots of power and then you got brake, at least some brake, but the whole thing was self-defeating, because the power you needed for braking action was enough to drag the airplane forward. Frustrating. The right engine had the hydraulic pump and it was a mess. Somehow, the throttles kept binding tighter and tighter in their slots, and just getting them to move at all took some real muscle, making the slight manipulations you need sometimes damned near impossible. But we rocked our way out of the grass at Aurora and made it to the runway and Bud went on the radio, which crackled like someone crushing eggshells magnified a thousand times.

"For the first time since I'd started taking a hard look at things, I realized that *Annie* had no workable radio gear of any kind *that was attached to the airplane*. All our communications were by a portable transceiver Bud kept in his lap, and visions of busted regulations began to play unhappily before my eyes. He did the transmitting and receiving and then shouted the information to me all between chomps on that dead stogie clamped between his teeth.

"Trying to do our run-up at Aurora gave *Annie* another opportunity to give me a warning. What little brakes we had left began to go some more, so that it was impossible to do the engine run-up and remain in one place. Annie would creep or turn this way or that no matter what I did on the brakes. I managed it without covering too much ground and kept trying to improve the wavelength that moved directly between me and the airplane, and then we taxied along to the active while Bud fumbled with that Mickey Mouse system he used to talk to the world outside the cockpit. The sun was hammering us through all the glass, and sweat was pouring off me and I was losing my temper and snapped at Bud about whether or not we had takeoff clearance. There were side windows in the cockpit, but

they were just about jammed shut and I knew if we opened them we'd never get them closed. My eyes stung with perspiration when Bud chuckled that we were clear to roll.

"We lumbered into the air and I climbed out at ninety and I was never sure of the rate of climb, because it was all in meters per second and I was sweaty and—well, hell, once we were flying it all went away and I was relaxed. Like getting a fix, I suppose. I worked the trim because this old girl flew more like a heavy single-engine than any multiengine transport. She was nose-heavy, and from everything I had experienced so far I had to judge that *Annie*'s weight and balance left something to be desired, and as long as I flew her in those days, I never did get accustomed to that nose-heavy characteristic.

"I wouldn't learn for a long time that it wasn't the airplane's fault. Her trim controls and indicators and a lot of other things were so screwed up that only the very docility of the airplane even let it fly at all.

"We made it to Polo, Illinois, where I refused Bud's request to fly low over the town—those restrictions on her operating limitations were red flags waving in my head all the time now. Bud accepted my refusal with a silent nod of his head. As I came to understand my partner in this clandestine branch of the long-gone Luftwaffe, though he was a hell of a nice guy that you just couldn't help but like, he had a propensity for operating on the ragged edge of the FARs. It wasn't with any malice or intent to bust the regs. I don't think Bud really knew the FARs and so he wasn't restricted by hewing to the line of those he might not like, if they were there at all, which he could ignore because he didn't even know of them. In any case, the man was personally a great guy and I liked him and had no desire to offend him in any way. But it was getting tougher not to clash, because I was getting stricter with myself every passing day about the regulations and I knew it could bring us into some head-butting.

"The radios were a good example. His portable transceiver worked, so what the hell did I have to bitch about? Because the regulations called for permanent equipment affixed to the machine. It could be regarded as a niggardly point, but there it was and it wouldn't go away by ignoring it.

"Look, the noise level in the cockpit was such an uproar and the reception of Bud's Mickey Mouse receiver so poor that when the two were together you just couldn't hear anything from the radio. The only way to get audible radio reception—and I know, I know what this sounds like—*was to pull all power back to idle, and while it was quiet and we were gliding earthward, get in all our radio communications, and then go back to power.* On top of this, the ignition harnesses in the engines were a disaster, and their interference was an ear-stabber of the worst kind. After a while, having to communicate made our flying something out of a comedy. But a comedy of errors, unfortunately.

"We made the flight to Oshkosh for the big flying convention in Wisconsin, the whole time *Annie* inching upward toward our cruise altitude of fifty-five hundred feet. The German instruments to me were not only unreadable but I would never have trusted them anyway. No one knew the last time

The airline captain on a busman's holiday: Scott Johnson in the left seat of N130LW. Bud Weaver took the picture. SCOTT JOHNSON COLLECTION

they'd been checked for accuracy, so to trust them was dangerous, and I was always down to the basics of needle, ball, and air speed. We got to fifty-five hundred feet and I set her up at eighteen hundred rpm which gave us twenty-three inches of manifold pressure, and it was cooler up there, and by the time our speed crawled up to a good cruise of 117 miles per hour (years later I would learn that air-speed indicator lied to us, and lied to us but good by being far too generous with speed), we grinned at one another and we lit up some horrible cigars, and it was wonderful. The feel of this

airplane in cruise is hard to describe. Beautiful, beautiful.

"Until the oil temp of number one began crawling up to the red line and I was bolt upright in my seat. I showed the gauge to Bud, who was completely unconcerned. It was running that way all the time, as far as he was concerned. But I didn't like two and three holding steady at fifty degrees while number one hung in there at ninety degrees. It gives me a high pucker factor.

"Let me go back to that balance of this ironmonger. Remember that I still didn't know this airplane or how many things really were wrong with her. When I flew the Ju-52, she wasn't all that stable around her lateral axis, most likely due to the weight and balance involved. She was always nose-heavy and it was necessary to retrim constantly, so our attitude kept changing all the time, and every time our attitude changed, so did the speed of the engines, but never at the same rate or instant. Thus our three-motored dragonfly cruised along with the props always out of synchronization, and that can set your teeth to dancing in your jawbone and turn loose some hornets in your ears.

"She had another strange habit: She would increase her speed to 120 miles per hour and then, without doing a thing, sag back to 110, and it kept changing, no matter what I did, and I was beginning to believe I'd finally met an airplane that was getting the best of my ability to fly straight and level. But it didn't fit with all I'd heard about the marvelous stability of this airplane, from German and British pilots who praised that stability to the skies. A British test pilot, Captain Eric Brown, with a list of credentials as long as your arm, had prepared a pilot report on a Ju-52 he flew at Farnborough, and what he experienced sure wasn't in the cards for this airplane I was flying.

"'If the Junkers climbed like the venerable old lady that she was,' reported Brown, 'she also possessed all the docility associated with the venerable, being beautifully stable and virtually capable of being flown hands-off in anything but really turbulent air . . . and I flew the Ju-52/3m in quite a lot of bad weather. . . .'

"Could this really be the same airplane?

"In addition to the strange quirks I had already discovered, as we continued to fly, *Iron Annie* exhibited a new bit of nonsense, and it seemed that the longer we subjected the old lady to the loads of flight—without having *rebuilt* this airplane—the more she was refusing to fly as Eric Brown had flown her. In fact, after a while *Annie* insisted upon taking up her own headings as the mood dictated. When I put in a corrected course, I discovered that to maintain that course I had to fly with one wing low. I couldn't believe the airplane was that far out of rig! And *Annie* didn't have an easy rudder trim, and what she did have was for engine-out procedures only (which is why the German airplanes had a rudder autopilot; smart, those guys at Dessau). Let me take that back. There were the big, T-shaped handles for the rudder, and maybe they would have worked okay, but in the years I flew this thing they resisted all efforts to move them and I never succeeded in budging them where they seemed to have been welded to the floorboards. I don't think they'd been moved in twenty years, and all this gave me new food for thought. What mechanic had signed off this airplane as airworthy when you couldn't move the rudder trim so much as the width of a hair?

"I didn't relish the idea of flying *Annie* with one engine out, because just to get our 117 miles per hour, our engines were pounding their hearts out. I finally solved the problem of the wandering by letting her wander and then brought in the needed corrections every now and then.

"I left *Annie* and Weaver at Oshkosh to return five days later, where Bud was waiting for me under the shade of the old Iron Cross; this was Oshkosh 1972. His rickety old lawn chair looked like it was going to collapse right beneath him. He had that baseball-type cap low over his forehead and one of those infernal dead cigars in his teeth. 'You'll never get rich that way,' I told him.

"He looked up at me and grinned. 'Wanna' bet?' Then I looked up at the first window behind the cockpit and there was a big FOR SALE sign right before my startled eyes. He was pushing to get $125,000 for the ironmonger, and I knew that in her present condition he was going to be a sorely disappointed man. A lot of people really wanted this airplane, but when it came to shelling out the long green—uh uh.

"As the months passed, *Annie*'s production time in the air diminished steadily, in direct proportion to her growing ills and aches and pains. Every time we flew, or tried to fly, it was a case of holding our breath, praying, hoping, and sacrificing horned toads to the gods. The tail-wheel tire was always going flat, and the next question was when the big

ones up front would follow suit. Did Bud have spares? I asked that question again and again, and he always gave me the same answer: 'They're coming. I'm getting some through the Spanish Air Force.' The truth was that Bud was just one more in a long line of people who'd attempted to deal with the Spanish Air Force who finally walked away muttering imprecations at their empty hands. And there wasn't any doubt now that the tires on *Annie* were really her last legs.

"As 1972 slipped into a frozen, storm-tossed 1973, I was taking very careful stock of what I was doing. The old girl had managed to stay in the air, but engine temps were getting chintzy, her wandering off course ever more pronounced, and her fabled stability was to me strictly a fable, because I hadn't found it yet. In every aspect, I was really becoming deeply concerned about *Annie*'s mechanical condition. We had flown her all summer with virtually no maintenance of any kind performed on her, and there was, by God, an awful lot that needed attention. Time was also inflicting its damage on the airplane, and the oncoming winter, with the airplane staked out in stinking weather, wasn't going to help any.

"I resisted temptation until the summer of 1973, when I just couldn't withstand that siren call any more, and I was on the phone with Bud and soon we were together, cleaning off the derelict of an airplane, clearing away dirt and grease and grime and filth, putting the batteries back in, doing what was necessary to see if we could drag her back to life. We got the engines running, but there was a new side to everything. *Annie* would need an annual relicensing, and this would give me the chance to talk to the FAA people, who knew her pretty well by now. As it turned out, the FAA inspector couldn't have been more cordial, and we finally got off by ourselves for the talk I wanted. The airplane had been inspected and signed off by a licensed mechanic, and in July of 1973 the FAA issued a year's ticket for the iron bird, although privately the FAA inspector felt there was damned good reason to be concerned. He was going by the books, and the books dictated a license could be issued, but he told me personally he wouldn't trust those old engines any more distant than any airfield still in eyeball range.

"I flew *Annie* a few more times in 1973, knowing I was at the breaking point every time I lifted those tires off the ground. I was truly worried

Typical view from N130LW: oil and heavy grease spattering the windshield. View from the left seat. SCOTT JOHNSON

about the airplane, but Bud? Never! He sat in that big cockpit and he grinned. There was a man who was superbly happy with himself. Not a care in the world. I admired his ability to take it easy and enjoy the world, a quality I found difficult to sustain with an airplane coming unglued all about me. Yet, as far as I must judge things *in the air,* Bud was overly nonchalant. I'd never seen him worry about anything, and I guess I've been flying too long and in too many kinds of airplanes and in too many tight situations not to pay the piper's tune of strict attention when called for. But . . . that's me, and if Bud wanted to wend his way through life grinning over a dead cigar, without a care in the world, it's not my place to be critical of a happy man.

129

"Coming out of Blakesburg in the latter half of 1973 was to be my last flight in 130LW. I knew it, and the airplane seemed to know it. The problems with mechanical systems had become so great that it was really a case of the airplane deteriorating right beneath our hands and feet, and every flight was a question mark, every engine start a wait for an explosion. I had already made my decision that dead cigars, grins, and lackadaisical attitudes do not make for decent longevity, and as long as Bud ran this airplane, that was to be its lot, and so this was the end of the line. *Annie* was sick and getting sicker, and she was getting close to being a basket case. That nose engine was starting to tear itself to pieces.

"My last flight brought home that fact with stark reality. I had the Mississippi River well in sight when the center engine began losing power. I thought for a while it was just this bad feeling I had, but after advancing the throttle for the second time to maintain manifold pressure, there wasn't any doubt. My bad feeling was alive and lurking in that nose engine. Soon the throttle was all the way forward, jammed against the stop, but it didn't do a bit of good. The engine still kept losing power and we were steadily losing air speed. At this point I didn't give a damn if it quit, just so long as the son of a bitch didn't catch fire. We dragged ourselves through the sky, and Polo, Illinois, was on the horizon and I knew we had it made. I let her descend slowly, gracefully, a stately return from the skies through which she had flown so long, and which her unattended ills were to keep from her. Down we went on final, and the fence at the east end of the airport disappeared under the nose and

then with a thump we were on the ground, the tail wheel and main gear touching together in a perfect finale. *Annie* rolled quickly to a stop without brakes in the tall grass of summer still uncut. I shut her down, each step in slow motion, and then left the airplane. Outside on the grass, I leaned back against her corrugated side and thought a lot about a lot of things that had happened with this incredible machine. In a way, I even felt a bit cheated, for I knew by now that I had never felt her vibrant with full power, never felt those wings grasp solidly at air, never experienced the whoops and joy as this machine rolled over steeply and went curving, whistling earthward.

"She had been worn and beat and tired and battered and aching from the day I first met her, and she had done her best, still flying when almost any other airplane I knew would have come apart by the seams and lay in a tangled heap of junk on the ground. Not *Iron Annie*. If you gave her even a gasp of life, she would try to fly and she did.

"I turned and walked toward my car, stopped by the door for a long and last look at this machine that had so captivated and enchanted me and still held such a tight grip on my heart. *If only you had half a chance, Old Girl . . . my God, the flying we could do together!*

"Two years of flying the Ju-52, right out of history.

"Two years—and averaging just over one hour every *month*, for the grand total of twenty-six hours and thirty minutes. An awful lot of work and sweat for not much time in the air.

"But it had been worth it."

Among all the many things to be said about the history of our *Iron Annie,* the period between late 1973 and the early spring of 1975 is clearly the time of the missing entries. By this, of course, we mean the aircraft log. The flights entered into the log are, to be very kind indeed on the subject, somewhat diluted. A modicum of entries were made to satisfy whatever prying eyes might officially demand to examine this document. But that was about all. There were flights made that never found their way to pen and paper. N130LW was to pass from the ownership of Bud Weaver, who never realized his dream of selling his airplane for $125,000 and finally was brought by the continuing breakdown of the airplane to get out from under while there was still scant time remaining to do so. On August 25, 1974, the airplane was listed for a flight of three hours and forty minutes from Rockford to Cape Girardo, Missouri, where she went on the auction block.

Salesmen in aviation are not always paragons of virtue. Do I hear groans from among the ranks of birdmen out there who have in their own pasts discovered that fleecing does not always apply to feathered wings? Ah, such is life. Medicine men and snake-oil salesmen are to be counted among all walks of life, and yet it is a good old American pastime to make the bread, man, while the door yawns wide. *Iron Annie* had moved through so many doors in her time they seemed almost to be countless, and then there was Cape Girardo and the auction block and—as best we can determine, a sales price of thirty-six thousand dollars put the big trimotor into the hands of Don Anklin, of Charlotte, North Carolina, whose company was known as Cannon Aircraft. Give the man credit. He took his shot. He bought the iron monster and had it flown from Cape Girardo to Charlotte. Sometime in September of 1974, it is shown in the less-than-bulging aircraft log of N130LW that a man by name of Bob

Evans flew the Ju-52 from Charleston to Salisbury to Lexington, all in North Carolina, and on the day following, with another capable gentleman by name of Frank Thompson, returned the ancient and wheezing giant to her berth in Charlotte. The two days totaled a logbook entry of three hours and forty-five minutes, and that was the last flying for another *entire winter* for the now sorrowful wonder of yesterday.

It is time to end 1974 with some spadework. At Confederate Air Force headquarters, in Texas, I had discussed the Ju-52 with a number of CAF colonels. We really didn't believe the airplane was available for sale, and when we confirmed that it was, we discovered *why* it was for sale. It was a wreck even though the wings were attached and the engines were still in their mounts. The spadework uncovered that Cannon Aircraft had wielded mops with paint onto the battered body and were laying lavish claim to the excellent condition of the airplane. I sent some people to Charlotte to study 130LW, and they came back with eyes rolled so far back in their heads it seemed I was facing a roomful of Little Orphan Annie posters.

But I wanted that damned airplane. It's like a disease, a fever that gets inside your skin and burns off your reason.

Still, a bit of caution. . . .

I talked with Don Anklin. I talked with him several times by telephone and in person. Anklin is a very smooth salesman, and he is also a very good pilot, and he flew down from North Carolina to Merritt Island Airport, in Florida, to do some more talking. I needed a big gun on my side and I called Ron Skipper, who has been driving large iron birds for a long time and with exacting skill and precision, to listen in on these conversations and give me his own opinions. Ron Skipper didn't go through military pilot school or any fancy flying academies. He crawled and slugged his way up the line to his air-transport rating, and he flew everywhere in the world, and it was his considered opinion that while 130LW *was* pretty much of a basket case, it could be rebuilt—if the man who bought the airplane was willing to make a staggering investment in time, money, and sweat. It seemed almost too much to handle on a basis of ownership by one person—who in this case was going to be myself—*but it could be done,* and I always did like the word challenge.

Then I had some talks with another very close friend, Sam Bothwell, vice-president of what is now the First National Bank of Brevard (at the time, the First National Bank of Merritt Island), and I told Sam I was thinking of buying the Ju-52 and wanted to finance it through his bank. Sam looked at me as if I'd carried a case of typhus and smallpox into his office. He blinked several times and didn't say a word. He didn't have to. The look on his face said it all. When he finally spoke, it was in his customary manner.

"How much?"

"About sixty long ones," I told him.

"Too much," he told me.

"Okay, then. *How* much?"

Sam studied me. I think he judged everything mechanical from the way he judged the man with him. "It's Don Anklin?"

"Uh huh."

"Offer him fifty even. He'll balk and we'll talk about it. In the meantime I'll find out what he paid for it. He's entitled to his profit, but we don't want it to be excessive, do we?"

"No, Sam, we don't."

"Get with it."

So I offered fifty instead of sixty and it came down to fifty-five and we shook our heads and then everyone smiled, because we agreed on a sales price of $52,500. Now, back in January of 1975, a number of weeks earlier, I had left a check for a thousand clams with Anklin to be held in the event I did buy the airplane. On the seventeenth of January, I received a telegram from Anklin: "As of [*sic*] our phone conversation, I am depositing your check on Ju-52 Junker [*sic*] N130LW confirming sale to Caidin Productions. Balance of $51,500 approximately 2,000 pounds of parts at purchase. It is our understanding you will give us drafting instructions to complete deal by approximately end of January."

Okay. I had a Ju-52 I had still never seen except in photographs, but I knew something of the airplane, and I started some very heavy homework on the corrugated mountain about to come winging into my life. I had also rebuilt a number of warbirds and I wasn't exactly green behind the ears on this subject. At the moment, however, I had a bitch of a writing schedule and I couldn't get away to North Carolina to get the airplane. But Ron Skipper could, and we called another old flying buddy of mine, Ted Anderson, with whom I faced getting killed more times than with anyone I've ever known in all my years of flying.

True to form, Ron Skipper and Ted Anderson wrangled a ferry job to take a Cessna 150 up to Charlotte. They got into Charlotte at night, on March 3, 1975, and promptly froze half to death from lack of warm clothing, a vicious cold wind, and being stranded on the bloody airport because of not being able to contact Anklin.

The next morning, still blue with cold and utterly pissed at the world but with Don Anklin in particular, the ferry team of Caidin Productions was pounding on Anklin's door. Was the airplane ready for a checkout flight? Anklin had passed on the word that Evans had a type rating in the Ju-52. Evans, according to Ron Skipper, is one hell of a great pilot, but we all knew that this report of a Ju-52 type rating was so much cockamamie, because *nobody* had such a rating, and without a rating you can't make a legal checkout, and . . .

The checkout consisted of going around the patch a couple of times and figuring out what did what, which control went where, and what *not* to move, because wherever it was at this moment, the damn thing worked, *so leave it alone. Iron Annie* is a taildragger, but Ron Skipper had been pushing around a lot of DC-3s and also the C-46, which is a grandmother of a taildragger, and he was right at home in 130LW. What Ted Anderson didn't like about the corrugated mountain was that it hadn't been fueled, the rocker-arm boxes needed grease, the oil tanks needed filling—twenty gallons, one quart at a time—all in a freezing wind, and Anklin and his employees vanished with all the swiftness of quail before a shotgun blast.

Finally they had the ironmonger fueled and gassed and greased. As had happened with George Hamilton and Scott Johnson, the airplane poured forth its magic and Ron and Ted were grinning like idiots as they fired up the airplane and taxied out to the active runway. There *was* a VHF radio

Ron Skipper, airline captain on another busman's holiday to deliver the "rambling wreck" from North Carolina to Florida, standing aft of the left wing and thinking it over *very* carefully. JULIAN LEEK

Coming into Ti-Co Airport on March 5, 1975—Ron Skipper and Ted Anderson at the controls of the big Ju-52. JULIAN LEEK

aboard, not a very good one and half dead from electrical leakage from the engines, but it was legal. So on the fourth of March, 1975, *Iron Annie* started her trek to her new home.

I received a telephone call from Brunswick the next morning that the gallant duo were on their way, and a small crowd collected at Titusville-Cocoa Airport (Ti-Co), and then we heard, for the first time, that utterly unmistakable drone of the Ju-52 wending its way slowly toward us from the north, flying along the western perimeter of the airfield. This was my first look at what was now my airplane, and I couldn't believe what I saw. God, she was *big*, and she was also flying at what appeared to be a reckless thirty miles per hour. She drifted, wafted, and sailed slowly through the air, a riverboat content to take forever to make a circuit around the airport, droning like some winged zeppelin. Ron brought her around to the south and set up his pattern, and with what seemed like a great sigh—relief, perhaps, because maybe *Iron Annie* knew that finally she had found the land of TLC—she drifted gently to the concrete of Runway 36. Ron and Ted brought her around and shut her down slowly. When the engines stopped and all was quiet and we heard hot metal creaking and crackling as it cooled, we stared in mixed disbelief and wonder at that scabbed elephant hide of blistered and peeling paint. Someone let out a great whoop of laughter and a shout of delight, and then Ron and Ted and I were pounding each other on the back and dancing up and down and enjoying the hell out of ourselves.

No waiting for *me*. Before the first hour was gone by, I was in the right seat and Ron was showing me this and that, and Ted was watching and he had a fistful of notes, and we fired up in that crazy

Cheers, whistles, shouts, and hoorahs for Skipper and Anderson as N130LW brings down her tail on the main runway of Ti-Co on her home-coming. JULIAN LEEK

Ron Skipper and Martin Caidin "doing the numbers" over Patrick Air Force Base on March 5, 1975—*Iron Annie*'s first local flight in her new home. U. S. AIR FORCE

fire drill of a start procedure, and down the runway we went with my first time on the controls, and Skipper playing mother hen, which he does so well. One hour in the air, some bumps and grinds and the first landing, with Ron talking me down and Ted shouting encouragement and laughing. One tire touched and squealed and we bounced, a long and gentle bounce, and then she was down on both wheels. "Hold the yoke forward, that's it, keep walking that rudder, you need a lot of rudder, keep flying her you dumb son of a bitch!" and we came to a stop. I couldn't believe it.

We flew once more with Ron in the left seat, on March 8, and that gave us the chance to take up Sam Bothwell, since we could legally take Sam along as a crew member, he being a pilot and financier and all that. There is that famous old saying of "What hath God wrought?" and Sam seemed to have a stricken look on his face that could have been read as *What the hell have I done!*

We poled our way down the Banana River and droned up the Indian River, and called Patrick Air Force Base for permission to do a low pass. We dropped the nose and rolled into a steep bank and down we went, tires just above the runway of the military field. Traffic stopped for miles as we thun-

dered along the runway and across Highway A1A. We were still in the control area of Patrick, so we slowed down to 80 miles per hour as we went up along the shoreline of Cocoa Beach. Ron Skipper opened the top hatch while I flew, and he stood up and waved merrily to all as they gaped and waved frantically back at us. Then full bore on the throttles and on to Merritt Island Airport, where we touched down on the eastern end. Ron did a wild pullup that I am sure would have turned anyone white who knew the record of this plane, but Ron had crawled through the wings, and he knew this thing was stronger than anything ever built.

We flew a total of ninety minutes on the eighth of March, and then Ron Skipper was off on another one of his global jaunts with Saturn Airways, for whom he captained a big Lockheed Electra. In the calm that followed, Ted and I had a hard look at the airplane. It was just the three of us—myself, Ted, and *Annie*, and there were a couple of immediate things to do with the machine. First, crawl through every part of her. We did. Second, identify everything we could in the cockpit and make Dymo tape identification tags and stick them where they belong. We did. We moved everything, tested everything, shook our heads and wondered

The front office of *Iron Annie*—subject of much study and groaning during the first days of "learning her inside and out" before even the checklist could be written. JULIAN LEEK

about things a lot more than we understood, but we were gaining.

There was no checklist.

No aircraft manual.

No engine manuals.

We'd have to start from scratch, and I mean the very first gentle scrape on virgin skin. For the next month, we didn't attempt to fly the airplane. We spent the month in poking and prying and learning and starting our tentative checklists, and doing a hell of a lot of research. Don Haynes, the resident mechanic at Ti-Co, marched bravely to the airplane and repaired and resealed the right-wheel cylinders, resealed the power-brake valve, installed a new bladder in the hydraulic accumulator, bled the brakes, checked and lubed all the control push-pull rods and bell cranks and cables, installed a

shock cord on the tail wheel, repaired the cable for the underwing landing light, cleaned the starter solenoid contacts, installed grease fittings for both main wheel bearings, and a whole big bunch of other things.

While Don Haynes wrestled with the airplane from his side of our needs, Ted and I were gathering information, getting accurate data on engines and aircraft performance and systems as best we could.

I mean, if I was going to fly this iron bridge I'd better get everything on my side that I could. The fact that I had never flown it from the left seat and that I'd never landed the airplane had to be considered, and those thoughts were kept very, very quiet between myself and Ted, for why give voice to what is patently absurd? Ted had a better way.

The "corrugated condominium. . . ." JULIAN LEEK

You want to know things about an airplane? *Work on it*. We did. We moved everything that could move, and saw what it did, and wondered and pondered, and very slowly, very surely, we began to put together a realistic checklist. Realistic in the sense that it covered everything in the cockpit that could move, so we wouldn't forget anything, and even more realistic in the knowledge that we would be changing it before almost every flight, because each flight would be an enormous learning process.

We kept finding more things for Don Haynes to do and made his days nightmares. But we worked with him, and we were all learning together, and just putting back parts and pieces that had come apart in the airplane was a major job unto itself.

And then I got my hands on the aircraft manual. Wonderful! Marvelous! Stupendous! *Ole!* It was for the CASA 352L and it was in Spanish, and I didn't read Spanish and neither did Ted. For that matter, we couldn't read German either, but if we could only find a German manual, somewhere, anywhere, there were enough German scientists at Cape Canaveral and the Kennedy Space Center to help out.

In the meantime, the month rolled by, and it was April 5 and my fingers and hands and feet were itching to *fly*. Ted knew all the signs of the dreaded disease, and he looked at me and he sighed. He remembered the time we were nearly killed in a howling storm in the Devil's Triangle, and another time when we were coming straight down from four thousand feet into a river and pulled out so wildly we blacked out and came to with the twin-engine airplane climbing almost straight up and— he didn't want to remember any more.

"Ted, my man," I said to him, "let us go out to the airport and talk to the airplane."

He nodded. "Right. But we follow Plan A." He was very firm on that point, because we had both agreed to it. Plan A was an old, self-taught lesson. The best way to learn your airplane is on the ground. Powered up, and taxiing, and high-speed runs on the ground, but you do not try to fly. You do not permit yourself to fly. You learn procedures with a bird hot and alive, and you experience what she does accelerating and decelerating, because that is where trouble lies. We had no doubts about flying, once we got into the air. In fact, getting up was easy.

Landing was going to be the *real* fun.

"Let's go," I said.

The New Age had begun.

There have been many strange sights about N52JU—and the diligent reader will notice that the designation N130LW disappeared almost as quickly as the airplane came into my hands. I like special numbers for my iron birds. That Twin Bonanza with 7777M. My Messerschmitt bf-108b carried the registration of 108U because someone had already hied off with 108B, and U was all that was available to me. When I signed the ownership papers, I called Mark Weaver, who has been one of the major factors in familiarizing the public with accurate portrayals of aviation for many years, out in Oklahoma City. That is where the FAA has their records division and assigns registration numbers, and of course I wanted JU-52 for my Ju-52, but ran into the implacable logic presented by Mark that American registrations begin with numbers and not letters, and it is all part of a very large and complicated international agreement, so, how about 52JU? Not bad, not bad. I knew immediately how that would sound when working towers and traffic control.

"Ah, Lauderdale tower, this is 52JU, over."

"Lauderdale, 52JU, go ahead."

"52JU is two zero miles out coming down through five grand and landing Lauderdale. Over."

"Okay, 52JU. What is your type of aircraft, please?"

"JU52."

Silence.

"Ah, 52JU, say again your type, please. Over."

"Roger, Lauderdale. Aircraft type is JU52."

"I think we got that, sir. What was your number again?"

"52JU."

"And, uh, your type?"

"JU52."

"Ah, aircraft working Lauderdale tower—"

"This is 52JU, JU52, and this is a recording. . . ."

Good thing that here in Florida I've got a lot of friends in the towers and the control rooms. They all know the airplane, *now,* anyway, and we've taken up a whole bunch of the FAA troops from around the state. When we rumble up and down the coastline or use Orlando as our pivotal point for cutting across the state, and identify ourselves, then it's *their* turn, and our call-in produces a different response.

"Hey, hey, hey! It's the sauerkraut crowd! You guys ever get that recording fixed, or are you still looking for land?"

But on the morning of April 5, 1975, that was still a mite in the future, and we were talking about strange sights connected with *Iron Annie.* The first was the gentle giant, Ted Anderson, who drove with me up to the airport to start our meaningful relationship with the corrugated condominium that I had willingly deposited into the mainstream of my life. Have you ever seen a 240-pound hound dog with a bristling beard and a toothy grin twice as wide as his face? A man with fingers thick and strong enough to tap holes through aluminum sheet, or to bend and twist and shape gold into the most fragile and beautiful jewelry you have ever seen. A contrast, a paradox, an outstanding pilot, and, as evidenced by his long association with me and the insane things we have done, quite pleasantly mad, too. But he also had that strange love, that tug at the heart, from this airplane, and among the things he knew so very well, far from the cluttered room where he wove magic with gold, was that he was also a duster pilot, a man who had flown single-engine planes across the Pacific and through typhoons to Singapore, and Cherokees the other way across another ocean to Israel, and that he had a sixth sense, a gut feeling, and a hard knowledge of radial engines. The man was Ted Anderson.

We needed magic with gold to weave the talis-

Martin Caidin starts the slow, careful learning process by talking to his airplane. *My God, look at that wing!* JULIAN LEEK

mans for our flying with *Annie* and his intimacy with the radial engines, to stay in the air. I know all this is irreverent and it is also on the thin edge of a most pleasant sort of madness, but this is the way it happened—and we brought new life to a magnificent, ancient machine, rather than stripping away its last, faded tatters of glory.

That's the difference.

———◆———

My initial flying in N52JU—and most of it was done with Ted Anderson in the cockpit with me, with both of us soon joined by Bob Bailey, a pilot for National Airlines who had a long period of

flying large jet iron birds with the Air Force—was never attempted with any concern but that we would always get through the mists of mystery that enveloped the airplane. The longer we flew the machine the better we would know her, of course, but in the early days we were as much pioneers because of all the things we didn't know, *and no one else knew*, that we not only felt but effectively shared a kinship with pilots of forty to fifty years ago, who plunged with the same blind faith as did we into situations that now render us tight-jawed.

Through her long decades of always-changing ownership, most of which used the airplane to squeeze the last hour of flight from her structure and return as little as possible to keep her airworthy, there had been so many internal acts of mad surgery performed that no one human being could honestly say he *knew* all her systems and how they worked. *Iron Annie* was a potpourri of nuts, bolts, wires, changes, and alterations. We would not only have to learn the procedures from which we would learn to fly the airplane, but we would have to unravel the effects of all the twisted minds that had visited their brand of madness on the machine. It meant knuckle-busting and wrench-twisting and crawling everywhere through the airplane. That was one of the negative advantages—and I intend those words exactly as they appear—of working with a basket case.

You could start anywhere and there was always some drastic, major, and necessary work to be done.

I began to produce a series of documents that ran in parallel. First, to gather as much information on the Ju-52/3m, as a type, that could be gathered. The conflicts of data were astonishing. Everyone was an expert, and that meant almost everyone else was wrong, so it was virtually impossible to select any one source as reliable. I wasted no time getting a copy of the manual for the CASA 352L through my Air Force contacts, for here we would at least have metric performance figures, and above all the

This can't be real . . . What am I doing here?
JULIAN LEEK

cutaways and diagrams would let us see into the basic structure without X-ray vision.

But first there was general information. History and development and use, thus gathering performance and other specifications as they applied to various series of Ju-52s with various engines, and separating from this conglomeration the details that applied to our airplane, or that could best be applied to N52JU as a rule of thumb, and from those data, and our actual experience, beginning to collect reliable information.

I wanted to know, for example, the basic dimensions of the airplane, and we used for our handbook various German combat references. When we got *Iron Annie,* and this is just one example, no one else knew the airplane fuselage was a Ju-52/3mg8e. We found out by scraping away a dozen layers of housepaint on a strange bulge on the nose of the airplane, under which—hooray!—was an identification plate with the serial number and the aircraft type spelled out to the last detail. It was like picking up a diamond in a field littered with rocks. *Now* we had a hard reference from which to gather other details that applied.

It was necessary to work out a checklist. This is the old procedures game, or, as it is known to pilots who have managed to survive various and sundry threats to life and limb, "doing it by the numbers." You establish your procedures by going one step at a time, and you do it by working through a checklist, and by God following that checklist. The problem was that there wasn't any checklist on the airplane that amounted to a damn, and the Spanish manual was filled with all sorts of homilies, such as the admonition to the pilot that if his mechanic was really a sloppy bastard, he was not to be trusted to do the preflight and the pilot should really get his hands and his magnificent uniform dirty by doing it himself.

The FAA, with a somewhat patronizing eye, wants pilots to know certain things about their airplanes. For starters, how big it is. You think that's ridiculous? No one knew the specifications of *Werke* Number 130714, because no one really knew if the serial number was accurate, and until we did some deep paint scraping, we didn't know the specific model of the airplane!

So we gathered our information slowly (a move I had started months before the airplane arrived, to give me something of a head start). We established certain specifications that would not change. For

The paint was peeling, the belly corroded, the cockput a derelict, the engines sick—but somehow she still looked beautiful. KEN BUCHANAN

example, the wingspan was 95 feet 11½ inches, and the length with the tail up measured out to 62 feet, and the height with the tail down was 14 feet 9 inches. The numbers worked out to a wing area of 1,189.4 square feet, and it was easy enough to know the size of the big German tires (which were Italian Pirellis made in Spain) as 300×1300 mm. There wasn't any exactly equivalent American-size tire, but it was big, about as tall as the tire for the C-46 (now on the airplane) but only about half as wide. Oh, yes, the tire was 12-ply, smooth when new but now just plain bald and severely weather-checked.

Some other numbers were easy, although in this area, the dimensions changed just as easily. The cabin was 21 feet long and 6 feet 3 inches high (the official book says 2.75 instead of 3 inches, but if we add carpet, or soundproof the overhead, the book is wrong) and 5 feet 3 inches wide.

Some other numbers started getting important. *If* the BMW radials still turned out 660 horsepower each, then the wing loading of this airplane at gross weight of 23,100 pounds came out to 19.42 pounds per square foot, and the power loading was 11.67 pounds per square foot. But were the engines still delivering 660 horsepower each? *No way.* What counted was that at least we had working, meaningful numbers. Those old BMWs just didn't have it any more, and how much was missing was yet to be determined, and it had to be determined, and quickly, because that's the starting point for working out takeoff speed and stall speeds and all those interesting facts of life.

Another point on those engines: we confirmed the Townend ring about the nose engine and the NACA cowlings out on the wings. By now I had collected stacks of magazine articles and a twelve-foot-high stack of historical reference books, most of them written by enthusiastic but woefully unin-formed amateurs who were overnight experts on the *meaningful* aspects of the Ju-52. *But most of them had photographs.* And photographs tell you many things that are revelant to what you have and what you're doing. For example, not one of about eight hundred photos of various Ju-52s showed the exhaust stacks on our airplane. Which meant ours were jury-rigged by someone who had the airplane between some undefined moment in the past and right *now*. Okay. We pushed that to

the side. As long as the stacks held in place, that was good enough for the moment.

The engines had superchargers. That was very important to know, because we were still thrashing around as to the exact identification of the engines. Sure, they were BMW 132 series. A or E? We didn't know for certain, and by God I didn't trust those logbooks worth a damn. Bud Weaver wrote down what he knew or what he thought he knew, but that was a long way from being accurate. The designations in his logs were misinterpreted scrib-

Looking straight down into the cockpit of the big iron bird—one of the worst airplane junkyards assembled within a single unit. JULIAN LEEK

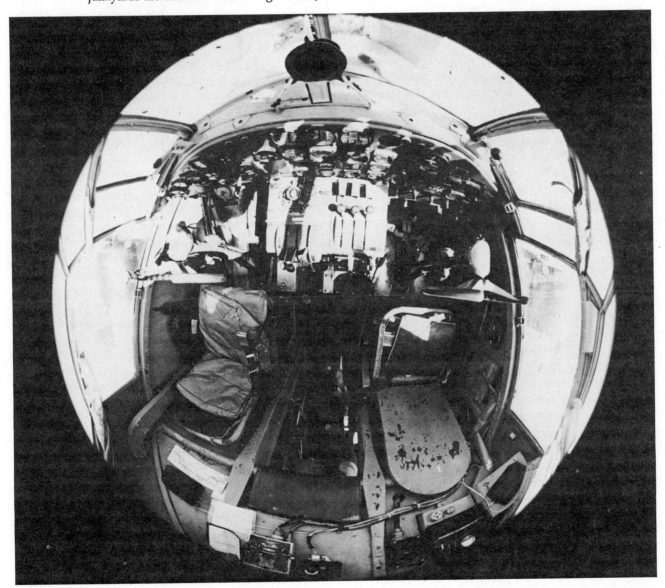

bles from somewhere, and that isn't good enough. It took longer than we expected to confirm that the engines were 132E models and were copies of a Hornet instead of a Wasp, and we went right to Pratt & Whitney for that, and found the old-timers who had actually worked on the 1690 series, and they found for us the licensing agreements between P&W and BMW. If you're getting the idea that this took an inordinate amount of time, you're right. About thirty-nine hours every day, all twelve days of every week.

Ted Anderson had flown these engines down from Charlotte and from their grumbling snarl had learned many things about them. The first order of the day, he announced, was *not* to use the over-boost or the superchargers. Their use was set for a flight of nine thousand feet or higher, above sea-level pressure, but the engines were so old and crotchety at this point that inflicting upon them the effect of going to overboost could literally send their internal pieces in many different directions all at the same time.

What confused us thoroughly was the indications that the engine controls marked OIL COOLER and CARBURETOR HEATERS (also often referred to as engine preheat) were intended for use only above nine thousand feet, only in conjunction with the superchargers, and—

"Hold it, HOLD IT!" I shouted in exasperation one day. "What the hell are we talking about here? Don't use the oil coolers below nine grand? What if the goddamned engines overheat!"

Ted tugged at his beard. "Throttle back and glide. Let the mothers cool off."

"Why?"

"Because no one seems to have used those controls for a hundred years and we're not sure what will happen if we touch them. They're probably going to come apart in little pieces on us and really screw up the engines. The same thing goes for the carb heat, because the way they are set now, they're working, and let's not press our luck."

"Sounds reasonable to me. Okay." So we made up those neat little plastic signs saying VERBOTEN! and plastered them everywhere we thought they belonged, and we ended up with a cockpit that had more "forbidden!" signs on it than a Yugoslavian minefield. What's crazy about this kind of situation is that the oil coolers were supposed to be left in the OPEN position all the time, to cool the engines (unless it was February in Stalingrad, and we

didn't plan to go that route), especially since we were flying in Florida, and they were in the full OPEN, or cooling, position, where they belonged for our kind of flying . . . only, we didn't yet know it. As we worked out the right engine temps and came to learn the systems and numbers, it dawned on us that we *were* right with our settings. Of course, had the engine temps gone the other way, such as run for the red line, we'd have worked those dudes and found out how to open the coolers much sooner than we did. The coolers, by the way, looked like stubby rocket launchers in twin cylinders suspended beneath each engine, and they were great for collecting grit and dragonflies and getting all clogged up. They required two basic kinds of maintenance: One was to wash off the blood and hair where we were always smacking our skulls against them, and two was to keep them clean so the airflow was unimpeded.

When we received the airplane, there were seventeen passenger seats in the cabin. That crowded things a bit, and we thought of all those bodies perspiring or throwing up and the charming perfume it would send wafting into the cockpit. So we reduced the number to nine seats, which gave a lot of stretching-out room, especially since the seats reclined. They were also of the original German leather and looked as if they'd been through a half-dozen wars, which, the more we thought about it, was certainly true. The cabin windows for the most part were scratched up and glazed and pretty cruddy, but attending to them would come later. We didn't look through those to fly—except that in many cases the cockpit windows weren't much better. The weather stripping was a gloppy mess, some windows were broken, none of them sealed properly, some windows kept falling out, and—well, you get the idea.

There were eight hundred pounds of radios and navigation equipment and antennas on that airplane—*none of which worked*. I think they had radios from every war since the charge of the light brigade, and their dials read in three languages. To me, all they spelled was FIRE! and we went wild with wire cutters and bolt cutters and quickly started stripping them from *Annie,* because they were just so much dead weight. The first time we turned them on, they emitted showers of sparks like a Fourth of July celebration, all within a very small room. Not conducive to relaxed flying.

We also removed those two small swinging

doors, saloon style, that led to the cockpit. First, they didn't accomplish much, they blocked off airflow for cooling down the cabin, and they also reduced the narrow space through which we would have to go like hell if it ever became necessary to abandon that airplane in a hurry.

The floorboards of the airplane resembled sawdust. I don't know what the material was, but it was moldy and soft and gave way beneath the pressure of a man's foot and sagged dangerously and unpredictably, and we knew it would be on the priority list to be exchanged. There were four big hatch covers between the rows of seats to be opened for cargo and baggage, and within which to wriggle your body into the Black Hole of Calcutta with a flashlight to inspect control rods, flaps springs, and the like. Ten minutes down there and you had the equivalent of a week's dieting, the way the sweat poured off your body.

We discovered that we had a twenty-eight-volt electrical system, and one generator that operated at sixty amps. Hah! *Sometimes* it operated at sixty amps. Not very often. It was hit or miss, and one out of every four times was an acceptable average.

The brake system, which in the ancient history of the airplane had been compressed-air, was now hydraulic and operating from the pump in the right engine. *Forget it.* The pump was wheezy and intermittent, the lines were corroded and leaked just about everywhere, and the pressure that got to the brakes announced its arrival by dribbling red hydraulic fluid over the wheels, tires, and ground. Only the pilot seat had brake pedals, and these had been stolen from a DC-3 and fitted into the Ju-52. The only way you got any brake pressure was by shoving with all your weight, so that your toes were scraping floorboard, your feet were twisted in grotesque fashion, and your heels were inches from your seat. When you climbed out of the seat, you staggered like a cripple with swollen ankles. I did not use or attempt to use brakes except when the moment was critical, like preventing the airplane from creeping into a ditch.

Those cockpit windows! The side windows slid fore and aft, usually at the cost of no more than two or three fingernails. There was a front-windshield window that pushed open by a metal bar, at the end of which was a large wooden ball you grasped to operate the window, and the first time we did this to get air, the only reason the window didn't fall out of the airplane was that air

pressure held it in place, for it had separated from all attachments. The cockpit windows were on our list to be thrown away and replaced with solid safety glass that did not move. The overhead exit hatch slid way back and gave delightful air conditioning. It was surprising to us, for when opened fully in flight it did not create a screaming gale, as we had imagined, and it certainly *did* suck up all dirt and debris and blow it away, and also cleared the cockpit from the storms of smoke the engines generated during starting. We were soon to learn something else about this sliding hatch: when fully open with the airplane being landed in a steep descent, it acted as an air brake and slowed down the iron machine by about ten miles per hour. Forget finding that item in a reference book; we got it from Wolfgang Wenck, who had been driving Ju-52s all over German combat fronts and told us about it.

There was a tail-wheel lock. When you moved it into the LOCK position by moving a handle on the lower-left quadrant, by the pilot, you released a cable, and this dropped a metal cylinder into the locking space to keep the tail wheel in place, so that taxiing was made easier and there was less tendency for the tail to wander from side to side. It also mitigated the effects of side winds on takeoff and landing. A very handy device and quite important to a large taildragger. The problem with our system was that the cockpit control jammed often, the cable was snarled, and the pin, broken unknown months or years before, was missing, and we would have to manufacture our own replacement. In the meantime, fast rudder movement, use of differential power, hard aileron, and the damping effect of thick bungees in the rudder/tail-wheel system would help. Oh, I forgot to mention that those bungees (shock cords) on the airplane were frayed so badly as to be useless.

Then there was fueling. The Spanish manual on which I had gotten my greedy hands delighted us with a cutaway of the wings, revealing the fuel-tank system in the Spanish airplane. But what was mounted in the 352L was *not* mounted in N52JU, because there had been some major adaptations in the system. The 352L still used a special blue gasoline and a white gasoline for an elaborate and cumbersome process of starting up and shutting down the engines, and none of this existed in our Ju-52. Cute. There were ten tanks instead of eleven (although there was space within each wing for an extra tank of 75-gallon capacity). The only thing for us to do was to Xerox the cutaway, crawl into the wings with the Xerox copy, a pen, and a flashlight, and go through the whole system, marking off the appropriate changes on the Xerox, then drawing up a new cutaway and writing a whole new technical description of the system. This was how we confirmed we could hold 620 gallons of gasoline. The next trick to learn—prompted by watching fuel cascade to the ground—was that you filled the tanks at not too rapid a rate or the fuel backed up and overflowed. The modern high-speed pumps were too much for a series of interconnected barrels and kegs. For maximum fuel, load her up gently, then wait a half hour for the fuel to settle, and then finish tanking, and you could get the total of 620 gallons into the wings—for a neat 3,720 pounds of fuel when you were full.

Then there was the oil, with twenty gallons for each engine, and that's a lot of oil for an airplane of this size—sixty gallons in all, with a weight of four hundred fifty pounds of oil. We learned *very* quickly not to fill those tanks all the way, because then they would vent and overflow and there'd be oil all over the mucking place. Not too bad for the wing engines, but when it came back from the center engine, it ended up on your windshield. A long time ago, we discovered, someone had sealed off the nose-engine oil vent, and since it still seemed to work okay, we left it as we found it and haven't changed that arrangement to this day. We carried fifteen gallons of hydraulic fluid, and lost no time in moving the tanks from the right engine to the nose engine, where there was plenty of room for the installation. We did this by removing the chemical tank for fire extinguishing. We wanted nothing to do with this system, since the chemical, when it mixed with flame, was converted instantly to a lethal poison gas, and that is not the way to go. You survive a fire and die from gas. Big deal.

Once we had the fire-wall section of the nose engine set up with the new hydraulic system, we discovered it still had many of its old quirks, among them a tendency of the airplane to celebrate its new home in America by emulating the Old Faithful geyser. Somehow the pressure in the system kept backing up, and the pressure-relief valve in the fluid-fill system would let go with a deep *whump!* and red hydraulic fluid would gush fifty feet above the ground until you could shut off the engine, which you could not do quickly without cutting off the electrical system, and in those old engines that always meant the chance of a fire, so when you geysered (that's got to be a new pattern for an airplane), you killed the mixture to FULL LEAN and shoved the fuel flow to SHUTDOWN, and then you waited for two minutes for the fuel to suck its way through the lines, at the end of which, of course, there wasn't any more geysering, simply because there wasn't any more hydraulic fluid in the tanks or the lines; it was everywhere else on the airplane and a considerable distance across the flight line.

The smartest thing we did was to throw out the batteries we found in the airplane: the batteries and the whole system were badly corroded and ready for a really bad fire. We cleaned up the works, installed new vent and dump lines, building a new battery retaining box in the number-two belly cargo hold and installing two Sears Diehards in tandem to get the twenty-four volts we needed for starting. It was the best battery system I've ever seen then or now, and hats off to Sears for incredible battery power performance, which has had all the pros shaking their heads, because what we have seems to outperform every other system known.

So we ended up soon with the right engine producing the electrical power we needed through a single generator, the nose engine running the hydraulic pump and the left engine operating the vacuum system—which never once, not for a single flight, ever managed to operate without balking in one way or another or crapping out completely.

I finally managed to obtain reasonably reliable performance figures—reliable in that they did apply to some late-model Ju-52 somewhere down the line, and while they might not have applied to N52JU, they did satisfy legal requirements in that we at least had numbers as a starting point.

The official figures called for a maximum speed, under full power, overboost on, at 10,725 feet, of 170 miles per hour. That is an absurdity of the worst kind. With engines running properly, that could have been possible, but in the airplane when I got my hands on it, you didn't dare go to full power except for takeoff, and then only *very* briefly (because Ted Anderson was *always* hauling back on the throttles so the engines might survive), and the idea of full bore at nearly eleven grand was horrifying. We would have blown engines all over the sky. The same for the published speeds of 156 miles per hour at 4,950 feet, and 145 at sea level. Those figures apply to a spanking-new Ju-52 with engines churning out full power, and that's something not too well understood outside this business. The rated power of an engine doesn't mean beans; what counts is what the engine really churns out, and listed and actual figures are often far apart.

Just as the above figures issued forth from some statistical fairyland, so were the cruise figures for the airplane as we received *Iron Annie*. The numbers of 142 miles per hour at 3,300 feet, 145 at 4,455 feet, and 144 at 6,600 feet just don't belong in our real world.

The book listed the rate of climb at takeoff as 871 feet per minute at 97 miles per hour. No way! We dragged upward at 500 feet per minute under the best of conditions, and that was with Anderson muttering darkly in his beard about mauling the engines.

The time-to-climb numbers were equally as absurd when they listed 10.4 minutes under full gross to reach an altitude of 9,900 feet from a standing start. To accomplish this in the Ju-52 with fixed-pitch props you would have to go to overboost, hammer on the throttles, and jam them halfway through the panel.

Strangely enough, the official figures *underestimated* the ability of the airplane to get off the ground. Using 25° flaps, the book stated, at sea level and the temperature at 59° F. the Ju-52 would become airborne at 72 miles per hour after a run of 1,231 feet in 26 seconds. At maximum gross weight with new engines the Ju-52 would easily cut short time, distance, and speed to get into the air.

The book listed the landing speed at 68 miles per hour—and that's always been a matter of dealer's choice, because you could do it from 62 to 80 miles per hour, depending upon attitude when touching down. No contest there.

And so it went, our collecting information and replacing all sorts of faulty data—on both sides of the fence—with reality, and rewriting our checklists constantly, and starting to write an aircraft manual and a pilot's operational handbook and everything else that was needed, and all *from scratch*. Because if we were learning anything, it was absolutely not, under any circumstances, to trust what was seeping into our hands and registering on our consciousness about this airplane. That is, if we wanted to stay in one piece long enough to continue to enjoy our flying, we would have to start at the very beginning, learn carefully and slowly, and establish meaningful procedures and become proficient in handling the airplane.

The books provide numbers; they don't tell you how to fly. And all the numbers don't mean a thing when you're landing ten tons of taildragger with full flaps in a really whomping crosswind. When *that* happens, it's all flying and the books are the last thing you ever want on your mind.

All this, of course, was still awaiting us as we went out to Ti-Co Airport for our first great adventure in flying the Ju-52—*on the ground.*

Iron Annie waited for us like a wounded elephant not knowing whether to trust the new hands that would be laid on her. There had been so much abuse and lack of minimum care that if an airplane truly could express its distrust, then this airplane would have to be approached with extreme care and gentleness or someone was going to get bitten. And that's precisely how we did it.

At the iron bird, the first thing is to open up every door and window, because a big airplane that's sealed off collects vast amounts of heat, and it's necessary to get some breeze moving through the cockpit and cabin. I unlocked the main cabin door, swung it around, and latched it against the fuselage, got the ladder and hooked it in place, climbed aboard, and nearly drowned in the wet heat. Up front, I opened the forward cabin door, which led to the right wing, then into the cockpit, where everything was soaked from a hard rain during the night. I opened the side windows, gaining a couple of scrapes and bruises in the process, cracked open the forward vents, and slid back the top hatch, feeling both a sudden breeze and a bucketful of water that had been collected from the rain. A hell of a start!

You didn't do anything in those days before you checked off the last time the engine rocker-arm boxes were serviced with grease, because if you went more than ten hours without a refill you'd have an engine full of friction and a lot of heat and very soon some eye-stabbing fire. They were okay, and they'd stay okay just so long as there was no more than ten hours' running time between greasings.

In the cockpit, I checked that all switches were off, removed the worthless cockpit cover and threw it onto the ground, then went back through the cabin to the ground. A fast glance to see that the chocks were in place, then back to the tail to remove the gust locks and move the big rudder

from side to side. All free. Inspect the tail area, the tail wheel, the fraying bungees, look for any broken safety wire, and try to find anything that might be loose. The elevators went up and down nicely, their interior sounding like a medicine man rattling bones in a gourd. That meant opening the elevators and getting inside to see what the hell was moving and scraping about in there. Some day soon, anyway.

I walked forward along the right fuselage, checking the security locks for the huge cargo door, looked under the belly for any signs of twisted or bent metal (I didn't need to look for corrosion; it was all along the belly). Then outward along the wing, checking flap attachments and where the flap and aileron separated. I removed the wooden gust locks that had been inserted between the flap and the aileron, inspected all attachments and fittings, groaned at the rust, moved the aileron full up and down, tugged and poked at all the underwing security attachments, and rapped on the access and service panels. Everything seemed pretty well glued together. I gave the aileron balance a long look for signs of cracks or corrosion, and looked at the wingtip light. Looking at it was about all I could do, for none of the navigation lights—wingtip or tail—worked.

Walking forward under that monster wing, I checked for general security: access-panel fastenings, any undue corrosion, the leading edge of the wing, then all about engine number three in a search for cracks, cowling security, attachments and fittings, exhaust stacks for cracking and security. You look for things that shouldn't be there. It's like a balancing act on skates or a tightrope. After a while the basic movements are all instinctive and it's the unusual that leaps out at you. You study the big propeller and look for anything that might jump out at you, such as a line. That could mean a crack and requires more investigation. And you always check the edges of the blades, because the nick of a pebble sucked up by turning props has to be smoothed out with a file or it can induce a far greater crack, vibration, and possibly throw the whole blade.

At the gear, you make sure the grease cups around the gear legs are properly packed, look for rust or breaks or cracks, inspect those tires (beaten and battered and so bloody *old*), look for breaks or frays in the hydraulic lines, any evidence of fluid, pressure, and appearance. At the nose engine, the same check as at the right engine, and at each engine one vital move: always to check the security of those oil coolers to be absolutely certain they are snug. If they come undone in flight it means a very hot engine and a damned fast landing.

There are two fuel drains beneath the wing center section, and for some reason this airplane simply doesn't seem to collect water. Since water is denser than gasoline, it settles at the bottom of tanks (from condensation) and works its way down to the lowest gravity point: the sumps. If there's water, it will show up in the fuel sample you study in the drain tube in your hand. We didn't find any now and were to remark on this one characteristic of the airplane; it just never showed (and never would, except for some fuel we once took on that already had water in it).

On to the left gear and tire for the check, to the left engine for a repeat of all that was done with the other engines, along the left wing to the long pitot tube. Remove the cover and make sure it's clear—no bugs taking up residence, for example. Tough to do from the ground, with the tube way over a man's head, but at least you can study the tube inlet. And on around to the end of the wing and repeat everything done with the right wing.

The routine called for climbing up the wing at the left cabin side to the number-one (left) engine. Open the covers and inspect the oil level; fifteen gallons is fine, and we use sixty-weight mineral oil. Check the fuel level. The tank dipstick goes up to about three hundred gallons, or, roughly, twelve hundred liters; we have two hundred gallons, which is fine. Then check all connections, covers, caps, everything, and have a good look into the engine from the open, back end. Then you go through the same routine all over again with the right engine, and when that's over, it's mountain-climbing time off the forward right wing, with various handgrips and footholds to get out to the nose

engine and, balanced carefully, opening hatch covers, unscrewing caps, and checking the oil level and then the level for hydraulic fluid. After crawling vertically back to the wing, a good eyeball scan of antennas.

Inside the airplane: Back through the cabin to the after bulkhead. Remove the big cargo hatch door and place it to the side, and with a bright flashlight, enter the cargo area (a bit tricky, with some neat body bending), into the cargo storage, with its top capacity of three hundred thirty pounds, then go through a swinging gate with a latch that's about frozen and tears more skin off fingers and hands, check the area, look back in the tail cone (you're under the old turret ring here) to check the bell cranks and cables. Be sure everything is secured by straps or bungees. Close the doors and hatches behind, replace the bulkhead door, and to the left, by the rearmost window on the right side of the cabin, check the ELT (emergency locator transmitter) battery date, be sure the thing is on ARM. Check the lavatory (*Krappenhausen*) for security, close the door, and you're free to breathe again. Then it's the ladder inside the cabin, close the cabin door, and lock securely.

Up front to the cockpit: Place a cushion over the waterlogged left seat, and climb into place. Ted Anderson comes up on the right wing and through that cabin door, closing it behind him, and stands in the cockpit, panting from the heat. "Okay, all tiedowns released and chocks in place."

Now, in this unmitigated disaster of a cockpit, with broken knobs and frozen handles and cracked leather and torn fabric and peeling paint and cracked glass and inoperative instruments, you're free to begin the cockpit check (which was much less complicated then than it is now . . .). Ted stands up in the open hatch and he looks, and looks carefully, for freedom of controls and their proper movement. Yoke full back and then forward for elevator movement, rudder pedals full deflection for rudder movement, ailerons left and right, and then simultaneous movement of all the controls to assure their freedom and proper movement, and you can never overdo this sort of thing, because forgetting one item with a locked control is begging for disaster. When it comes to something of this nature, I am a combination of a worrisome little old lady and an absolute bastard where everyone, including myself, is concerned. More damn fools, who have been otherwise brilliant and experienced pilots, have taken off without performing this check as a religious matter, and climbed up, and then crashed almost at once, because their controls were locked.

I check out the T-handle rudder trim on each side of the pilot's yoke—those that Scott Johnson found always frozen. We unfroze the goodies and in the process snapped the bungees and broke the cables and their attachments, and we're going to rebuild this system at the first chance. In the meantime, we can always use a heavy foot if we lose a wing engine. The elevator trim is set at neutral by a gauge to my left. I reach down to the right side of my seat to the Mighty Wheel, as large as the steering wheel of a truck, and move the trim just to be certain it *is* moving, and with one eye scan the needle indicator of the trim gauges. It moves freely both up and down.

Okay. Now, in the center of the wheel is a vertical handle with a wooden ball on it. The handle is depressed into its slot, which means moving the wheel moves only the trim. Up with the ball, and now trim and flaps are engaged and move together, and I start the flaps down to check their movement and be certain they both go down at the same time. Then roll them back up. That wheel gives you mighty muscles, because you're pushing against those massive coiled springs that handle the flaps. We leave the flaps up. Don't need them. I'm still not that sure of the trim, because I've never flown in the left seat, but it can't be too far outside its limits if it's a zero, or neutral. I'll find out fast enough and soon enough the first time we push upstairs.

Then there's the instrument check. The eight-day clock is frozen; forget it. Altimeters are set to field elevation. Directional gyros can be forgotten; they don't work. There's one radio, sort of sick, and I check that the switch is OFF, and dial in Ti-Co ground-control frequency, which at Ti-Co Airport is like having traffic lights at a Sahara oasis. Vacuum pump is off. There are oddball switches here and there, like the cockpit lights (dead), the navigation lights (dead), the rotating beacon and strobes (dreaming for the future). Tail wheel in the unlocked position; that's for practice, because there ain't no locking pin there, friend. Fire extinguisher controls: all three to SECURE. Another exercise, because it's all disconnected and that deadly carbon tetrachloride tank is empty. The fuel-selector switch to the right-wing position, then to the left-wing position, and back to center for drawing fuel from both wings. Oil coolers to OPEN, carburetor heat to COLD (wind them around to be sure they work; okay), primer to SECURE, primer secondary system (Snapsebensin) to SECURE. It's Norwegian and we don't know what the hell it does, so secure it. The windows are open and the fire guard outside is asleep on his feet, waiting for us, and Ted bellows at him and he waves at us. If only he knew how these things started . . . oh, well, when he sees all that raw fuel, he'll come alert damned fast.

Now we're ready to bring *Annie* to life. . . .

Ted pumps up the hydraulic pressure to a reading of 1,000 psi and we pray it doesn't break the accumulator bladder wide open (it's been doing this for a while and it's a bitch to replace). We need the 1,000 psi to be sure that what little brakes we have—and we're still guessing about this—are ready to work. Remember that this is my first time in the left seat.

We'll leave the mixtures in the LEAN position. No one is certain about that, but Ron Skipper said he got his best starts by cranking up and then moving the mixtures from LEAN to FULL RICH. Okay; we buy that. The props are fixed, so there aren't any prop controls to worry about. The supercharger control is set to below nine thousand feet so we don't overboost and blow the engines.

Spark advance, and—

Spark advance?

"They're supposed to be in the RETARD position for starting," Ted murmurs.

"What the hell is this? A Model-A Ford?"

Ted grins wolfishly. "Someone disconnected them a long time ago. Forget 'em."

Gladly.

Bulkhead master switches up and behind the copilot seat to my right, and three more switches on the right bulkhead, by Ted, all to ON. Then the quadrant master on the console before me and to my right up to ON. There are three fuel selectors on the right side of the console, and I move the selector for number-three engine back into the OPEN, or center, setting. Number-three ignition switch up to ON, magneto selector for number three centered to BOTH.

Now it's Ted's turn to work, which means grasping the wobble pump by the left side of his seat and moving it up and down in a steady, fast motion. Faster, more; faster, faster, damn it, until the fire guard outside stares in disbelief as fuel cascades from the engine onto the tarmac. Ted yells to him. "We got fuel yet?"

"You guys sprung a leak!" he shouts back.

To hell we have. That's how you start this thing. Ted stops pumping for a moment, reaches to the forward part of the console on his side, flips away a protective covering so he can reach the T handle for the Bendix inertial starter, and shoves it down hard, holding it for a count of fifteen. We hear the system winding up from a groan into a whine and then the shriek we want to hear and Ted hauls up on the T handle. There's a wheezing, grinding moan, and then a groan, and all sorts of clanking noises as the prop turns and huge clouds of white smoke belch from the stacks. The engine is just catching. I move the mixture into FULL RICH and do a finger dance with the throttle to number three, and she's trying to really light off. I yell for Ted to pump some more, and his hand is going up and down on the wobble pump because if the engine doesn't start now, we've got to do it all over again. But she's catching, and I jerk the fuel flow from OPEN to RUNNING position, full back, and there's a throaty roar and number three is turning. Ted gasps as sweat collects all over him.

I'm working the throttle. The generator should come in at 700 rpm but it doesn't, and I go up to 900 and then there's the indication that *Annie* is now generating her own current. Back on the throttle to check the generator charge and advance it again to 700 and hold it there and check oil temperature and oil pressure and fuel pressure and carburetor heat and the cylinder-head temp and see what the manifold pressure reads. We can't do a thing about manifold pressure, but it does work as a crosscheck for any problems. It's on the money. I let her warm up briefly and pull the throttle full back into a spring detent for dead idle and she continues running.

Damn! There's a side-bulkhead master switch that should have been turned on, and I hit it to its UP position and still can't figure how the engine started. I also forgot the generator relay, pushed in to ON, but because we're generating it means Ted has done it. I check the after-bulkhead voltmeter to ON, and we're getting the proper indication. Okay, number three is running and everything's in the green. Now it's time to start the center engine, number two, and it is the wicked one, because that wobble pump has to haul the fuel a long way upward into the nose-engine carburetor. First I

depress both brake pedals to reduce any hydraulic pressure in the system, because the automatic safety cutout at 1,000 psi doesn't work and we can blow the accumulator bladder.

We go through the same Chinese fire drill to start number two, with the exception of Ted's working ten times as hard to keep that wobble pump going, but we've got smoke billowing back and the whole airplane shaking madly as I try to "catch" number two. It won't, and I shove the throttle full forward for a moment, bring it back, crack it a half inch, and then start in with the mixture to the RICH position. She catches, and we repeat everything and number two is running, and okay, we've got a thousand pounds showing on the hydraulic-pressure gauge.

It's time to start up number one, to my left, but she balks, and it takes four complete exercises of the starting sequence before she catches with her throaty roar and everything is running. The airplane is rumbling and snarling, popping through the exhausts, and I'm soaking wet. Ted's arm is in a cramp and looks like a claw, and he also looks ten feet underwater, with the sweat plastering his clothes to his body everywhere. His seat is wet and the floor about him is wet and I hand him a towel and in a few moments that's soaked also. I check the vacuum pressure for the engine-driven pump and the outside venturi and they're both working. We each set the directional gyros and laugh hollowly as they turn willy-nilly and not even full vacuum will bring the artificial horizons to any more sense than rolling like a pencil in zero g within their instrument mounts.

I signal the fire guard to pull the chocks, and hold full brake pressure and it works, and I release the left brake and stand on the right brake and bring in the power on the left engine to swing her around to the right. Slowly, ever so slowly, because right here and now is where she can get away from me, and these brakes are unpredictable and you never know what they're going to do. It takes some good throttle to get *Annie* rolling, and the right brake suddenly isn't worth a damn and I'm mashing my foot, toe down, as hard as I can with my leg muscle already cramping, and *Annie* wheels about ever so slowly and ponderously. I let her turn and straighten her out and let her roll a bit, holding the yoke full back, all three throttles now in dead idle, and try to drag her to a stop. Being able to stop is our whole world now. The taxiway

Okay, we've got three churning, flaps down, ready to move out for the first high-speed runs on the main runway of Ti-Co. Martin Caidin and Ted Anderson carrying on their "conversation" with Iron Annie. JULIAN LEEK

is too damn narrow and *Annie* has so much mass she wants to keep moving. I'm really doing a dance on these brakes and working the throttles and trying to make sure the left wingtip doesn't cream a big light pole. Ted is gazing with one eye at a row of planes to our right. The idea is to get to a sharp turn, swing the airplane about one hundred twenty degrees into another taxiway, and get her to a closed runway that's five thousand feet long and one hundred fifty feet wide, where we can practice this sort of nonsense.

The radio stinks, but we can make out the tower —barely—and we're doing some heavy shouting to one another, sort of trying to justify what the hell we're doing here. We creep along, we've *got* to creep along, because one moment the brakes work and then they don't and then one or the other comes in squealing like a ten-ton sow being raped by Godzilla. Before long I'd be writing up not a pilot note but literally a warning for the operational handbook that the "brakes for this aircraft operate in a manner unique to this design. Unless the pilot, who from the left seat is the only crew member who can apply brake pressure, is aware of the unusual brake operation characteristics, he can easily find himself in a situation where he loses stopping ability entirely."

That would be putting it mildly, because braking action in this machine *was differential only*. If you lead with right rudder and apply right brake,

there's braking action but on the right brake only. The same with the left rudder and left brake.

But I discovered immediately that *if I depressed both brake pedals there was no braking action whatsoever*. That is the goddamnedest arrangement I have ever run into. It meant I had to use the brakes when taxiing with a sidestepping toe dance of differential engine power and one brake at a time or control was lost. If the brake pressure was low and we decided to pump the manual system, it didn't do a thing except rupture that accursed bladder. We'd learn that, when we started the engines, the pilot had to depress the right rudder pedal and press down at the top of the pedal for braking action, and this would provide right brake *only* until number-one engine, to my left, was running, and then I had the choice of either brake.

Good God. . . .

We made it, us sweating and the airplane squealing, perspiration and leg cramps the order of the day, out to that inactive runway, and we spent the next several hours practicing. Little by little, we increased the speed until I had the tail up and could feel the yaw and compensate for it with right rudder as *Annie* started to run. I'd chop power and hold up the tail with forward yoke until she came down by herself, and then holding her straight was a matter of whipping my feet back and forth on those rudder pedals to keep the barn door far

She's going good, DON'T LET HER FLY, DAMN IT! That's it, kick that rudder, kick it, boot it, keep her straight.... The process of learning an airplane comes best through high-speed taxiing, *not* flying. JULIAN LEEK

Okay, tail's down, full back on the yoke to keep her planted, WALK THAT RUDDER! Iron Annie rolls straight and true. They're learning. JULIAN LEEK

"WE'RE FLYING, DAMN IT!" Iron Annie thunders into the air—Caidin at the controls in the left seat for his first flight as captain. JULIAN LEEK

behind us, working for directional control. It didn't take long to learn not to trust those brakes for stopping action. We ran up and down the runway without flaps, with 25° flaps for takeoff position, and down to 40° in landing configuration. This is the *only* way to feel the bird. Up and down the runway, throttles full bore for maximum power, tail up and the feeling lighter and lighter on the controls, and then chop everything, yoke full back, and see how long she takes to stop, if the brakes work, or whatever.

Then we did the run-ups before takeoff. Not just to get used to them but to see if we could hold the bloody airplane still long enough to do the pretakeoff checks without sliding around when the brakes just decided to quit. We learned that, whenever it was possible, the idea was to roll off the runway and put her on grass, and the softer the ground the better, because that had a braking effect all its own.

For the run-up, we turned into the wind, applied maximum braking pressure (hah!), and held the yoke full back. Check fuel selector to BOTH. Advance the number three throttle to 1,500 rpm, and then check each mag, left and right, with an acceptable drop of 50–125 rpm. Throttle back to 500 rpm idle, then advance to 700 rpm, repeat for the nose engine, recheck the hydraulic pressure, and repeat the entire sequence for the number-one engine. All the time, the airplane is creeping about, trying to sniggle its way forward and *fly*. But there was the vacuum system to check, all the engine gauges to recheck, controls free movement again, fuel selector confirmed to BOTH, recheck flap and trim position, forget the passengers (ain't none), get tower to clear the airplane for takeoff. We did this several times, and the last time, sitting on the edge of the inactive runway, at the edge of the *active* runway, the tower operator comes back with: "Ju-five-two, what are your intentions?"

We hadn't planned to fly this thing. Not yet, anyway, but Ted looked at me and I looked back at him, and we both agreed without saying a word. Hell, we had to fly her sooner or later, and it was nice weather out there and the wind was right down the active, and Ted picked up his microphone, and he couldn't help the grin and he said, "Big Daddy, we is ready to fu-lye!"

"You is cleared for takeoff," came back the chuckle with the words, and we inched out onto the active, hating the turn, my leg all twisted and cramped, and straightened her out. One brake squealed her crawl to a stop, the engines back to dead idle. There wasn't any tail-wheel lock to work, but we did a fast scan of the mixtures—FULL RICH—and then started forward. We knew the engines were supposed to deliver 2,100 rpm and somewhere about thirty-two inches manifold pressure, but that was just a big yuk and we would be happy to see 1,900 rpm on the gauges, and we had it. Ted hollered he'd take the power and for me to fly the damn thing, and he brought in the power slowly and steadily, babying the engines, and I kept the yoke back until I could feel her lighter and lighter, and then I went forward on the yoke, bringing in right rudder to compensate for yaw from those props, and she was holding down the centerline, her attitude absolutely level, accelerating steadily, the noise in the cockpit absolute bedlam, and then, faster than I thought it would happen, she was indicating 70 mph and just like that we were at 80 on the needle and I eased back with no more than finger pressure on the yoke and it was just *unbelievable.*

It was the first flight, the first solo all over again, the heady exhilaration of a once-in-a-lifetime moment. She took off and flew with a pounding and steady grace that defied everything I had expected. It was an incredible moment; here, in the left seat, this was *my* airplane, not in the sense of ownership but as a pilot. Finally it was go or no-go strictly on the basis of what she and I were doing together, and as we lifted up and climbed away straight ahead, Ted's always-ready hands were coming back on the throttles, babying the engines, he was talking to them, feeling them, and he never hesitated a moment to respond to whatever message those pounding radials gave to him. The harsher vibrations eased away. I was climbing at ninety and put the nose down slightly and adjusted the Mighty Wheel for the trim. Ted had the power back to 1,750 rpm as we climbed to three thousand feet, and I eased into level flight and retrimmed; he came back some more until the engines were loafing at 1,650 rpm. By now I had eased into the first turns, holding the right rudder through the climb to center the ball, and the rudder pressure was gone, once we were level. The Atlantic Ocean spread forever to the east, and the Florida coast had its usual cumulus buildups along the mainland, providing us with a marvelous corridor of beautiful sky in which to get acquainted with the old girl.

As soon as we had her level and trimmed out, Ted caressed the center throttle to exactly 1,650 rpm—I think he may have changed 10 or 15 rpm to meet his standards—and then we each took the wing-engine throttle on our respective sides, looking into the polished aluminum mirrors on the inside of the engine cowls. There, that gleaming shadow line spinning around slowly toward me meant that number-one engine was slightly faster in its turn than the nose engine. Squeeze back the throttle gently and the shadow slowed in its movement and finally disappeared. The same on the

other side until Ted and I lost the shadows and the three props were in perfect synchronization. I felt her out in turns to the left and to the right, glued one eyeball to the air speed, and went through the introductory waltz of climbs and descents and then rolled into steep turns, and she was remarkably, unbelievably stable.

Down the Indian River, heading south from Ti-Co—and it didn't take Caidin and Anderson long to see that those rocker-arm boxes in the nose engine were going to be a problem. JULIAN LEEK

Certain things became evident at once. This was a rudder airplane, and if you wanted a co-ordinated turn, man, you led just a hair first with rudder pressure and then brought in aileron, and, as steady as a rock, that big nose engine would sweep along the horizon. Aha! You do need back pressure if the angle of bank goes to fifteen degrees, and at thirty some good pressure, and at forty-five you're really holding it in there. Good. The ailerons in gentle turns were featherweights. With any tight turns they demanded some muscle. On a smooth cross-country flight you could fly her

153

like a baby carriage, but with any turbulence you used a lot of strength to bring up a wing.

The turns had their own special characteristics. The ailerons were so bloody big that if you rolled in aileron for a turn to the left and failed to use rudder, the adverse yaw of the interrupted airflow would swing the nose slightly to the right, the nose then going through some sort of gentle Dutch roll as she lumbered around to the left. But if you coordinated the controls, she flew right on the mark and with absolute precision.

Holding a course cross country was far easier than I had expected. The key was to walk the rudder tight, sharp, and with brief movements. You could fingertip the ailerons for lateral stability, and if the nose wandered at all, rudder would hold her where you wanted her to be. There was a tendency to drift off to one side, and this could have come from a dozen things. First, the aileron trim and wing trim were movable trim tabs but worked from outside the airplane on the ground and had to be preset. Second, the fuel that went to the engines as overflow, and returned to the tanks, always dumped into the right wing so that even if you took off with the wings level in fuel, pretty soon there'd be more fuel in the right wing than the left and you were heavy on the right side. The cure was to shove the fuel selector over to the right wing so that you burned out of that side and began to balance off the weight in the wings. This can get to be a severe problem if you forget your fuel management. I once had to take off with eight hundred pounds more fuel in the left wing than in the right because of a screwup in refueling, and it got *very* interesting as we reached about sixty and were getting flying speed. The only thing more interesting was landing, and the first touch of brakes brought the mass of the left wing into an inertial moment and *Annie* wanted to *swerve*.

Keep in mind that, while we were doing all this let's-get-to-know-one-another serenade, we were still reading most of the gauges, those that worked, anyway, in meters per second and kilometers per hour and God knows what else. The few we could read were not that accurate, but if we could define what they indicated at various points in flight we'd at least have guidelines. The busiest man aboard the airplane wasn't yours truly—it was Ted, writing notes furiously to record what was happening, and marking off with a grease pencil every gauge that so much as trembled, so that it was a definite refer-

ence point for a definite happening, and even if we couldn't read the numbers we would know where, at what point, an event would occur. If there are no numbers on a dial and the needle moves, then at the moment the airplane lifts from the ground you mark the dial and you know where to look the next time for your takeoff and approach to landing. You've found a valid and viable reference point.

Ted flew her for a while so he could get the feel of the bird. This would let us compare notes later, and I could also observe what was happening. I learned immediately that having the nose engine uncowled and covered only with the speed ring was a definite advantage, because you could see through those spaces between the cylinders and you had an unexpected visual advantage that way. It didn't matter very much in the air, because of all the big airplanes in which I have ever had cockpit time, none matches the greenhouse of the Ju-52, and with the overhead panels covering the entire cockpit, rolling into a steep turn doesn't burden you with a single blind spot—you see just as clearly in a forty-five- or sixty-degree bank as you do straight and level and looking directly ahead.

We went through stalls and approaches to stalls and hanging on the edge of stalls. The book says that the airplane will stall out at just about 100 kilometers per hour; the exact number is 62.2 mph, but percentages like that (again) are just so much conjecture. At those speeds, the air-speed indicator isn't worth a dime for a really accurate reading. If you want an accurate reading, the guy sitting next to you is the one for that.

We put down full flaps for landing configuration —and this was my first airborne experience with the mighty wheel, the biceps flexer, the master of muscle, the exhauster, and its interesting characteristics (it's easier putting the flaps *up*, because of air blast)—because the nicest place to screw up on an approach is four thousand feet above the ground. The airplane had not stalled until the needle was reading below sixty miles per hour, and then she entered the stall regime with a pronounced rumble and shake. It took a lot of back yoke to hold her up, and when she fell through it was gentle and smooth, without breaking off on one wing. Okay; now we set her up with forty degrees of flaps and let's see how she handles. Ted is doing everything but waving a baton as he calls out the routine, the mixtures to FULL RICH and the power back and the yoke back to maintain five

Martin Caidin brings her in for his first landing in *Iron Annie*—and the Pumphouse and Locomotive Gang is on the scene to record it all. JULIAN LEEK

"Watch that crosswind. More rudder, you blind idiot. Swing her around. Where'd you learn to fly? Dummy! *Oh, my, that's just bee-yoot-iful!*" The vocal orchestration of Anderson to Caidin on the first landing. JULIAN LEEK

hundred feet per minute rate of descent, and we bring in flaps, first to 25° down to observe the trim changes, and then to 40°. Ted scribbles down precisely what throttle setting is needed to maintain ninety miles per hour and five hundred feet per minute on the way down, because these are now *the* guidelines for landing. Our early routine, still flying at four thousand feet and aiming for a flareout at three thousand, was to set 10° flaps at downwind, go to 25° for base, and full 40° on final, but before long we dispensed with the 10° and went directly to the 25°. The rest of it was game-playing and unnecessary.

She held her approach right on the money. We knew we had a high-drag configuration in the airplane, and the key was to maintain a minimum of 80 mph and aim for a 500-fpm rate of descent on a long approach to the runway, playing with yoke and/or power as needed. It didn't take long to realize you could fly her down without any power

just so long as you kept these figures in the ball park. She came downstairs as if she were on a rail, locked tight as a drum. Rudder corrections took a lot of foot movement. The immediate response at cruise speed was gone, and, as expected, to get immediate and strong rudder response you needed a lot of heavy foot in there and then she'd answer.

The pitch control was completely unexpected. In cruise she responded at once to any fore or aft movement of the yoke, but this didn't seem to change even with power way back and the speed reduced, mainly because of those angled props, I guess. Whatever it was, you didn't need much elevator and you needed it smoothly or else you'd jerk the airplane up and down in a porpoising effect. On our practice landings a half mile up, we went through the whole drill of feeling out trim and playing with the airplane, and learning that with 25° flaps and full power applied suddenly for a simulated go-around she leaped back upstairs. We

155

didn't know if she would even hold her altitude with 40°, and we were amazed, and delighted, to find the airplane climbing steadily even with maximum flaps down. That kind of extra joy we just didn't expect.

Then it was time to commit to the *big* one, to getting her on the ground without rolling her up in a ball. We went through the drill on a nice, wide, and extended landing pattern to give me plenty of time for any surprises. It is difficult to explain how utterly different the feeling was in a multiengine airplane with that huge engine out there in front instead of just open space, but looking between the cylinders for runway references did help. Also, when you touched down, the pilot was more than two stories above the ground, and with the nose engine blocking off half the world, the depth perception cues were all to hell and gone in a basket. The first time I came across the fence it was going very well, but a slick landing vanished with a sudden crosswind and—

You got eighty, hold the eighty, back on the yoke for the flare, not too much, damn it! kick in rudder, straighten her out, you dumb ass, don't let her touch down with any side motion! Good speed, now hold her off, don't jerk back on that elevator! Hold her off, that's good, let her ease down, you're overcontrolling, you bloody nit! She flared and came down on one tire and there was a gentle but don't-mess-with-me bounce right back into the air and *keep the yoke forward, flare her again, easy, gently, you've got her now!* She was down on both main gears and I went forward on the yoke, shoving hard and fast and constantly on the rudder pedals and she ran straight and true. Then I brought back the yoke gently until I felt the tail wheel touch, and held the yoke back, and within three thousand feet of the end of the runway we had come to a stop, with *no* brakes even being applied. *Hot damn, we'd done it!*

We didn't quit there, oh no, there were more things to try, and before the afternoon ended I had six takeoffs and landings under my belt and I was learning fast, very fast. Above all, there were certain idiosyncrasies about this airplane that must be observed. Because before the day was out I tried a direct-crosswind landing, and in that instant the Ju-52 turned into a beast, and I mean with horns and fangs. That old lady turned right around snarling and bit deeply and never let go.

There are a couple of ways to handle a cross-wind landing in a taildragger, and it begins with the old argument about using flaps or not. Well, in *Annie* speed control had a lot to do with the flaps, and when they went down 40° and the ailerons came down 15° you had both enormous drag *and* lift and you could play one off against the other, and without brakes you sure as hell wanted all the drag you could get with the tail wheel down or you might not stop while the iron bird was still heading for the boonies. In the twins I'd flown, such as the Apache, Aztec, Twin Bonanza, 310, and birds of that nature, the wingspan was always short enough so I could cross-control and fly down on one wheel; slipping into the wind, in terms of flight through the air, so that I balanced out and held my course along the runway. Any good pilot, and the woods are filled with them, does this. But in *Annie* we had a full-size airliner with an enormous wing, and as I kept slipping into the wind, my wingtip would lower to within inches of the ground and I had a lot of round-eyed people in the bird with me. We played around with the approaches a lot, and I learned that in a taildragger this big, and with flaps you CANNOT get up in a hurry and must leave down, *you fly the airplane very carefully and on the tips of your toes right down to a full stop, because at any instant, she can get away from you.*

Annie had a nasty habit in a crosswind of weathervaning as if it were her last chance in life. I'd bring her down, crabbing on the approach; then, as I flared I'd roll in a cross-control effect and, if the wind was too strong, even use upwind engine for directional control. The moment she touched, if the wind was from the left, the great barn door of a rudder would try to swing to the right. So if you used upwind engine, the left engine, this would help compensate for this effect. But you had to do a rugged tap dance with the rudder and play wildly with the aileron and wish you had brakes. Then, *then* came the most critical of moments, when you were running out of speed and you had a lot of lift and the tail was coming down. *Annie* would then begin a pivot into the wind on the upwind wheel and you fought her like mad to stop that, because you were rushing right into a wild ground loop that would spin her about like a top. Knock on wood, that's never happened to me in the Ju-52 (or the bf-108b, either, with its incredibly narrow gear width of four feet ten inches), but I fly scared, and that sort of keeps me alert.

But those crosswind landings are tough in *Annie,*

It was all too marvelous to believe . . . and there's no use wasting good sky by staying on the ground. Flaps up, trim set, everything in the green, and another takeoff, letting her swing into the crosswind as soon as the wheels are up. JULIAN LEEK

because her gear really isn't all that wide (much narrower than a DC-3), and you can't get the flaps up and out of the way before putting down the tail (we could go to a power system but that would take some of the fun out of it, I suppose).

Using full flaps reduces your touchdown speed. It demands more skill and attention, but it's worth it. If you swerve on touching down or while you're rolling out, this opens the cage doors and the fire-breathing dragon is running wild among us. The dragon is none other than unfriendly centrifugal force, and in a swerve, centrifugal force increases "as the square of the speed" at which the swerve started. So the key is to land as slowly as possible, unless it's one of those very, very, rare situations when you have to punch through turbulent, rolling crosswinds, and even then it's a dealer's choice. But in the crosswind landing we're talking about, the key to success is *not letting the swerve start.* If you could touch down, let's say at 50 mph, and you drop her in at 70 mph, what you've done, if you let the swerve really get going, is to *double* the centrifugal force that you get at 50 mph. The faster or the tighter the swerve the wilder the dragon gets until you reach a point of no return.

Now, *Annie* gave us fits because we couldn't get her flaps up in a crosswind landing, and during those early flights especially I was a rubber-legged lunatic on a trampoline trying to keep everything, including the airplane, where she belonged on landing. The more flaps you set the more surface you offer the crosswind and the stronger the effect of the wind on the airplane, once you're on the ground. And where are the flaps situated? Behind the main wheels, so that any crosswind acting on them is like a huge cable trying to tug the airplane around into the wind—that so-called tendency of the airplane to act as a weathervane. The upwind wing also wants to lift up, and that same tire wants to pivot, and you've got a half dozen forces all acting at the same time on the airplane, and it is a lovely and frenzied mess indeed. There's no one answer, because, each time, the wind is different, and I would be landing *Annie* with all manner of crosswinds, even quartering tail winds, which are the all-time worst in this sort of airplane. There would be times when I'd be forced to put her down in a howling crosswind of up to 40 mph because of a storm and the need to get it down *now.*

After that first day, we spent three days on the

Flying down the Indian River—and there comes Leo Kerwin in his Skylane, just off the right wing. JULIAN LEEK

ground sort of mulling things over (while Don Haynes and Ted Anderson and myself and a few other friendly volunteers tightened things, did a hundred necessary small repairs, ad infinitum) and writing new checklists and cursing strong winds, low clouds, and heavy rain. Then, on the fourth day, the weather broke in our favor and we were off and running once more, this time to set up cruise numbers and to test engine-off emergency procedures. I didn't believe how well she behaved with a wing engine out. There was no sharp swerve, but a good pull to one side that could be and was countered immediately by rudder into the working engine, then setting up some nose-up trim and flying her one-engine-out by hand. We pulled the power all the way back to simulate zero thrust for these tests (we didn't want to chance shutting down and starting up in the air with *these* engines), and chopping the nose engine simply reduced speed to about eighty-five miles per hour, and that meant cranking in nose-up trim and just flying. There wasn't any doubt whatsoever that she'd keep right on flying with two engines instead of three. What we liked most of all was pulling one engine and slowing down to see what minimum-control speed would be and, joy of joys, she held straight and true, with a lot of rudder, until she started breaking into the stall, which meant that with one engine dead there wasn't any minimum engine-out control speed. Vmc (velocity minimum control) with two engines only was less than stall speed. Hooray for you, Kirt Weil! (and Zindel!).

There was another period of a few days when I couldn't fly because of a workload on the ground, and Ron Skipper and Bob Bailey were in town and how about their taking up the ironmonger? I told them to go have at it, and while I banged on typewriter keys they took *Annie* up to six thousand feet and put her through a whole series of stalls. Just two kids out for a great afternoon. They gave me a bunch of notes on the stall tests, which is a neat package to get from two guys who had been driving large airplanes for a long time, and another few pages of the growing pilot's manual were soon in place. They went into turns with the power *off* and the aircraft clean (flaps up) and whomped into stall entry at an indicated air speed of 80 mph. The bank angle was 30°.

Then they did the same thing with a bank angle of 60°, and the aircraft was into its built-in warning rumble and shake so badly they could only guess the stall at between eighty-four and eighty-eight miles per hour indicated.

They cranked in 20° flaps, power off, came back steadily on the yoke, and got the stall at 75 mph. They were surprised to find that rolling the airplane into a 30° bank under these same settings didn't change the stall speed.

With landing flaps at 40° the stall came in at 65 mph. When they banked to 30°, they got the stall (without power) at 75 mph. From this series of tests it became unquestioned that so long as you were holding 100 mph you could do about anything you wanted where a steep bank was concerned and that if you flew a pattern with your steepest turns always backed up by 90 mph you had plenty of money in the air-speed bank.

They also stalled the big bird with full power, and it proved almost impossible, because *Annie* was wallowing up an invisible wall in the sky, the air-speed indicator flopping around the 55–58-mph mark. According to the regulations, a nose pitchup at 30° is the limit you go before you get into an aerobatic maneuver, and the Ju-52 would hang right in there with the engines howling and refuse to stall.

Good girl. . . .

During these few days, we were attending to another problem. Ted Anderson, despite all his flying, had never bothered to get his multiengine rating, and so while I thumped on the typewriter to muffle the screams of an upset editor on Madison Avenue, and the team of Skipper and Bailey dragged and clunked *Annie* through her stalls, Ted hied off to

Is it a phantom? A glob of oil? A splatter of grease? No, it's Leo Kerwin in his Skylane, visible in the copilot window. JULIAN LEEK

Early days of the Flying Pumphouse and Locomotive Gang at Ti-Co Airport. From left to right, Jay Barbree of NBC, Billy Wiggins, Martin Caidin, Dempsey Blanton (who insures *Iron Annie*), Bill Bagwell, Dale Holzen. JULIAN LEEK

Melbourne early in the morning and came back later that same afternoon with his new multiengine ticket folded neatly in his wallet. Before the next day showed the sun at high noon, he had run that airplane through its paces from the left seat, with me in the right, and grateful for the deafening roar of the engines, because he was very happy and when he's happy he sings and when he sings it sounds like a chorus of hound dogs all huddled together on a sinking raft.

———◆———

While all these happy events were going on, there were the realistic and very dark clouds to face. We never landed without long notations on the squawk sheets. We never had a flight without something going wrong, something breaking, something failing, something (in quantity) needing repair. We flew an air show at Patrick Air Force Base in mid-April 1975, and it took an hour and a half to get the balky engines started, and we were all weary by the time we rolled into the air. By some miracle, that same day, on departing Patrick, she fired up three-two-one, *zango!* Go figure out a lady.

But we couldn't get away from the enormous amount of work in the start-up procedures, and the engines were starting to make all sorts of strange clanking and strangling sounds. We were throwing

oil like mad from the engines, and we knew the gaskets and seals were really in their last moments of life and the lines and the tanks were leaking. But I wanted desperately to get this machine through a complete weighing and balancing, and so a bunch of us, myself and Ted Anderson and Bob Bailey and Leo Kerwin and two others who were along to watch pieces fall off as we flew and mark down the general area of their fall (for later retrieval), made the cross-country across the Florida Peninsula to St. Petersburg to visit Spadco, a company that

Iron Annie makes a flyby along the main runway of Patrick Air Force Base in April 1975 for her first public appearance at a military open house. JULIAN LEEK

160

works on aircraft; once there, we finally did the complete scene that had been pushed off for twenty or thirty years or for however long. When we got back, we knew we would be able to reduce the empty weight a great deal more simply by getting all that housepaint off the airplane. Ron Skipper took all the details of the weight and balance and charted them out and made it clear that to put this airplane out of its CG range was a task at which you would have to work very hard and on overtime.

So we were learning it all and unraveling the mysteries, and the fuel-flow levers, the wobble pump, spark advance, autorich-on-power-reduction, and the meters per second and kilometers began to lose their alien flavor and began to fit into the scheme of things we could understand and with which we could work. Because of those brakes and no tail-wheel lock, we learned that taxiing in a stiff crosswind was an insane game of chasing squirrels. It went slowly and the repairs were endless. The trim was loosened and broken lines replaced, corrosion cut away for new metal and gadgets and gidgies and glonks or whatever were all

being repaired or modified. The flaps were transformed from creaking drawbridge muscle breakers into an assembly that worked. It began to look good, except for those engines.

On April 24, we ran what we all dreaded but knew was absolutely necessary: a complete engine compression check. I don't know how this had been avoided since the airplane arrived in the United States. The sad part about it is that this sort of thing is flirting with fire, breakdown, and disaster. There's really no future in being stupid—and this airplane had had its share of stupidity.

So we ran the engine compression check and the results were disastrous. Eleven cylinders were below average and two were completely dead (and both were in the nose engine). Nine cylinders had a burnt exhaust valve or seating, two had a burnt intake valve or seating, and seven cylinders had pressure leaks.

What it all meant was that the airplane had all this time been flying with the equivalent of only two engines operating, in terms of horsepower produced. There was thrust from all three propellers, but the combined output was no more than two en-

It was like old home week with the Thunderbirds also on the flight line. *Annie's* first public showing was an overwhelming success. The Air Force counted sixteen hundred people going through the Ju-52 during the day. JULIAN LEEK

gines at full power. We had been flying with a maximum of 1,200 horsepower at takeoff—which was utterly ridiculous. The situation could only get worse instead of better, and it was time to bite the bullet.

I grounded *Iron Annie*.

———◆———

She would be on the ground the next six months, but those were going to be damned fruitful months. We investigated every possible way of overhauling the BMW engines but finally had to admit it was a lost cause. Too many cylinders had given up the ghost and were beyond repair. They couldn't be chromed. Many parts were metric, and replacements weren't available anywhere. I dealt for a while with officials in Spain and concluded that continuing that Alice in Wonderland relationship was just another brand of insanity. So the way to solve the engine problem was to take the best of the three engines and combine them into the two best possible BMWs. The question that remained unanswered was what the hell did I do about the third engine? Spain was out. A search in Germany produced mournful sounds. There was always the route of buying 1340 engines, but that was staggeringly expensive, because the Pratt & Whitney R1340 was in screaming demand by crop-dusters all over the country. Besides, I wanted the flavor the 132E radials with their 1690 cubic inches gave me.

I'm not certain to this day what sorcery or leger-demain Ted and I pulled off, but there were a lot of telephone calls, and sleuthing of all sorts, and upsetting many people, and getting those hollow questions: "A 1690? What the hell is a 1690? There ain't no such animal."

Would you believe we found one? More power to Ted Anderson, for he badgered, bullied, and cajoled his way around a whole bunch of people and had someone out in Oklahoma do some go-phering for us. There the miracle happened, and out in a cornfield, in its original container, was a spanking-new, never-turned R1690-42, which we managed through nefarious means and a cashier's check to buy, along with many parts and two ancient 1690s. We shipped them all to Ti-Co. Don Haynes wanted to weep with the job he faced, but he did it, with a great, heaping dose of assistance from Ted. We threw out the cracked impeller housing of the never-used 1690 and slipped in the

one from the BMW and we were in business. There was much more to do, of course; we had to swap carburetors and ancillary equipment and work out a new spline for the prop and adapt the BMW ignition harness to the P&W, and matching up American and metric measurements and connections was a dandy brainbuster for a while. But the end result was that N52JU was coming together with a brand-new 1690 engine and two 132E engines that were far better than they'd been in a long time.

We ripped out the entire instrument panel, throwing away just about every instrument and gauge in the airplane and replacing them with new or rebuilt instrumentation. The Narco company came through with some beautiful transceivers and VORs and an encoding altimeter and a transponder. We sealed most of the cabin leaks and ripped out the old floorboards, while a husky enthusiast by name of Steve Allen hammered in a thick new floor of three-quarter-inch marine plywood. A police lieutenant from Cocoa Beach, Larry Urback, my favoritest Polack friend from eighteen years of boozing together, came up and grabbed all our seats and took them to downtown Cocoa Beach, had them all re-covered, and then brought them back and installed them snugly. We tried everything with the brakes and managed, by God, to improve them. They were still on the minus side of being decent but so far better than before that we had no complaints. We moved things around in the cockpit and set up a call light and bell for a crew chief back in the fuselage and went through an impressive program of covering tears and holes and gashes and cracks and splits everywhere we found them. We changed oil lines and hydraulic lines and fuel lines and vacuum lines and did what we could to clean up the horrors of the electrical system that had been so mangled. Volunteers from Patrick Air Force Base showed up to work on the iron bird. It went on like this for months, and I took the time to set up letters and discussions with German museums and pilots and institutions and officials to learn everything I could and get everything I could.

This was the time that I met Kurt Streit by mail, and although we would correspond steadily and make long-distance phone calls between Florida and Germany for three years before we finally shared the cockpit of N52JU, it was the single most marvelous break of all. A Florida newspaper had done a big story on me and even plastered my face, in the cockpit of the Ju-52, in blazing color all over their cover. This could be seen three miles away on a dark afternoon and it caught Streit's attention. He just happened to be visiting this country and was flying north in a small plane from Key West. He bought the paper, tucked it away, and wrote me from Germany. Instantly we were friends, and that friendship kept getting better and better. He found the German manual for me through friends. He told me things about the Ju-52 that were confidence-building and inspiring. He taught me to fly the airplane by mail, and that is one hell of a correspondence course.

The flight manual, aircraft manual, and service manual kept growing, and the checklists began to attain some real meaning. It was obvious, even sitting out there on the line and being poked and prodded and riveted and welded, that *Iron Annie* was beginning to regain some of her old spirit.

Another marvelous break. One of my closest friends was Vern Renaud, who drives big airliners for Eastern, and Vern is as much of an aviation enthusiast outside of his jetliner seat as he is at that yoke. We had done a lot of flying and had many long sessions of airplane talk into the wee hours of the night. I discussed with him many of the problems we had with the airplane, and his help consisted of crawling all through the bird and offering advice that had meaning behind it. He loved to fly small airplanes as well as those turbine monsters, and way back in his flight history was a time when he skinned knuckles and wore shining grease all over his body. He had a thick shock of white-gray hair that had often been soaked with oil because he had been a B-29 engine mechanic and knew whereof he spoke. One of the things he did was far-reaching. He understood our needs and he knew the federal regulations. He recommended we get in touch immediately with Red Gargaly, of the FAA office of Miami, then ensconced at Opa-locka Airport. Since N52JU was officially quartered at Fort Lauderdale Executive Airport, in the area run by Ben Bradley, where I'd kept my bf-108b for some time, and I maintained a business office with John Hawke, a wonderfully mad British test pilot and international adventurer, we legally came under GADO-5 jurisdiction. I had at least two or three hundred questions to put to Red, who I heard was very tough indeed and also one of the fairest and most sensible men ever to grace a federal personnel roster.

It was then that I learned I didn't have to explain about the Ju-52 to Red Gargaly, for the intertwining of many lives and many new friendships was being worked by this eerie touch of *Iron Annie* —and it was Red Gargaly who had signed off the ferry permit for George Hamilton to fly the airplane into the United States from Ecuador. He had seen the airplane back in 1970, and after our long discussions he knew that it would be a far better Junkers than he had seen five years earlier. We would need a new annual inspection and issuance of an airworthiness certificate and a letter of operating limitations, and I would need a pilot-in-command authorization, and much, much more, all of which Red handled in a style that belies the abilities of a single individual. Strange how that intertwining would work, for after we met and had shared a pot of coffee, it turned out we had a whole mob of mutual friends. Red had been a flight instructor in piston-engine jobs and in jets, and we had actually flown from the same field at the time without ever having met in those earlier years. He had eaten many meals in a restaurant I frequented, owned by another instructor, Ed Keyes, and we were all three of us good friends with that international master of aerobatics, none other than the famed Bevo Howard.

On October 3, 1975, a worn and exhausted Don Haynes completed his grueling finishing work on the airplane. For two weeks, Ted Anderson had been living with the machine, as I was, day and night and night and day, cleaning and washing and touching up and wrapping up. Don Haynes signed off the airplane as meeting every requirement in accordance with every regulation and was in airworthy condition, and then he signed off all instruments as tested and repaired or overhauled, that our altimeters were certified to twenty thousand feet, and we were ready to have a go at it.

It was just in time. We—Caidin, Anderson, and Bailey—planned to roar off to the great annual bash of the Confederate Air Force in Harlingen, Texas. We had been asked a thousand times if we would bring the Ju-52 to the air show. A whole contingent of the Florida Wing of the CAF, under the guidance of one El Supremo Colonel Leo Kerwin, would be there, and *Iron Annie* was our big gun for the event. In fact, the CAF called every day, almost every hour, to check on our progress, and it was a close shave all the way. During the six months of working on the Ju-52, I'd banged around the country with Leo Kerwin in his Skylane, and while in Texas as the guest of John Stokes, had flown with astronaut Joe Engle and some other live cats in a Messerschmitt bf-108b like my old bird, and there had been some flying in T-6s, and Arrows, and all sorts of Piper and Beech spam cans, but that was all whittling idly at wood while waiting for the big event.

Don Haynes staggered out of his workshop to stare hollow-eyed at two grimy figures: myself and Ted Anderson. Don's voice was a hoarse memory of what it had been. It was a momentous moment, the evening of October 4, the day after he'd signed all the papers. "Tomorrow," he said in a strangled, oxygen-starved voice. "You can fly it tomorrow."

It looked like *Iron Annie* was back in business. The next morning would tell.

Ted Anderson (left) and Martin Caidin just before departure for the air bash in Texas in October 1975. DON COLE

She hadn't flown this well in *years. Iron Annie* from the outside was still shabby, but that's not where it counted. Beneath the skin and the corrugated shell and the dimples of repairs and the rash of patches is what counted. We really had no way of knowing how well those old engines would do. Sure, now they ran and the compression was up, but the cylinders and valves and pistons and rings and the whole shebang within each BMW 132E was one huge question mark. That 1690-42 was beautiful, but she was running with a German carburetor, generator, ignition harness, and various and sundry other pieces of auxiliary equipment, and a fact of life is that your main source of power is successful only in direct proportion to the rest of the hardware. That's what we had to discover as we went along: the new hoses, lines, electrical connections, fuel system, instruments, all of it, had to be proved in actual use.

But the first indications were to inspire us to whoops of delight. We kept *Annie* low in weight, that old "just in case" routine, and she came off the ground sprightly and steadily, and the engines banged away, and number one was too rich (we kept Don Haynes standing by, gaunt and hollow-eyed though he might be, for immediate corrections to whatever we put on the squawk sheets). More than that, the next morning, if all went well, we were bound for the south to meet with the FAA and get all our new papers on the bird and whatever other documents were required to make us and the world legal.

So it was a good day, eight takeoffs and landings, climbing out and descending, and although the brakes were still something on the soggy side and a bit unpredictable, we at least had a fighting chance with them. When we got down to Texas and the sky and flight ramp would be choked just full of warbirds and people who took care of them, maybe we'd find someone who could unravel the mysteries of our balky system. It was certainly worth the shot. All else went well. Then we went cross country for a while to check out the VOR navigation system and it, by God, worked. The radios still left us less than happy. Nothing wrong with the Narco transceivers, and Haynes had done his best to shield the ignition harnesses of the engines, but it was impossible with those worn-out old systems to eliminate all the hash. We'd find out as we went along. By nightfall we were done, even to the point of watching our wingtip and tail lights come on, and the rotating beacon atop the after fuselage flash, and even the underwing landing light poked its Cyclopean beam into the darkness. We kept Haynes up to three in the morning, and Ted Anderson was absolutely tireless, although he'd left about two pounds of scraped skin and pieces of his anatomy littering the flight line from last-minute chores.

Early on the morning of October 6, I took off from Ti-Co with a yawning Ted Anderson in the right seat. He slouched down and chewed a bit on his mustache, belched, and scratched his belly with immense self-satisfaction. When I came back on the power and the noise was about a half shade below intolerable, he leaned over and said: "Just fly south. Don't turn left and don't turn right and don't pass Go and don't collect no goddamned two hundred green ones, just go on up to six thousand feet like a nice fella' and when we get to Lauderdale Exec wake me up." *Whomp*, just like that, he was fast asleep. What really put him out, I think, was his shouting that message to me. We lacked an intercom system in the airplane, and to talk to one another you needed a combination of a scream, bellow, and roar. What wore you out more than anything else was the breathlessness from shouting to one another. If you had to talk for a while, the easiest thing to do was for one pilot to stand up between the two pilot seats so you could each shout

Martin Caidin (left) and Ted Anderson in a typical pose of benevolent belligerence with Sam Bothwell (right) just before their departure for Fort Lauderdale Executive Airport for FAA inspection and documents. Whatever it is they're selling, Bothwell is giving back with interest.
JULIAN LEEK

with only a reasonable thunder in your voice to be heard.

Behind us in the cabin, Don Haynes, of course, feet propped up on the seat before him, was dead to the world and sound asleep. I drove on, following the coastline, not even bothering to navigate. It was clear and the beaches formed a perfect curving line directly south, and as I started down I shook Ted awake. We made one low pass down the runway, pulled her up in what amounted to a very respectable zoom, and I rolled into the pattern and started cranking on the Mighty Wheel, much to the amusement of Anderson, who peered at me through sleepy eyes. He came awake when the tires squealed on the runway and we taxied off the active. Ted stood up between the seats, hauled the flaps back up, slid open the top hatch, and jammed a huge Confederate flag into its slot on the left side of the cockpit exterior.

We taxied up to Bradley's operation, stopped while I jammed my feet desperately on the brakes, and Ted shoved the fuel-flow levers to the number-

one position. This kept oil flowing through the engines but shut off the fuel supply at the tanks. You sat and waited until the engines ran themselves dry by sucking out every last drop of gasoline from the lines. This could take thirty seconds or it could take three minutes, and every shutdown was accompanied by my staying in the seat and Ted signaling frantically for everyone else to stay the hell away from those great whirling propellers until they groaned to a fuel-starved halt on their own.

We climbed down and there was Bob Bailey, grinning hugely, and with him Red Gargaly and Jaime Serra and some other people from the FAA shops to see this incredible thing out of time. Standing by Ben Bradley was none other than The Man. Beefy, huge, lovable George Hamilton, who five years before this moment had landed this same airplane at this same airport and shut down on this very same spot with the same FAA crowd there to shake their heads in wonder at George having taken leave of all his senses. But nothing could have been better for us, for George climbed all

Plenty of reason to grin: the FAA has just finished its inspection of *Iron Annie* (now N52JU) and disbursed all necessary documents, and the new pilot-in-command, *Oberst* Martin von Caidin, has plenty to smile about. TED ANDERSON

through N52JU, shaking his head constantly, murmuring words of delight to one and all that came out as, "I don't believe it. I just don't believe it. My God, they've turned this thing into an *airplane*." For the FAA this was the best possible of all inspections and vindications, and the man who had signed it all off and busted his back and nearly wrecked his marriage was there to back it all up and answer all questions. Jaime Serra and Red Gargaly had a lot of questions, and we all answered them and their smiles grew broader and so did ours as they handed over to me all those vital documents—Special Airworthiness Certificate, Letter of Authorization as Pilot in Command, Letter of Operating Limitations—that would release us for the long trek westward the next morning. All that was missing was the long and loud cry of, "*Wagons, hooooo!*"

Dinner that night brought with it abnormal consumption of fiery alcoholic goodies, all richly de-

served and more richly consumed. With the Ju-52 in obviously remarkable shape, with nothing having broken or split or burned or collapsed or exploded on the way down to Fort Lauderdale Exec, there was good reason to believe our good fortune would be repeated going the other way. We were waved off from Exec with Don Haynes and Ted Anderson sound asleep in the cabin and with Bob Bailey in the right seat showing an exuberant grin and fondling his wooden yoke as if this were the first airplane he had ever flown. From a pilot who flew jets for National Airlines, who had cruised over much of the planet in great Lockheed C-141 Starlifters in the Air Force, and who had hovered and darted and skidded under heavy enemy gunfire in a chopper in Vietnam, that was high praise indeed. To Bob, flying the corrugated hulk all the way to Harlingen, Texas, for the Confederate Air Force bash was heaven itself. It was a clock-stopper and one that hurled backward the hands of time, that made us all barnstormers, that defied modern tradition and loss of identity to a computerized world. We climbed to forty-five hundred feet and wrapped up about two hours for the flight, including the steady climb and landing at Ti-Co.

Now it was hurry-up time for another reason. We wanted to get on our way *now*. This was the early afternoon of the seventh of October, and the air show was getting under way in about forty-eight hours, some twelve to fourteen hundred miles distant, depending upon routing and weather and mechanical reliability. We made it. Luggage was tossed aboard. Some vital spare parts went into the cargo holds. The tanks were filled to their absolute load of 620 gallons. The oil tanks sucked up their twenty gallons of oil—each. The hydraulic tank was right on the money.

My God, everything was working. We'd flown two hours down to Lauderdale and stayed overnight and flown another two hours back, and there had been three and a half hours of checkout test flying the day before that. Over seven hours of non-disaster in the air. It was incredible. Every gauge, every wire, every hose, everything that moved was all moving in concert. Don Haynes was close to tears at our departure—because now he could sleep, his wife would talk with him again, he could resume a normal life. He saw us load up, he helped with the luggage, he helped lock the door, he stood fire guard, he pulled the chocks, he waved good-by to us. Lord, but that man was justifiably pleased to see the Ju-52 lift from the runway, bank on her climbout, and slowly diminish to a pinpoint as it departed to the northwest.

In that cockpit, there were three grinning idiots, slapping each other on the back, chortling with glee, bursting with the joys of life. We'd had perfect communications with the tower at Ti-Co, everything was in the green, *Iron Annie* was purring like a big kitten. Ahead of us was a gray sky with scattered thunderstorms, but they were localized and we could see around and beyond and between them and there wasn't any sweat at all in working steadily to the northwest. We really had it knocked. Seven hours of preparatory flying and virtual perfection had been the result. We even sang in that cockpit, which, fortunately for each other, could not be heard by each other because of that deafening thunder. We had headsets and earplugs and everything was—well, it was all Cheshire Cat grin.

Ernest Gann said, in *Fate Is the Hunter,* and he said it very well, that a great deity resides in the clouds and the heavens through which we mortals fly. And every now and then this godlike creature of the ethereal domain gets a half-assed grin on his face and he lets down his trousers and he pisses all over the sacred pillars of science.

In this case, smack into the electrical system of one 3-engine airplane with the registration of N52JU. Our brand-new communications system, a whole six days in age and use, crapped out. Just *like that.* The Narco radio popped its circuit breaker and our radios went dead. Oh, just great. I popped it back in and the deity smiled and popped it back out again. A dozen ins and outs made the point. No radio. That's all there was to it.

The grins diminished somewhat. We got serious. Let's get the hell up past Tallahassee, because there's a vicious storm line coming through the Florida panhandle, and we sure as hell don't want to get caught in that thing. So on we went, flying

The first leg of the flight to Harlingen, Texas, in October 1975—and the grease is already splattering. Moments later, the radios went dead. BOB BAILEY

low, waiting to hear an engine come unglued after our warning from the radios. But none of that happened. The engines rumbled and thundered happily with the sound only a radial engine can make and that a pilot can love. Those engines were running like dreams.

But, halfway up the Florida Peninsula, the vacuum system swallowed itself and the beautiful new artificial horizons and the directional gyros turned instantly into brand-new warranteed, guaranteed-for-life junk. Well, at least the transponder was working and we were squawking. Let's see. We thumbed the book. If your radio fails, squawk 7700 for one minute and then switch to 7600. Whoever picks up the transponder knows the radios are out and won't expect to be able to scream threats and curses at us.

We rumbled northward, dodging more and more thunderstorm cells. The thunderboomies were getting too numerous for comfort. Ted Anderson stabbed toward the horizon and cried, "Onward!"

Tallahassee lay off to our right. It looked inviting as hell. Bob and I agreed several times rapidly that it was looking more inviting with every passing moment. We were getting scud below us. The radios were dead, the horizons rolling around insanely, and the directional gyros spinning like pinball machines gone ape. Surely this was not the time to continue. Ahead of us, the sky was filled from the surface to a height Bob and I estimated as halfway to the moon. "Let's get out of here," I told them. "We'll put down for the night and see if they can work on the radios and the vacuum system and maybe even get another generator."

"Onward!" cried Anderson.

The black wall kept getting closer, punctuated by great slashes of evil lightning in the form of enormous fangs waiting to chew on our bodies. "Keep going!" cried Anderson.

"Jesus Christ, Ted, we have no radios, no horizons, and no DG's, and you expect us to fly into *that?*" Fire spilled hysterically through a maw as dark as a shark's gizzard.

"I know this country like the back of my hand," Ted sneered. "Dusted and sprayed this whole area. Friendly country. Never let you down. We just follow that thar road and it'll take us right through that itty-bitty storm. You're acting like a chicken."

Lightning speared the sky and smashed into the earth all about the ground before us and to our left and the clouds turned into the darkest tunnel I had ever seen. "Just follow the yellow brick road," sang Ted. "Right through there."

"*The god-damned clouds are down to the deck!*" I screamed at him, and just as I said that it also occurred to me that I was insane even to be talking about it. I grabbed the yoke. "We're getting the hell out of here," I snarled, and at the same moment, I started into a steep right turn. Of course, what was happening was that the ground level had been rising and we had been descending to stay below the lowering cloud deck and the storm was also moving toward us and just as I made my move I was in the blinding stuff. Bob Bailey, just a few feet to my right, could see clearly and he stomped rudder, shoved the yoke forward and hard over, and we went into a smooth, wicked turn. All I saw for a moment was clouds, and a moment later I saw a great big mass of trees rushing up at us—at least a hundred *feet* away.

We're going in!

But Bob had been right on top of it; he'd judged everything that was happening, and without saying a word he overrode me on the controls. He was on top of it all the way through and he got us out of there, and headed back for Tallahassee—through scud that in scant minutes was thick, but *very* thick, and we ran for Tallahassee, not knowing that their radar was out and no one was paying a damn bit of attention to our squawking dead-radio signals. We got to Tallahassee with the stuff at three hundred feet above the deck and I ducked under it while we still had a chance. Trying to keep the field in sight, I came around, whee, we were *low*, and flat-hatted it right on down to the runway and set her down. We taxied in and got on the flight line to find a bunch of Mustang fighters with Don Plumb and Johnny Bolton and some other friends.

They had hit that same storm and turned back and landed, because even with all their performance they weren't about to fight a thunderboomie that topped out somewhere above seventy-five thousand feet and was over a hundred miles wide and forty miles deep.

Ted listened to it all and his lips pursed a bit and he said, "Oh."

That night, after we'd roused a wonderful radio crew who would spend hours working on our brand-new but dead electronics, and while mechanics wrestled with the generator and the vacuum system, we joined the gang at a local motel and settled down for good food and wine. After our first clink of glasses, I looked at Ted out of the corner of my eye. "Do you remember that slight noise when we made that turn away from that storm? You know, that road you know like the back of your hand?"

"Can't say that I do," he remarked, stuffing hot bread into his mouth with his wine. "Why?"

"It was by that farmhouse." The one I could describe in great detail as Bob rushed over it and the trees came up to meet us.

"Well, what about it?" Ted asked, refilling his glass. He was happy with the world. Good wine, good food, lots of airplanes. What more could a man ask?

"It was their television antenna," I said.

"Who's television antenna?" he asked.

"The same one we knocked down with our wing."

There was some quiet and Bob Bailey blinked.

"Pass the wine," Ted said.

Safely on the ground at Tallahassee—and Anderson waves hello to the world. CAIDIN ARCHIVES

We drove out to the airport early in the morning in a screaming rain. Clouds down to four hundred feet and whipping by at thirty miles per hour or better. The world was water, the earth was soggy, our spirits were at best questioning. Oh, well, we'd find out about radios and vacuum systems and the generator. The Mustang gang were by their fighters, and there were some other warbirds, a couple of the guys part of the Florida Wing of the Confederate Air Force, to which we all belonged, and we had a big halloo and said inane things about the weather. Our radios had been repaired and now they worked, the vacuum system was a question, and the German generator had left the mechanics scratching their heads and butts and they had tried but they wouldn't promise a thing. While we were working on the corrugated condominium, there were some breaks in the weather. The rain quit and the ceiling lifted and some people flew away to the south, but to the west it still looked horrible. Plumb and Bolton gave it a shot with their Mustangs but they turned around and came back in. It was solid and black and mean out there, and the next few hours went by with a wild gin game beneath a Mustang wing.

We began to see some blue sky, patches in a huge sky-covering blanket of gray and dark. The Mustangs had their hole and they whipped away into the sky, arrowing upward at a steep angle, and we heard them call in to us that they were in the clear and were going on. We fired up the Ju-52 and waddled out to the active and took off. "We'll use Plan B," Ted remarked through the chewy sounds of a candy bar being masticated with gusto. "We don't go west."

"Oh?" I said.

"Uh uh. See that road. It goes right on down to the coast and it's supposed to be good there. If it ain't we can go right down to the deck along the beach and pick up a field along the way. Smart,

ain't I?" He licked his fingers and gave us that hound-tooth grin of his and we nodded and followed the yellow brick road.

Green forest stretched forever, cut every now and then with winding rivers and streams, but there was that road Ted knew so well, and we stayed at eight hundred feet, bouncing easily in some chop that made the trip interesting. By the time we reached the coastline we were down to four hundred feet, but Ted was right. The scud was hanging along the coast and we pushed out over the waters of the Gulf a bit and were in clear sky, and we were able to climb up to three thousand feet. It was a long way to go, for Ted had his sights set on Houma, Louisiana, and the winds were against us, and there was no way Ted would let us run those engines at any more than 1,600 rpm. We climbed to sixty-five hundred feet and Ted played with the throttles and the mixtures like an accordionist. We droned along indicating 95 mph and if we were getting any more than 105 mph true air speed it would have been more than a small miracle. But we continued flying, and we didn't need the directional gyros (we told ourselves), the VOR worked, and the navigation went along as neatly as could be, considering a thick gummy haze that began to fill the entire world. We had no complaints—except for the rocker-arm boxes of that nose engine.

Three hours after takeoff, we were looking through a thick film of grease splotches mixed with oil across the windshield. It was absolute crud. It cut our forward vision all to hell. On we went. Four hours in the air and still we droned on, still the engines turned faithfully. I was developing a nervous tic in one cheek because blind flying isn't my most favorite cup of tea. Just after the four-hour mark, Ted cried out, "There!" pointing straight ahead into a world of oil, grease, and thick smog, which resembled the inside of an eggnog container.

The VOR needle was hanging tight and Ted recognized shimmering lines of rivers, and he chortled happily while Bob and I looked at one another from the pilots' seats. Ted stood between us, his fingers caressing his beloved throttles and mixtures and I followed his hand, waving about us like a baton. "Got the field in sight," he said in triumph.

"Do you see it, Bob?" I asked.

"Uh uh."

"I don't see it either. What I see is as blank as a whore's memory."

"*I* see it, you idiots!" Ted reprimanded us. "Right —over—thataway!"

"What the hell do you see?" I snarled.

"Houma, m'boy. The airfield at Houma in the greeaat state of Louisiana. Where I learned my trade as a cropduster. Yep, did m'thing right here. Killed boll weevils and all sorts of evil critters by the millions. We land here. Take her down."

I swung into a wide turn to the left so I could look through the open space where I'd pulled back the side window. Damn if he wasn't right. Houma lay flat on the ground, pressed down hard by oppressive heat and humidity. I eased back and continued in a wide, circling descent to keep the field in sight.

"Why are you flying in circles?" Ted demanded.

"Because I can't see ahead of us, that's why."

"No need, no need," he said expansively, patting Bob's shoulder and then mine in his ultimate reassurance. "Just follow the yellow brick road."

"There ain't none," I spat.

"Figure of speech. Come around thirty degrees to the left, there you are, hold that heading. We'll make a long straight-in to the runway."

"You idiot, *I can't see the freaking runway!*"

"I'll guide you in." Ted stood straight in the cockpit. Among the seventeen windows of the front office of *Annie* were two wide but thin horizontal sheets of curving plexiglas. Standing up, Ted *could* see. I couldn't and Bob couldn't. "Just like radar," came the singsong from Ted. "Beep-beep and a zap or two. Come right five degrees. Good. Hold it right there. Back on the power, the mixtures are rich, fuel selector in center position, I've got everything under control, all you've got to do is go where I tell you. Very nice, you've got eight hundred feet, we're doing ninety, and time for the flaps." His big paw grasped the Mighty Wheel and there was a groaning and creaking through the whole airplane as he brought them full down to

forty degrees. I retrimmed to keep the rate of descent at five hundred feet per minute.

"Very neat. See how easy it is? Continue straight ahead, couple of degrees to the right, the wind's right down the runway, ain't a thing to it, you got eighty, you got eighty, keep her at eighty, touch of power there, very nice, very nice, ease off the descent, that's it, give me three hundred a minute down, the runway's just ahead of us, come left a hair, hold it, hold her straight, you got money in the bank, seventy-five, very nice, start coming back on the yoke for your flare, very nice indeed—"

I couldn't see a thing. Only eggnog and black splotches, and I wanted *so* desperately to have just one glimpse of the ground.

"—you got her right, flare some more, back on the yoke, back, back, chop the power, very good, very good, hold her off, back on the yoke some more, hold it right there, get ready to keep her straight, ah, nice. . . ."

I felt two tires kissing concrete.

"See what I told you? It's the best landing you ever made in your life. Keep her going, lots of room, *walk that rudder—*"

Through the side window I finally had a clear view of trees going by and the edge of the runway and I had it all back now, and I eased down the tail and Ted hauled back on the top hatch and stood outside, wind blasting in his face and then easing off as we slowed and maneuvered with the wing engines only. Only then did it dawn on me that Ted had been shouting above the engines—and, of course, with reduced power it was possible to communicate without strangling your own vocal cords.

Something else dawned on me. I *had* landed the damned thing without ever seeing ground until well after we were rolling on the runway. Ted slid down, stuck a cigar in his face, lit up, and blew evil smoke at me and Bob, and we grinned together to the flight line and finally shut down. We began refueling—the airplane and ourselves—and by the time we were rolling for takeoff more than five hundred people had come to the field to watch that impossible machine. Tired, worn out from *Annie's* pounding engines, eyes squinting from that bloody haze, we flew on to Lake Charles in a two-hour hop, and just as the sun was touching the horizon I rolled her out of base onto final. With all that had gone on through the day, the old girl was running sweetly. We shut her down, filled her tanks, and replenished those seemingly ever-growing vast oil tanks, cleaned off her windshield, and put *Annie* to bed. That night, at the Hilton's Cajun Kitchen, Bob and I watched in awe and wonder as Ted Anderson demolished three entire meals—by himself—and then maneuvered himself with the tread of King Kong, shaking earth and buildings, back to the motel. The smile of gastronomical bliss on his face alone would have made the flight worthwhile.

———◆———

Early the next morning, the day the Confederate Air Force bash was beginning, we stared morosely at a sky filled with low scud. It was lifting steadily but with terrible slowness. Could we get a special clearance for takeoff? The tower said no, the field was officially closed. Then the airport manager came to see this great hulk of an airplane from out of time, and we knew right away this man had for many decades of his own life been borne on old wings. We sat under *Annie's* own great wing and drank coffee and we all looked at watches, and he thought about the old days and the restrictions and regulations of now, and he must have imagined all those waiting warbirds, and well, whatever went on in his mind he went suddenly to his airport car and got on the radio. "As soon as this airplane is at the end of the runway," we heard him say, "there'll be a break in the ceiling and the field will be open for at least ten minutes."

Someone must have whispered in the old girl's ear, for fuel-flow levers and throttles and mixture and mags and switches and wobble pump and inertial starters all came together in a sweet symphony of parts and pieces meshing together, and *Iron Annie* sang her throaty thunder as if she had emerged from the Dessau factory only that same morning. The miracle happened: We were waiting just short of the active and lo! by the magic words of the tower the ceiling "lifted." The field was open and away we went, working our path upward through the lower stuff and then marching between the fast-growing pillars of cumulus, and there was no outclimbing those in *Annie,* so Bailey, whose fingers had been itching terribly anyway, took the yoke with a nod from me. He threaded the needle and we danced along the vertical edges of great cloud mountains and skimmed our wheels in shining vapor. There was one last, yawning space that was closing together, and an ancient machine from time *almost* forgotten rode through, with even Ted

grudgingly allowing more than his usual allowance of engine power. No sooner had we pushed through this last tunnel than the world behind us and below and in all directions became a dazzling carpet of eye-stabbing whiteness. Time stood still and we climbed slowly and steadily, seeming to drift, a speck in an endless ocean of white below and dark blue above. We eased out of the climb at twelve thousand five hundred feet and it was everything the poets write about. We flew that way for nearly five hours, and then Harlingen and Rebel Field were coming into sight and down we started, a steady five hundred feet per minute. It was a damn good thing we had good visibility on each side and above us, because once again *Annie* had done her thing and turned the windshield into an opaque mess. At four thousand feet I had the runways of Rebel Field in sight through my side window and I could see a P-38 going straight up at the end of the runway. That would be Lefty Gardner, and then there were a whole mob of fighters and bombers in the sky, milling around like a swarm of gnats. We tried to reach Rebel Control by radio and the electrical interference was absolutely awful. *Annie* had flown like a queen, but those harnesses were coming apart and we had eighty per cent hash and twenty per cent talk.

I looked over at Bob and Ted and pointed. "There ain't no way, *no way* in the bloody world, I am going to fly into that mess down there with all those iron birds, and not being able to see out of this thing!"

Bob looked at me and shook his head. "What are you going to do? Climb outside and clean the windshield?"

Perfect! "Damn right I am," I told him. "Take it. I'm going back to get the helmet and goggles."

Ted looked at me as if I were mad. He shoved me back into my seat. "Uh uh. This is *your* arrival. It's *your show. You* fly. You made all this possible. If you can go outside, then so can I."

He disappeared into the cabin and returned with a leather helmet and skydiver goggles on his face and a big towel in his right hand. "Cut the goddamned nose engine!" he bellowed.

I pulled back power and slowed her to eighty indicated, and Ted shoved the upper hatch all the way back and stuck his head and shoulders outside the airplane. We guided one foot to the armrest of Bob's seat and his other foot to the right edge of the quadrant, and then he was swinging his right leg through the upper hatch, resting that foot on the after-cowl of the nose engine. In the meantime his foot on the quadrant had slipped and kicked the right throttle forward, and I was desperately trying to pull it out of the way, because *Annie* wanted to slew around. Bob and I were standing on right rudder to keep her straight. Above everything else, the noise and thunder and engines and wind, we could hear what I swore was a long Tarzan yell. Ted was doing everything but beating his chest out there, and then he leaned down and began to clean the windshield until it absolutely glistened in the late afternoon sun.

I saw something off to my right. A Mustang fighter, the gear full down and the flaps down and holding a ridiculous angle of attack, the canopy back and the pilot staring wide-eyed at us. Then he couldn't hold that speed any more and stalled and fell off. Ted finished the windshield and waved at a

T-34 off to our right that was also coming in with gear and flaps down, only he held formation. The guy in the back seat was taking pictures like mad and there stood Ted, triumphant, waving that greasy towel like a banner of glory. He finally came back inside and we got the power set straight and downstairs we went. It was exactly four-thirty in the afternoon of October 9, 1975, and the first day of the air show of the Confederate Air Force was coming to its close, and baby, down we went. Ancient clanking airplane or not, by God, this was our moment. The air-speed needle came around and *Annie* shuddered and shook from nose to tail, her wings trembled, and we went down, right to the deck, the tires almost kissing concrete, and flew down the runway before a hundred thousand people. I hauled her up in a tight climbing turn to the left and rolled her into a wide pattern, and before we knew what was happening, there came the

On the ground at Rebel Field, and the Confederate Air Force meets the airplane in a mob. Facing the camera at far left is Randy Sohn, a master at flying any kind of warbird. Standing before the door with goggles raised is Ted Anderson, behind him is Martin Caidin in his helmet, and under that big white hat is the master of air shows himself, Bob Hoover. VERN RENAUD

Florida gang. Pete Sherman hit us in his P-51 and we could have seen his grin for a hundred miles, and Don Plumb and Johnny Bolton, with Norm Danielson in his back seat, flashed their wings as they shot past us, and there were Leo Kerwin and Jack Kehoe in their silver T-6, and hey! George Morris and Chip Deems and Denny Sherman and George Baker and there were more guys waiting on the ground for us: Doug Clark and the Martin brothers, Tom Reilly and Ted Votoe, and Dennis Bradley down from Canada in his Corsair and whee-hoo, but the whole gang was there. We came around and landed in a stiff crosswind and *Annie* was all lady, prim and proper. We parked in a row along with Mitchells, the Marauder, the Fortress, the Liberator, the Invader, and the Super Fortress, and there were the Havoc and the Dragon and the Gooney Bird and the Commando and the Airacobra and the Kingcobra and Bearcats and Furies and Helldivers and Dauntlesses and—we were surrounded by history. We shut her down and climbed out, and a great mob surrounded *Annie*. Lefty Gardner parked his P-38 and joined us, and there were Ronnie Round and Harry Sletner, Larry Irvine and Billy Boyer, Bill Childers and Walt Estridge, Harold Fenner and Vince Hinds and Walt Tierney, Lash Lashbrook and John Stover and Lloyd Nolen, who had started the Confederate Air Force, and Revis Sirmon and Ed Messick, and the whole gang.

When we climbed down, Bob Hoover and Art Scholl, the all-time greats of air-show flying, came up to us and Hoover grinned hugely under his big

Virtue triumphs; Caidin standing through the cockpit hatch of *Iron Annie* on arrival at Rebel Field, in Harlingen, Texas, for the CAF air show.
VERN RENAUD

straw hat and turned to the crowd and said, "I always thought he was a crazy son of a bitch." He looked at *Annie*, engines creaking and crackling as they cooled, and he studied the bald tires and saw the scabrous paint peeling and tearing, and in a single long glance he understood it all. "I always thought so," he said, and his grin grew wider, "and now I *know* he's a crazy son of a bitch to fly this thing down here!"

Friend, there ain't a better compliment in the whole world than that.

I guess she'd flown her heart out to make it down to Rebel Field just in time to close the first day of the air show. That night, while the merrymaking and the annual meeting of old friends thundered to the mellow sounds of exploding volcanoes and raucous uproars, I drove from our motel back to Rebel Field. It was quiet now. There was a thin, high mist, through which the moon cast a pale, silvery glow, and I spent the next two hours walking slowly along the flight line, beneath the wings of the machines in which so many men had flown and fought and so many had died. I saw the Avenger I'd missed before, and the Spitfire and the Messerschmitt Me-109G, and there was the Mosquito and there were rows of trainers in which so many of us had learned how to move stick and rudder and gentle the throttle and watch the needle and ball and air speed, and done oh, so many things so sweet to the novice. As the years accumulated, why, the wine was still as fresh as ever and here we all were, together, with so many deep things behind the singing and shouting going on at the clubhouse. The parties were everywhere in Harlingen, but I wanted this moment, and I went to *Iron Annie* and sat down on the concrete beneath her wing, leaning back up against a tire, smoking a cigar, quiet, restful, immersed and enveloped in history. Maybe an hour later, a form approached from the darkness, and it was another one of the gang from Florida, my old friend Bill Bagwell, who had been one of the first to fly *Annie* earlier that year. He sat down by my side, and we hadn't said a word, and we didn't need to, because a long time ago, when he was only twelve years old, Bill had lived on this same airfield, and then it was all military and his father was stationed here and the place was filled with B-29s and the world was at war.

This was a hell of a far sight better, this gathering of warbirds from a dozen countries, and all the insignia that once meant a killing dive and chattering roar of machine guns and cannon now meant the sound of friends drinking and laughing and sharing together.

It was a good moment.

We flew the air show for the next three days, and we flew every one of our slots on schedule. I wish I could say it was a lot of fun, and I will, because it's true, but it was a backbreaker of the worst kind. *Annie* had flown her heart out, and all those systems we had put together were now coming unglued. The vacuum system and the generator and the oil lines and the radios—jeez, it was all going to hell. On the third day of the show, after we taxied in and just made it off the runway, we blew a tire. The next bunch of hours were the wildest one might imagine. We towed *Annie* off the active by her tail and then began the miracle of miracles. Ted Votoe, of Eastern Air Lines, my flying brother if ever I've had one, was on the phone and getting people out of bed back in Florida. Tires and tubes were loaded into a Lincoln Continental and driven to McCoy Jetport, in Orlando. Walt Estridge, commander of the Confederate Air Force, was in civilian life the top gun of all pilots of American Airlines and he had a gate ready and waiting, with Votoe giving up his last day of the show to fly to Dallas with Don Whittington, bless him, in his magnificent A-26 bomber, to get those tires and tubes to us on the flight line of Rebel Field. We got them on the morning of the fourth and last day of the air show, and this was to be the Big Event. We didn't know how to pull the damned wheels off the airplane and break them down or *what*. We'd never done it before. Jack Kehoe was the man of the hour, absolutely incredible, and he and Ted Anderson and Bob Bailey and Ronnie Round and Billy Boyce and myself, and the

Colonel Billy Boyer, Confederate Air Force, grins with delight as *Annie* runs up her engines before an air-show takeoff at Rebel Field—a task necessary every day of the four-day bash. VERN RENAUD

Daily Ministrations, Repairs and Fixit Program takes a respite to watch CAF colonels fly. Standing at left is Golden Gopher Ted Votoe, seated with parts he's repairing is Ted Anderson, and the Beer Pouch to his left is a weary Martin Caidin. VERN RENAUD

whole gang from the Florida Wing, just busted their knuckles changing those tires. I still don't know how, but that crazy, impossible, marvelous bunch of madmen did it. Rebel Control kept asking us if we would get into the air on schedule and we were racing the clock, so they moved up Lloyd Nolen in his Bearcat and he went out and thrilled the mob with spectacular and honey-smooth aerobatics. He was still cutting up sky when we towed *Annie* off the workstand we'd "borrowed" from an Air Force C-130. Ted was up in the cockpit with his hands a blur, and Bailey and I were moving things, and then we had all three engines burning and turning. Rebel Control asked us to get out in a hurry, and there were Jack Kehoe and a couple of the guys in the cabin behind us, because this was *their* flight and they weren't going to miss a thing about it. We had the whole air-show schedule in front of us as we started down the runway and broke out in a wide left turn with Lefty Gardner right alongside us, *inverted*, in his gleaming red-and-white P-38 with the sharks' teeth, and he flew that way for a while. Rebel Control called and said to forget the schedule, the B-29 was about to take off, and they'd like us to make a pass, an honor flyby, as the B-29 lifted from the ground, Vic Agather and Randy Sohn on the controls. Well, we threw away the schedule and I cut the pattern in tight, watching that B-29, and Rebel Control was telling us to bring it on down. But I waited, and when the 29 was rolling I dropped the nose and brought her over in a steep right turn, the wing lifting higher and higher until we were part-way over on our back in some sort of bastardized split S. *Annie* just dropped out of the sky and I came back hard and steady on the yoke and we crossed right over the 29, sliding at an angle, lifting up, and then back, skidding the other way right to the very edge of the runway, squeezing into another tight bank just as the 29 lifted from the ground. Back in the cabin, they said that Jack Kehoe was looking out his window at the ground and shouted, "I can read the numbers on the goddamned lights below us!" We pulled up steeply, and the B-29 flew off to join up with a mob of other bombers, and we went back and did our bombing attacks and the fighters had a grand old time. It was going beautifully, and we were swinging around in the pattern to put *Annie* to rest when Ted tapped me on the shoulder and pointed. "Look at the oil pressure on number three." He said a lot of other very nasty words, be-

cause the needle was swinging to the left and we were already down to forty pounds. We were losing pressure steadily. I cut back on numbers one and three to keep the load off the bad engine and whacked the power to the nose engine and we brought her in like that, nobody outside the airplane having any idea anything was wrong.

When we parked, Ted looked at me. "She's coming apart inside, and we'll never make it home with that engine." The big radials talk to this man, remember, and I listened carefully. "You'll have to get it fixed here."

The next morning, with most of the flight line empty and a strong wind blowing across the field, we fired her up and taxied to the main hangar of the Confederate Air Force, and we sat there, waiting, while the engines ran, and then it happened. I heard it the instant it started, a whistling, fluttering sound from number-three engine, and the oil pressure dropped and that was *it*. I jerked the mixture to FULL LEAN and didn't even wait, but punched off all the right electrical switches and killed the engine before she started to tear herself apart. Then we shut down the other two, and sat in the cockpit and talked about it. The CAF didn't have a single certified A&P (airframe and power plant) mechanic of its own, but they did have people locally who worked for them, and one of them had helped us out during certain tribulations of the past few days. We went into headquarters and worked out a deal with him. I figured, what the hell, they rebuild warbirds here, right? I told him and the other people to go all out, don't spare *anything*. Fix it and fix it right, and the whole thing was a blank check. At least *Annie* was now in good company, and I felt lots better about leaving her behind. It was necessary to get back to Cocoa Beach and a waiting typewriter and those demanding deadlines, but we figured we'd be back in a month or so and bring her home.

Never has a man so underestimated the colossal incompetence of another man to perform mechanical acts on an innocent airplane. But this was yet to be discovered, and on the morning of October 14, with Rebel Field largely deserted, Ted, Bob, and myself climbed aboard a commercial jet in Harlingen and began the trek home—making sure, uncomfortable as we were not to be doing the flying, that we were laced stiffly with shocking mixtures of vodka and tequila.

It was quite a trip. You should understand that

Bob Bailey is a very rugged and clean-cut and handsome cat, who is the perfect image of the guy who drives airliners for a living, as well as enjoying every moment in the seat. Understand that, and also that Ted Anderson and myself are pretty much on the grungy side. We're addicted to old T shirts and boots and jeans and vests with a few years' collection of oil and grease, and the things we wear atop our heads sometimes have been classified as hats, or whatever, and here was Bailey with me on one side and Ted on the other, and we were in Dallas, changing planes, sort of standing in line to get aboard our airliner, and reminiscing on our flight because with all our ills it had been absolutely magnificent, and we were talking about coming back to get *Annie* and our plans for the big bird. During the air show, I asked Ted Votoe to *quickly* find me a Mauser rifle, and how in God's name he accomplished this, I'll never know, but he did, and we kidnaped Art Scholl and ran him half naked down the flight line before that hysterical crowd—in a motorcycle and sidecar—and then Ted took the Mauser with him into the airplane and when we made our bombing passes and were jumped, literally, by a crowd of Mustangs and two P-38s and a Thunderbolt and a Spitfire and a Fury and an Airacobra and a Kingcobra, and while the fighters worked us over, Ted shoved back the top hatch and climbed halfway outside again and began going bang-bang with the Mauser at the fighters, and since we were only about ten feet off the deck while this was going on, it broke up the crowd.

"I can't wait until next time," Ted told us while we shuffled to the gate at Dallas. "Get that turret put in, and I'll have my hands on that machine gun and we'll blast 'em out of the sky." No more than sixty seconds went by after he spoke those words when three very large people with guns in their hands and badges on their shirts arrested the ass of one Ted A. Anderson. Those were the days of the hijacking scares and realities, and someone had heard the words "machine gun" and parts of the rest and they just *panicked.*

They hauled Ted off to a security room and I tried to find out what was going on, and some guard sneered and told me: "Your buddy is in real trouble, so you watch it too." That was one man who came very close to wearing his .38 as far up his butt as his biological structure would allow, but Bob stepped between us. I told Bob to get on the airliner and hold three seats together, and I'd wait out Ted. Minutes went by. Nothing. Time was running out, and then someone told me they were going to take Ted off to jail.

"Not by himself he ain't," I told the guard, and he was a mean and unfriendly son of a bitch, and told me they could accommodate me, too, if only they had a charge. So I told him, "Friend, he misses this airplane and he goes off to the cooler, I am going to be with him, and the charge will be beating the absolute living hell out of you, and I hope you go for that popgun, because you just ain't that fast." I stepped out of line and went to find Ted, who by now had thrown the entire security system into bedlam. He did it all seated very quietly.

"You were making jokes about a machine gun. We don't think it's funny."

Ted cleaned his nails. "Wasn't joking."

"And you were going to use it in a German bomber?"

"Yep."

"With *three* engines?"

"Uh huh."

"That Hitler used to fly in?"

"By golly, that's right."

"And you're the gunner?"

"Gonna be. Right now I fly it and I got to use that measly little old Mauser. Popgun. Ain't worth a turd in a windstorm."

"You know, Mr. Anderson, we're checking you out in Washington?"

"Yep."

"You don't seem very disturbed."

"Ain't."

"You could be in a great deal of trouble, Mr. Anderson."

"Ain't and ain't gonna be."

"Who's this fellow who owns this, ah, three-engined German bomber you're talking about?"

"Martin Caidin. He's a maniac."

"We already assumed that. Has he been in trouble before?"

Ted laughed. "Last one worth recalling was in Portugal. Secret police threw him in jail. He'd been in a fight with some Russians couple days before that up in Newfoundland, in Canada. Then he went to Lisbon."

"What was the charge?"

"Starting a war."

Silence for a while. "And, did he?"

"Nice feller. He wasn't mad at nobody. Of course not."

In the meantime the security check on Ted had come back from Washington and the security people gaped at one Ted A. Anderson. His security clearance went all the way past Top Secret. They found out he'd been in a crack, selected crew of the Strategic Air Command as a B-29 tail gunner, he handled atomic bombs, he'd bailed out of B-29s twice and. . . .

"You're clean," they said, dragging out the words like pulling nails from oak wood.

A voice bellowed from the hall. "Anderson, where the hell are you!"

Ted smiled. "That's him."

"The pilot? Owner of this German bomber?"

"Yep. Tell you what. You think you're confused about me? You check *him* out in Washington and you ain't gonna be the same for a month."

They escorted the both of us back to the airplane with only thirty seconds to spare, and we took our seats, one to each side of Bob Bailey, who was now doing his best to slide under the seat as we regaled him with the details of what had happened. I do think we were being stared at; after all, we'd had an armed escort getting into this airliner. Finally Bob got up for a drink of water, and the stewardess took him to the side. She had no idea we were together.

"Sir," she whispered, "I'm *so* sorry about those two rowdies you're sitting between. I can change your seat for you."

Bob patted her on the shoulder. "That's very kind of you, miss." She started to melt before his eyes. "But you see, they're my half-wit brothers, and I promised Mom I'd personally bring them home safely."

"You poor dear," she told him.

The pattern had been established. You can repair an airplane and give it all sorts of TLC, but if, before you get your hands on that machine, certain elements have really gone beyond the point of no return, you're never going to get your bird out of the pits. Whatever you do is really a stopgap operation. The engines were the best example. We had combined the best of the three BMW radials into two engines and turned to the R1690-42 for our main, dependable power supply. We have already entered into our record that even though we had a zero-time engine in the number-three slot, the reliability of that engine was no greater than the reliability of the systems that were added onto the engines, such as the ignition harness, carburetor, generator, tachometer drive, and so on. As far as the BMWs were concerned, our worst fears were that even the best parts of those engines simply weren't good enough. There had been so much wear and tear on the engines that performing maintenance simply wasn't enough, and therein lies one of the great truths in maintaining aircraft and most especially in bringing abandoned machines back to life. You've got to rebuild the airplane, and the only way you do that is to start at the beginning: you take it apart and go into every system. You drop the idea of fixing and patching, and go all the way down to the basic elements.

When number one lost oil pressure, we knew that our repairs were only of a temporary nature and that a major overhaul was really the answer. That meant, possibly, chroming the cylinders and going through an engine rebuild. The problem was twofold. The engine was metric and we couldn't exchange cylinders and some other vital parts. And the chrome shop in San Antonio, where we sent a batch of cylinders, said the parts were so badly worn they wouldn't guarantee the job. So right there we had a "no go."

The pattern, as I said, was being established.

The airplane had been left to fall apart before I bought it, and then I flew the Ju-52 for approximately a month before accepting reality, and I grounded it for six months for the engine work already described and the many other repairs, changes, and modifications. We flew local test flights, went to and from Fort Lauderdale Exec, and boomed our way down to the Ghost Squadron air bash in Texas, and saw number-one engine coming unglued as the oil pressure began to give up the ghost. We'd never gotten rid of our problems; *we were just better equipped to handle them.* That was the heart of the matter. We still had a flying wreck on our hands, no matter how many times we flew, and the game had become one of sweating out every flight, of waiting for something to go wrong. And that is not conducive to good flying and it gives you too many points for a high pucker factor.

The immediate problem was to get the airplane the hell out of Texas. I tried working with a bunch of the Confederate Air Force members in Harlingen, but camaraderie was apparently something reserved only for the big air shows, when we were marching before the face of the public. With the shouting and awed throngs gone, we faced the everyday problems of personal interests and disregard, and it was not the most pleasant discovery in the world. My estimate of the Confederate Air Force—the concept of which was brilliant and the execution of which for years *had been* exemplary—went into a downhill slide. By now I had to recognize another reality: *What I was told by Harlingen was not what was really happening with the airplane.* I had accorded the people running the outfit complete confidence, and the long and short of it was that they couldn't get out of their own way in doing the job they promised to do. There were a number of these people totally dedicated to warbirds and keeping them in the best possible condition, and there were an equal number of people who, flat out, were mealy-mouthed nothings who put up a good front and never deserved to wear the colors of the Confederate Air Force.

By mid-December, two months after I had left the airplane for the all-out program of rebuilding it to flyable condition, I began to hear disquieting reports, and soon I knew I'd been suckered. Oh, some work had been done but none of it necessary to get the airplane back into the air. Indeed, the aircraft log entry of December 9, 1975, reported everything that had been done to the airplane in those two months:

> Installed radio jacks, installed throttle knobs, installed clock, installed vacuum directional gyro, installed landing light, installed tail light, installed rotating beacon and strobe light [the new bulbs were already shot because of electrical problems], installed grease deflector on nose of aircraft [it was worthless], installed American sockets and lights in cabin of aircraft, installed vacuum hose on vacuum directional gyro, repaired corrosion on belley [sic], repaired cabin door, repaired lavatory floor.

I had called and demanded a reading of the aircraft log and a recitation of everything that had happened. I received a reading of the above and a great deal of mumbling about the engines, all of which amounted to nothing. I spoke to the front office of the CAF and received some absolutely honest confusion. They were of the opinion that the mechanic was handling everything to my satisfaction, which sure as hell he wasn't, and I tried to get them to assume at least some *direction* of the affairs with the Ju-52. During the next month, Jack Kehoe flew into Harlingen and did his own private study of what was going on, and he came back with a summary of the whole job.

"You're getting screwed," he told me. Jack was the flight safety officer of the Florida Wing of the Confederate Air Force and an impeccable civilian and warbird pilot with a towering honesty and a blunt approach to living through whatever flying you do. If Jack Kehoe said this was a shaft job then that was the crux of it all.

Sometimes you can't get away to handle things, and time slipped by before I could take any action. Four months later, I threw in the towel when I learned that the airplane hadn't moved an inch.

The engines had never turned over, and that is death personified for power plants. What I was getting for my money—oh, yes, the bills rolled in regularly—was just what Jack Kehoe reported: a royal shafting.

I have my own personal way of handling such matters and they're not always what other people like, but by this time I really didn't much give a damn who liked what. One of my associates was Terry Ritter, who is a (1) physically huge hulk of a man, (2) of incredible strength, and (3) an auto mechanic. Now, consider that Terry had flown in an airplane only with me and no one else. He had never ever *seen* the Ju-52 and he had never worked on an airplane before. But he seemed a bear for work and for getting other people all in a row and he knew how to cut the mustard. I sent him to Harlingen with absolute power to do whatever was necessary—including my assurance that we'd get him out of the slammer just as fast as he got into it if that proved necessary. That he was not a certified A&P didn't matter. The mechanic had been living off my wallet for some time now and I was bloody well going to get my bread back one way or the other. The regulations state that a man who doesn't carry his A&P card can do a lot of work on a large iron bird, and if it's done under the supervision of an A&P, then the latter can watch and inspect and if he's satisfied he signs off the books. That was the route I was going to go, because Terry Ritter's basic instincts and mechanical touch were worth a hundred A&P's to me. Terry has driven screaming race cars and hydroplane racers and for the fun of it takes engines apart and puts them back together, and he and mechanical objects have this strange affinity for one another.

Terry's commercial flight to Harlingen left much to be desired. The final run down the Texas coast was through a violent thunderstorm line, and the DC-9 was hammered up and down and all over the place and Terry was hanging on for dear life while all about him people were filling the empty spaces in burp bags. They emerged from lightning-filled clouds to a *whump!* (as Terry described it) of a landing, and as they slowed their roll along the runway Terry looked out at the warbirds by the CAF ramp and his eyes glued to the gray-white hulk of a three-engine airplane and he wanted to gnash his teeth in frustration or weep or what. "That thing looked as if it had as much life in it as the underside of a dead fish's belly," he said.

"I couldn't believe it. It was ghastly. A horror. It hadn't moved an inch in six months."

I knew *that.* In fact, this was April 1976 and just one year since I had bought *Iron Annie,* and she had already spent at least 90 per cent of her time welded to the ground, and this crap was just going to have to come to an end. Terry's first few hours were spent crawling through the airplane with the mechanic moving silently with him, answering questions as they were asked. When it got about four in the afternoon, the mechanic told Terry he had to leave because it was quitting time.

That, dear friends, was one of the worst mistakes he ever made. I shall spare you the sordid, crunching details, but visions of his anatomy being sundered in slow and painful ways brought to him a sudden, fiery enthusiasm to work seven days a week, starting at the crack of dawn and continuing until such time as Terry said, "Okay, knock it off until the morning." Terry also visited the front office of the CAF, looming in the doorway and darkening the interior of the building and, having thus quietly but effectively commanded attention, made a brief and to-the-point speech that within ten days at the outside he expected to have that airplane alive and in flying condition, with or without assistance, but that he, and I through his representation, would welcome the latter. And above all, he added as his final fillip, whoever and whatever got in the way would do well to stock up on iodine and large rolls of bandage.

He called me. "Kehoe was very kind to these people when he told you it was a screw job," Terry announced in his usual no-nonsense report. "I have never seen so much CENSORED by so many CENSORED in so many CENSORED ways in all my life."

"Can you get it flying?" I pressed.

"It'll fly," he growled. "Gimme two days to learn what makes it tick, maybe a week after that, and you get your ass down here." There was a brief silence; then he continued. "They say that number-one engine will never turn. It's finished, *Kaput.* A basket case. Junk."

"What's your opinion?"

CENSORED.

"Okay. How about the headquarters people?"

"It's half and half. The first half are embarrassed by it all. They're good people. The second half are CENSORED. The way I look at it, they'd love to see you give up and just leave the airplane here."

"Will they co-operate with you?"

"We had a little talk. They will, *now.*"

"Have at it. Call me day or night with what you need."

"Keep your lawyer handy. 'By."

———◆———

The CAF invited Terry, in a move made with good intentions, to live at the visiting quarters directly on the flight line. This would keep him close to the airplane and save money. Hard to argue with that. The problem was that the quarters were ancient, in a condition somewhat paralleling the sordid disrepair of the Ju-52, without a telephone, and lacking any means of providing one's necessary life sustenance such as food—which Terry consumes in great quantities. He also failed to get his hands on a rental car that first night, everything having shut down. When he went back to headquarters, it was closed tighter than a call girl's private address book. The nearest place to eat was miles away and there wasn't any telephone available. So Terry decided to enjoy what he might not have time for again. He walked the deserted flight line, awed by the great and legendary warbirds of the past, and he was completely unbelieving of the fact that not a single security guard was present, none showed up, and that security for these irreplaceable machines was nonexistent—and that the static display of great warbirds, past and present, was a disaster of vandalism and utter disregard for the condition of those aircraft. Before he quit for the night, he wrenched some spotlights around and played them on the Ju-52 for a modicum of security, a situation he would attend to the next day. That evening he had a friend in the hollow, isolated quarters—a mouse with which he shared a few packages of cheese crackers.

As an idea of what continued to befall our attempts to get life back into the carcass of N52JU, the next morning Terry got his rental car, moved into a motel, and was frozen to the floor by an enormous bolt of lightning that smashed into the ground just outside his motel room. This was the opening gambit in a huge storm line rolling into Harlingen, and Terry took off for the airfield and the airplane, and was just in time to watch *as eight inches of rain fell in the next forty-five minutes.* He also stared at an amphibian that broke its tie-down lines and floated clear across Rebel Field to the other side of the airport and, closer to home, saw water rising to the door level of a line of aircraft.

He called me that night to tell me what he thought of me, my airplane, Harlingen, Texas weather, and the Confederate Air Force, and none of it is printable in these pages.

One week later, to the day of his arrival at Harlingen, he phoned me. "C'mon down," he growled. "We're ready. It's done."

"How'd the engines do?"

"They haven't done anything yet. This whole crowd of geniuses hasn't got anyone among them who knows how to start your airplane."

"I'll be down tomorrow." And the next day, I was on my way to Harlingen with Dee Dee, my wife, another pilot, Chuck Kendron; and a promise from Vern Renaud, that Eastern Airlines captain, to join us in a few days for the flight back to Florida.

I was in Harlingen the next afternoon and I went through the airplane, saying little except to ask questions and get instant answers.

Of course, no one in CAF headquarters believed the airplane would even turn an engine, let alone fly. But we didn't much care at this point what *anyone* thought. Terry said it was all systems go.

"Okay. Let me see the log," I said. Terry handed it to me and I went through each line carefully.

———◆———

May 7, 1976. Overhaul, repair, and maintenance program of several months at completion: (1) modified VHF radio system, (2) installed second VHF radio, leads, jacks, power and antenna system, (3) repaired number-three oil-temperature gauge, (4) performed complete check of flaps and trim system, internal and external, (5) completed corrosion repairs and replacement of skin on forward and aft belly sections, (6) repaired right-wing skin corrosion, upper surface, (7) completed sheet-metal repairs flap and aileron trailing edges, (8) performed complete control-system check including hinges and bell cranks, (9) inspected tires, inflation-tested mains and tail-wheel, (10) installed new window and hatch handles and locks in cockpit, (11) overhauled wobble pump, checkout okay, (12) inspected all fuel tanks, lines, and supports, (13) performed inside wing inspection, (14) performed hydraulic-system inspection, (15) installed second venturi tube for vacuum system, (16) tail-wheel lock system repaired—new pin

installed and checkout okay, (17) removed German external power plug and replaced with US AN type, (18) greased all three engines' rocker-arm boxes, (19) completed master weight-and-balance reference charts for this aircraft, (20) inspected pitot-static system, (21) checked out batteries, connections, and electrical system.

Complied with FAR 91.217 (B) (5) Aircraft Inspection Program for 25, 50, 75 and 100 hour periods; and all FAR 43 Appendix D—inspections and servicing completed; and complete FAR 91.217 (B) (5) Annual Inspection Program. This aircraft certified airworthy.

———◆———

And we hadn't yet gone to the engine logs. Well, one way to tell: If Terry was right, then he deserved a medal for Miracle, One, 18-Karat Gold.

I went through the checklist and we pushed and pulled and turned all the right things in the proper order, *and on the first shot that number-three engine turned over with a thundering roar.* I couldn't believe it. We started winding up number two, and the nose engine belched and hurled out great gobs of water in all directions and groaned and backfired and spat and then caught and the prop was a marvelous blur in front of us. We went to number one and had the same routine. Water exploded out in all directions from the engine and we cranked and primed and worked that wobble pump to death and had to do the bit with the inertial starter four times, and then *that* engine caught, and we sat there with all three turning—and Terry was right, and everyone else was full of crap.

I called the so-called mechanic into the cockpit, for the vacuum gauge readout was a blur of the needle moving back and forth so fast you couldn't *see* the needle. I pointed it out to him and he sort of turned pale. I hadn't said a word, but then pointed to the electrical-system gauge, which showed the generator was running only intermittently; Terry stared at him with a face full of fury, and I knew someone would be working the whole night through. Well, we had her running, and a taxi test is the best way to find out things. I eased the power to her slowly, and we even had some brakes, and that was a small miracle in itself. We pulled away from the CAF ramp, went over a slight bump, and the right tire went flat.

I shut her down in the center of the taxiway, and

the silence inside that airplane was death itself. We inspected the tire. Flatter than yesterday's pancakes. Harry Sletner and Walt Wootten, two CAF colonels who believed in airplanes and working with your fellow pilot, came to our rescue with jacks and tools and more helping hands. Just before we pulled the wheel, I turned to the mechanic. "You told me you jacked up this airplane and changed the tubes, right? You remember that?"

He allowed that he remembered it.

Which was cause for another long silence when we pulled the wheel and removed the tube from the tire and found it filled with dust and a gaping, four-inch hole in the tube. The only thing that had kept that tire from going flat was the tight seal of the tire to the wheel rim.

"You're a goddamned liar," I told this paragon of mechanical genius.

Colonel Ronnie Round, of Round Tires, came to the runway with a truck filled with workers. He picked up the tube and shook his head. "Damn thing ain't held air for six months. Looks like the boll weevils got into this here tube." He turned to me. "Thought you'd had all these changed?"

Well, screw the recriminations. "Ronnie, you got something that will fit inside these tires?"

"Sure do. Tractor tubes. We'll have to get the valve stems off your tubes, though."

It was a weekend. They charged me only cost. They did the job in three hours—five hours after that flat; and to be on the safe side, we changed the tubes of both tires, with tractor tubes that fit within 99 per cent of the Pirelli tubes. Those CAF colonels were just the greatest.

There was still daylight and the air was calm, and although the vacuum gauges fluttered like a hummingbird's wings and the generator was screwed up and we knew we had an engine tach drive slipping, those were minor points. I took her up with Kendron in the right seat and Terry Ritter riding herd on everything as flight engineer—which was an auspicious moment, since this was the first flight he'd ever made in the Ju-52! Nothing burned or exploded or fell apart, and we logged seven takeoffs and landings for the remainder of the day. The next morning, the ninth of May, I put in four more flights, and then we spent the rest of the day trying to repair all the things that were supposed to have been repaired months before.

Vern Renaud arrived on the tenth, and we wasted no time getting him out to the airplane, so he could spend an hour just sitting in the cockpit and learning the gadgets and the procedures. A pro always goes this route, and Vern was one of the best in the business and a natural-born flier. While he and I played catchup in the Ju-52, Dee Dee and Terry went out for a flight in a Messerschmitt bf-108b, with Walt Wootten in the left seat, and they were having a blast, doing fighter passes over some cotton fields, when at four hundred feet the engine quit cold. They got thumped about a bit, but Walt did a masterful job, skidded the 108b along some trees and flat-hatted the bird on the ground in a wild, sideways slide. Before she left the field in a pickup truck, Dee Dee made sure to get some cotton leaves, which still adorn her logbook.

They weren't back at the field more than an hour when I told them to climb aboard *Annie* for her first checkouts with Vern. Dee Dee looked at me wide-eyed and half turned and pointed off in the distance. "Don't you believe me? *We just crashed out there!*"

"You hurt?"

"Why . . . not really."

"Then, get aboard, damn it. You're crew and we're flying."

Vern took to *Annie* as if he'd flown her all his life. He did six in the pattern and stalled her and rumbled and droned around the sky, and we put the big bird to bed for the night and got ready to leave the next morning. We loaded up with 620 gallons of fuel and stuffed the oil tanks and had all sorts of equipment and spare parts aboard.

Early the next morning, the engines that would never turn started up with the usual arm-smashing and body-twisting procedures. We were pretty confident. If the vacuum system went out, hell, we'd fly eyeball all the way home. If the electrical system went out, we'd land at uncontrolled fields and use the batteries when they were needed and charge them on the ground. During the preceding few days, we had made seventeen takeoffs and landings, and our crossed fingers held good promise.

We taxied out to the active and, wonder of wonders, even the radios worked, and Harlingen tower cleared us for takeoff. I held brakes as long as I could, we watched the gauges carefully, I looked at the windsock and a stiff crosswind from my left, and then we let her go. We were finally on the way home—*seven months* after the Ju-52 had landed at Rebel Field.

We were just over 22,000 pounds and going like gangbusters down the runway and I was holding full left aileron into that crosswind. The tail came up slowly by itself and she felt good and we had nearly 2,000 rpm going for all three engines, and we had about 50 mph on the gauge when the left engine lost power. Not all power, but the rpm dropped to about 1,300, and with that crosswind, oh, good damn, *because* the wind was blowing the tail to the right and the asymmetrical power was tugging the Ju-52 nose to the left, and I was trying to get some nose-up trim in there and I was so spitting mad I took my eyes off the runway for a moment and of course that swerve was really getting the upper hand. Like a snake, Vern's hand was out there to pull power from the right engine until I had her straightened out. I had full right rudder, right on down to the bloody floorboards in a foot-stomping effort to hold her straight, and I let her build speed slowly, with only the nose engine full bore, and she was swerving from all the oddball forces on her. I brought in full power on the right engine and kept tapping right brake. I was so burned and determined to keep her going straight, it never occurred to me to fly; I just wanted her going right down that centerline. Vern pointed to the air speed, we had ninety, and the easiest tug on the yoke, and no matter about that crippled left engine, she soared into the air. The faster we went the more power we got and finally the rpm came up to 1,550. We figured we'd keep on going to Galveston and get out of the bottom of Texas, and for fifty miles it looked as if we were going to make it. We kept in some right rudder trim with that weak left engine, and Terry ventured it was the carburetor that was letting go and not the engine itself, and then we were about sixty miles out from Harlingen at sixteen hundred feet when it all fell apart.

Terry proved to be right. The carburetor broke something and fire blossomed into the stack. We were lucky, for flame shot back from the left-engine exhaust to fifty or sixty feet behind the wing, so that it was trailing well behind the airplane. We decided to let her keep operating, because obviously the fuel was being consumed in that fire and it wasn't burning anywhere but the stack. Even though the power kept dropping, down to about 1,100 rpm, it was better than shutting down a system we couldn't trust and possibly getting a worse mess on our hands. We drove north along the coastline so that we could always dump the bird on the beach if it turned out this was the way to go. Our destination now was Corpus Christi Naval Air Station (which doubled as a Coast Guard Station), because there we knew we could get help, once we were on the ground in one piece.

Five minutes later, the right engine lost oil pressure and began severe backfiring that became so violent we thought we'd blow the stacks clear off the airplane. Number three was now torching wildly from two cylinders. We drove through the sky with flame blazing from the stack of number one, fire sprouting from number three, and the explosions so violent the entire airplane shook with each blast. We learned later that we could be seen and heard for more than fifty miles because of our unusual pyrotechnics and sound effects.

Our troubles weren't over, as the generator quit completely and we lost all electrical power. Kendron lost no time in activating the mayday signal on the Emergency Locator Transmitter (which went nowhere, because the battery, exactly three days new in the airplane, also went dead). Without the generator, no power; the VOR needle did everything but go limp. I called in mayday on 121.5 and 126.2 and nobody heard us anywhere. We had the nose engine jammed forward, the left engine flaming with 1,100 rpm and the right engine torching and backfiring with 1,200 rpm, and we dragged ourselves through the air at 90 mph and, by God, *she was hanging in there.*

We passed over an auxiliary field and I determined not to take her down, because there weren't any facilities and Corpus Christi NAS was only five miles ahead of us, and if it fell apart on the landing I wanted crash trucks and the meat wagon right where we were instead of five miles across a body of water. We droned on, unaware that our flight had generated a full-scale emergency and that we'd been declared a UFO. The navy radar was skin-tracking us, and the corrugated skin returned a huge oval blob on the scope. We were throwing so much electrical signal from the wing engines, and people were reporting fire and explosions, that the radar crew in their sealed room literally declared us an unknown, a huge shape drifting along the coast at ninety miles per hour. They reported this to the Corpus Christi tower and asked them if they could spot the unknown object.

"We've got a visual on it," the tower reported back, "but you'll never believe it." The tower immediately notified a whole swarm of training aircraft in the airfield pattern to be ready for anything.

I dragged *Annie* along just below a broken cloud deck at sixteen hundred feet, and then we were over the middle of the airport and starting a swing to the west, and I was rocking the wings to signal them we were in trouble and needed to land, and suddenly every one of about thirty or forty trainers broke off from their positions and headed for the boonies, leaving us a clear field. I brought her downwind, started a long base, came around on a long final, right down the centerline of the runway, and holding altitude. Vern watched the end of the runway disappear beneath the nose of the Ju-52 and concluded I'd gone mad, because at that same moment I killed all three engines, moved the mixtures all the way to CUTOFF, cut off the electrical switches, and shouted to Terry for full flaps, all the way down to forty degrees.

The nose went down, and I think Vern thought I'd died on the spot, because I wasn't moving, just holding that yoke in both hands and driving her downstairs. Vern looked from me to the gauges and saw 95 on the air speed and the descent rate pegged at 600 feet per minute, and *Annie* rode down as if she were on rails, incredibly silent with the engines shut down. I aimed five hundred feet beyond the numbers at the end of the runway,

started the flare with plenty of time, and held her off. She touched down right where she belonged— and rolled two thousand feet into a good wind, no brakes, and stopped off the active as I managed one last turn onto the nearest taxiway.

The United States Coast Guard, bless 'em, towed us all the way down the main taxi ramp, past every hangar on the field, with Terry Ritter sitting on the wingtip and me in the cockpit smoking a cigar and Vern riding up ahead on the towtruck, and Chuck Kendron looking over my shoulder.

Dee Dee had fallen asleep.

◆

Jim Marcotte and Ken Stallings, of the Coast Guard, pulled off one of the neatest miracles of all time. They got official permission to give us all the help we needed, and *Annie* rested within a huge hangar while coast-guard and no small number of navy mechanics pondered her aches and pains— and scratched their heads trying to figure out what to do. I concluded that with so many military types watching and riding herd on things, we could go back to Florida and ship off every spare part we had in the hangar. We were on our way before the day was ended.

One week later, four of us were on the trip back to Corpus Christi. With me came Terry Ritter and Ted Anderson and a fourth madman, Major Frank Urbanic of the Air Force, who had flown a couple of hundred low-level support missions in Vietnam and thought the idea of flying right seat in the Ju-52 was a gas. All the parts had arrived before us, and a lot of work remained to be done. The Coast Guard and the Navy had been busy, and they'd tried their best without any knowledge of the airplane, with its metric measurements, to patch it up. They'd even put great bandages of asbestos material on the exhaust stacks, which by now were so thin they'd never bring us home. Anderson and Ritter and yours truly went to work, while Urbanic collected people and parts and kept other things going for us by using his own uniform to its best advantage.

After all that had been done to the airplane, you can better appreciate the aircraft log entry of May 21, 1975:

Entire flap and trim system inspected, greased, lubed, and tested satisfactorily. Hydraulic system purged, B-nuts cleaned and tightened,

The miracle workers of the U. S. Coast Guard: Commanders Ken Stallings (left) and Jim Marcotte, who pulled off one of the neatest stopgap mechanical miracles in getting *Iron Annie* back into the air for her flight home. Marcotte is probably the only man in the world to have had a Ju-52 fall on him. u. s. COAST GUARD

pressure established both brake pedals. Fire bottle filled with nitrogen. Rebuilt German carburetor installed number-one engine. All plugs all three engines replaced. All exhaust systems checked, cracks stop-drilled, asbestos and metal patches installed. Vacuum system number-one engine cleaned and purged. Carburetor heat gauge cleaned and tested. Voltage regulator and generator for number-three engine cleaned and reinstalled. All external hatches drilled, new screws installed. Tach generator number-three engine modified, new shafts installed, replaced on aircraft. Installed all-new carburetor heat ducting all three engines. Oil-pressure relief valve number-one engine purged and cleaned. Anti-skid strips placed on both wings. Rocker-arm boxes greased.

We towed the airplane from the hangar, and the tail-gear assembly cracked in three places and the tail fell onto the arm of Jim Marcotte and we were sure we had severed the arm. Anderson's voice bellowed out like a foghorn. "He's pinned! *Get that tail up!*" Without thinking about it, Urbanic and I, who were the closest, lifted up the entire airplane by putting our backs beneath the horizontal stabilizers, and they pulled Marcotte free and rushed him to the infirmary. The tail had crushed itself around his arm in the only place it could do so by metal yielding instead of crushing bone—but he still wears a permanent crease in his arm from that moment. We got the tail repaired, cheered lustily when Marcotte showed up, two hours later, with his arm in a sling, bellowing orders at a hugely grinning crew.

That night we stayed in a motel that had been

condemned a year before but was the only place in town with rooms. We slept with open doors and windows for any respite from the temperature in the nineties, no air conditioning, and not even any cold water for a shower. I kept a .38 automatic by my hand in case we had any sudden visitors, and woke up to find the weapon in Terry's hand as he was taking dead aim *on a mosquito.* I grabbed the gun and he looked sheepishly at me.

We took off early the next morning (we were to fly with Marcotte and Stallings many times in the future in a friendship stronger today than it was in those hectic times) bound for Lake Charles, but, two hours out from Corpus Christi, we already had a bucketful of problems and a new one that scared hell out of us. Right after takeoff, the electrical system failed immediately, the vacuum system never did work, but we were ready and we operated that airplane all the way home on the power of those Sears Diehard batteries.

But the problem that had our pucker factor at full bore was the series of explosions that began again with number-three engine. We couldn't figure it out. They came more and more frequently, and then they were so violent they felt as if we were taking direct hits from anti-aircraft fire. Ted Anderson babied the power controls and pointed to Galveston, but I was already on the way down there so we could figure out the problem on the ground.

This was one of those impossible journeys on which everything goes berserk. We taxied up to the ramp at Galveston, opened the door, and stared at four stunning, amply endowed beauties, the first of whom in an impeccable British accent, screamed, *"Frankie! How wonderful!"* and threw her arms about Urbanic.

Terry and Ted huddled over the engine while I sulked in the cockpit until Frank led his charges up the cabin and I was surrounded by bodies beautiful. I kept a vision of Dee Dee clear and bright in the dead center of my skull. We were being invited to a barbecue party when Ted came up to me. "Think I got it figured out. When the engine heats up after a while, it wears down the electrical resistance of the system, and the harness sets up a predetonation condition. If it happens, we just land, let it cool off, and get going again. If I'm right, we'll get a little more flying in each time before the detonation starts up."

Ted's analysis was good enough for me and I

hollered for the guys to go. They looked at us as if we were mad to turn down those luscious forms and I guess they were right, but they returned and we fired up and off we went. We flew for an hour and twenty minutes to Lake Charles, and that night again did our destruction act at the Cajun Kitchen. Frank Urbanic, bless his pea-picking, romantic soul, wept his way to slumberland between belches.

The next day, we were out on the flight line just as quickly as we could get going and headed for Tallahassee, hoping the harness would hold together long enough for us to make it. It didn't. Soon after the takeoff, we started getting detonation. We also saw one of those giant black walls in the sky ahead of us. We punched in the radios by using the batteries, and weather told us the storm system was moving north, so to the south we went. *But the weather advisers had the movement reversed.* Twenty minutes later, well out over the Gulf of Mexico, we were right in the middle of the storm and nowhere to go. We were without artificial horizons, directional gyros, and turn indicators. I kept flying as long as I could by staring at a sliver of orange in the midst of the storm, and then that disappeared. I set up a steady rate of descent at four hundred feet per minute, put the magnetic compass on 9 (we were lucky; it was mounted on shock cords and, within ten degrees of any turn, didn't process but held position) for a due-east heading. If the numbers drifted to 8, to the north, I eased in right rudder, and when they drifted to 10, I eased in left rudder, and that's how we flew the next forty minutes in thundering rain and ink-black skies and cloud, and came out of it about six hundred feet above the waters of the Gulf, looking down on a big tanker. Ted stabbed his hand to the left and I was already in a north turn to get us to land. By the time we saw the shoreline, we were up to a towering eight hundred feet above the ground, slipping beneath the cloud bases. Frank Urbanic was talking to Air Force radar along the coastline, because that predetonation was wild by now and jarring our teeth with every blast, and it had been nearly four hours in the air. We got a direct steer to Sikes Field, at Crestview, Florida, and gratefully put her on the ground on the long, single runway.

Sandwich and Coke time while they refueled *Annie,* and then a race against the clock and the setting sun for an hour and forty minutes to put us on the ground at Tallahassee. Ted had the batteries charged up during the night, and early the next morning there we were again, staring morosely into a thick, blinding haze. Ted went to the tower and came back grinning. "Let's go. We got a special VFR departure cleared for us."

"In this mess?" I asked. "It would be like taking off into yellow pea soup."

"They said we could go."

We went. I wasn't a hundred feet in the air when I thought I'd gone blind. I used ground reference for flying, because the only direction in which I could see anything at all was straight down. We climbed up to seven thousand, *Annie* dragging her weary metal bones to that altitude, and the haze got worse. At seven thousand, I couldn't see the wingtips and I said to hell with this, I'm going down for contact flying, because if there was another aircraft up here heading our way we'd never see it until we tangled, and I wanted none of that nonsense. We were flying straight into another storm system, and this was the most vicious one we'd seen yet, with lightning all over the damned place and clouds down to the deck. Tampa was closed, Ocala was closed, and Urbanic went back to his magic with radios and got us a radar steer to Brooksville. Ted was annoyed and he wanted us to continue the flight on the deck all the way across Florida. In one way he was right—it was open country and we could do the whole thing lower than three hundred feet. In the other way he was dead wrong. The weather was horrible and we didn't know what was ahead of us, and I thought his idea of cutting toward Tampa and doing an end run around a storm line we could see from eighty

miles away just stank. I wheeled into a ninety-degree turn to the left, due east, and there, under the only patch of sun in the whole bloody state, was Hernando County Airport, at Brooksville. Ted showed complete disbelief at my decision to land, and I told him to stuff it, and put her down in that glorious, warm sunshine. On the ground, Ted stalked off angrily and, engine genius or none, I couldn't have cared less. The end run he insisted we should have made was hit by a mass of tornado funnels. At the time we would have arrived on the east coast of Florida, a violent hailstorm with fifty-mile-per-hour winds was in progress, while *we* basked in sunshine and drank coffee and smoked cigars. We finally got the all clear from Patrick Air Force Base, and we flew the last leg across Florida under scattered clouds.

On the afternoon of May 24, I put her down at Merritt Island Airport and taxied into the greatest greeting we'd ever had. Dee Dee was jumping up and down, and our entire gang had prepared a huge Welcome Home banner for *Iron Annie* and her motley crew.

The round trip had taken from October 7, 1975, to May 24, 1976.

———◆———

We need a certain postscript here, and it involves the Confederate Air Force. On August 12, 1976, Colonel James P. Hill, Executive Director of the CAF, sent me a letter in which he wiped out any and all bills I had accumulated with the CAF at Harlingen during the period when I believed the airplane was being repaired.

We were home—at long, long last. Yet there was no question, and it didn't take hindsight to understand it, that *Iron Annie* in her present shape was living—and flying—on borrowed time.

We needed a new direction, and I had just the place in mind. It would eliminate once and for all the staggering cost in time, effort, and hard cash I had endured since *Iron Annie* came into my life. For months, Bob Bailey had been trying to get me together with Dan Freeman, who ran the working section of Aero Facilities Corporation, at Miami International Airport. He wanted me to talk to Dan and his boss, Nick Silverio, about doing a *professional* job of rebuilding *Iron Annie*. I asked Bob to set it up as soon as possible, and that same afternoon of my return from Texas, Dan was on the phone.

"Where and when can I see the bird?" he queried.

"Merritt Island Airport. Any time after the next few days."

"What's the next two days?"

"I got an air show to fly. Florida Wing of the Confederate Air Force. Big harooh at Ti-Co Airport. Then we're going to open the Bicentennial Exposition at the Kennedy Space Center with the Ju-52 leading a pack of warbirds."

Silence for a few moments. "I, uh, thought, you know, from what Bailey told me, your airplane was pretty well worn out."

"It is. In fact, it stinks. That's why we need you and Nick."

"And you're going to do an *air show?*"

"Yeah. My father-in-law will be pissed at me if I don't go through with it."

More silence. "Your, uh, father-in-law, huh?"

"Right."

"And you want to keep him happy?"

"He's a detective in Cocoa Beach. You come up here, *you're* gonna want to keep him happy too."

Chick Autry had been waiting too long for this moment to let it go by—if he had to start those engines by hand-propping them on his own. Of course that would have been a bit difficult with the center engine, but he'd even figured out what to do with that. "I can't reach the damn' thing," he said with unquenchable enthusiasm, "but I can wrap a rope around the wing props and haul them through and let you catch them real quick to get the engines running."

"But what about the nose engine?" I insisted.

"Simple," he said, stealing a cigar from my pocket. "We take off on the two wing engines, get upstairs, push over into a dive, and let the wind turn the nose prop over until we get it started."

I stared at him. "You're *serious?*"

"Damn' right."

I shook my head. "Sounds pretty hairy to me, Chick."

"Call me Daddy."

"Up yours, Daddy." I sighed. "It's still hairy. But you'd want to do it anyway, wouldn't you?"

He looked at me as if I were mad. "To fly *that* airplane? I'd do just about anything."

"What if I say no?"

"You want to go to jail?"

"What in the hell for?"

He smiled with his sharp, legal teeth. "For breaking a poor old cop's heart, that's what for."

"Okay. We fly."

"Goody," he chortled.

We flew. Indeed, we flew the very next morning. Chick was out to Merritt Island Airport at dawn, wearing an ancient flight jacket from days of yore, when the big airplanes in his life were Stinsons and T-6s. He had polished the windshield until it gleamed, done the preflight three times, and drummed his fingers impatiently on the wing a couple of hundred more times. Daddy-O wasn't a very big man, about five foot eight, but he was about as wide as he was tall and he had forearms that approximated the size of my thighs. A very solid keg of nails if ever there was one.

Terry didn't want to fly the air show without spending a couple of days on the airplane. I said you can work on it all you want at Ti-Co, which was about twenty miles upriver from Merritt Island Airport. "Why Ti-Co?" he demanded.

By now I had learned the nature of the winged beast. "Because if it all comes apart and we're at Ti-Co we'll at least have the airplane there for a static display. Load up. We're flying."

Her exhausts taped with asbestos bandages, U. S. Coast Guard stripes on the after fuselage and tail, her exterior shabby, generators and vacuum systems dead, operating on batteries alone, *Iron Annie* pounds along the runway for the big Valiant Air Command Air Show in 1976 at Ti-Co Airport. JULIAN LEEK

Chick took the right seat and I let him do his first takeoff in an airplane that made everything else he'd ever flown a Tinker Toy. I rode with him on the rudder because of the torque he couldn't anticipate without experience, and he sort of wobbled a bit getting into the air, but within five minutes he was right at home and singing and bellowing with pure, pasteurized, and unmitigated joy. We cut short that ear-shattering uproar by landing at Ti-Co twenty minutes after takeoff and turning the

airplane over to a ground team for the next three days. We were to be ready to go for the festivities on the morning of May 29.

And fly she did. I still don't know how it all happened, but maybe *Annie* sensed those tens of thousands of people gathering, and she certainly was in good company, because the Kerwin Gang began showing up with T-6s and F4U Corsairs, P-51 Mustangs, and B-25 Mitchells, the T-33 jet, T-28 Trojans, and the sharkmouth P-40N Warhawk, and our A-26 Invader, a Gooney Bird, and a bunch of helicopters. There were also some good stuff from the Coast Guard and some choppers and close-support birds from the Air Force. Allan Wise showed up in his delightful Pietenpol, and there was Bud Clark with his gleaming Lockheed 10. A bunch of the boys flew in with their venerable Stearmans and a couple of T-34s. We had a mob of guys throwing themselves out of airplanes to land their chutes all over the place. And there were popcorn and cotton candy, hot dogs and hamburgers, and soft drinks and beer, and it was a high old time.

Annie flew three days of air shows with the Florida Wing and earned star status by leading a formation over the Kennedy Space Center and circling the huge Vehicle Assembly Building, where NASA had assembled the monster lunar rockets, and then we went back for the bombing attacks and low passes and getting shot down by the whole gaggle of fighters. On the last day of the air show, Chick and I—by now he had passed into heaven and beyond from three days of hard air-show flying—watched a heavy thunderstorm rolling into the runway at Ti-Co, and I said to hell with that, because I've had enough of beating out storms for a while, and we took *Annie* down to Merritt Island and put her to bed.

There was one more flight to be made. Not yet. But soon. . . .

◆

Nick Silverio sent Dan Freeman up from Aero Facilities to look at the winged locomotive about which he'd heard so much from Bob Bailey. Dan couldn't believe what he saw. I opened the wing panels and Dan stuck his head inside and looked at those massive spars and cross sections, playing a bright light out to the wingtip and I heard the muffled explosion of "Jesus Christ! This is a *bridge* in here!" He ducked under the wing and came around to look at me and said, "I can hardly

Her greatest moment of glory after her return from near death in Texas: *Iron Annie* leads a contingent of warbirds of the Valiant Air Command, on invitation of the U. S. Government, to open the Bicentennial Exposition of the Kennedy Space Center, in 1976. Two great shots of the huge Vehicle Assembly Building at KSC, where NASA assembled its giant Saturn V moon rockets. JULIAN LEEK

Where warbirds aren't birds of war: two exciting moments during the Valiant Air Command Air Show of 1976. In the top picture, a simulated bomb drop from the JU-52 rips up the field—and a joke becomes a roaring fire, seen behind the British biplane. No damage and no casualties, and score a great time for all. PAUL BROWN

Colonel Ted Anderson narrating the air-show combat sequences for the crowd during a Valiant Air Command air demonstration. Anderson is now known on the circuit as "Old Spellbinder."
PAUL BROWN

believe it. That's the strongest damn' wing I've ever seen in my life. Now, tell me what you want to do."

"I want to make her an airplane again. No short cuts. No crap. No restrictions. I want this bird brought back to zero time. I want her better than new."

Dan's face went serious, and we had a long talk, sitting beneath the wing and sucking beer and puffing on good cigars.

By now I was *feeling* the weariness in the metal bones of old and tired N52JU. An airplane talks to you if only you know how to listen, and *Annie* was just about ready to give up. There were no more patches to make, and the next fixes were about to be her last. After a while, even metal gets so tired it starts coming apart, and internal systems are so worn that they simply cannot be rebuilt. You've got to get down to bare bones and start from scratch. I told all this to Dan Freeman, how I wanted it all done the right way.

"I can do it," he said, looking up at that giant wing, "and I'd love to do it. You'll need new engines and you'll need American propellers with them, and I'd recommend constant-speed props."

"I know. That's the way it's got to go."

"It's going to cost you, friend," Dan said softly.

"Resurrecting the dead never did come cheap," I

told him, and he understood and smiled, and we shook hands and made the contract right then and there with that handshake.

I called Bob Bailey and told him to come up about the middle of the month. Since he'd set it all up, he was going to play midwife, and the last flight of the old airplane was to be his right and privilege.

"Terry, you go over this bird with a fine-toothed comb," I told my stolid giant of a mechanic, "because she's more tired than even you know, and she's about ready to quit, and if she starts coming unglued we're going to have to set down in a hurry. I don't think she has more than this one last shot left in her."

He nodded. He'd felt it also. We both knew the engines were coming apart deep inside. We knew some cylinders were dead. We knew the electrical system throughout the entire airplane was shot, the vacuum system was a joke, the brakes were in the final act of expiring—well, it was a long and sordid list, and the only real question we asked ourselves, so convinced were we that this was the flight west for the old girl, was whether or not to take parachutes, because engine fires were now definitely a real danger. We went against the chutes—and gambled on *Annie* and our ability to get her downstairs in a hurry. I already knew I could dump her onto a road or a cow pasture or a beach if necessary.

But we *planned* for the worst, and that's the key to making it. If you expect things to go wrong, when they do you're only a hair trigger away from the right corrective action. Ours must have been one of the strangest crew briefings ever performed. I got together with Bob and Terry and laid it out. "No passengers and no other crew. Nobody. This to me is a risk flight, and that's all there is to it." They nodded agreement. "Okay. We're loaded up with three hundred gallons. It's two hundred miles to Miami International, so we have plenty of time to stay legal for an alternate with extra fuel, but we're going to Miami if this thing stays together in the air. Our weight will be well down, I've worked it out to eighteen thousand pounds or so, which helps. The brakes are about to go if they haven't already let loose, and we can't count on them. I don't trust those engines. They're dying on us. Which means, among other things, that, once we start our takeoff and really get going, there's no stopping. We're flat committed."

I gestured across the field. "We'll do our takeoff

to the east from the grass overrun. That gives us about a thousand feet, maybe only eight hundred or so, *before* we even reach the paved runway. That's another thirty-six hundred feet and right over the river after that, so no need to climb upstairs in a hurry if we're losing power. If we lose one, we keep flying. If we lose two, we slow down and roll into the river as easy as possible. If we lose three, cut the deck and deal a new hand.

"If we make it off this field okay, we climb right away and we get plenty of altitude before we leave gliding distance of this runway. If we get off and we lose power, we'll stay on the river, right on the deck, and try to use ground effect to get to the golf course in Cocoa Beach and set her down there. If we got enough speed going, we can push it a bit farther, over to Patrick, and visit the Air Force. That's it, then. Bob, I'll make the takeoff and then the airplane is yours."

On the morning of June 17, 1976, we fired her up. She fought coming alive, and deep down inside me I heard a voice saying, "Oh, oh. It's the last shot, all right." She didn't want any more. She was too tired.

"Come on, baby," I whispered. "Just this one last time . . ." and finally all three were turning and I swung around on the grass and, sure as hell, the brakes were going. The right brake was completely gone and the left brake was maybe or yes or no, and you found out only when your foot went hard down on the pedal. We bumped over the grass, moving slowly and carefully, and I did everything I could to hold her with the brakes, but it was no go. Terry climbed outside and put some heavy chocks under the tires and came back in and I did the run-up slowly and carefully. Somehow it all worked, and while the mag drops were a bit on the raggedy side, they were still *just* on the acceptable margins of safety and legality. Out went Terry for the chocks, and we felt the cabin door close, and he came up front, and we checked one more time, flaps down to 25° and trim set at minus 1.5°, and I turned her toward the runway, and by God, I had right brake suddenly, a last-gasp measure that joined with the left and I seized the moment to stand on the brakes and run those engines as hard as they would go, and that's all the brakes gave me, they died, but we were rolling along the grass and I had the tail coming up and three guys were in the cockpit silently saying, "Come on, *come on*, baby, you can do it. . . ." Our speed built ever so slowly

but faster than we realized. The end of the grass strip was coming up, and we already were moving the needle past sixty, which meant we had it made, because there were another three and a half thousand feet beyond that. Just before we reached the end of the grass, a dull explosion shook the airplane; people watching the takeoff saw a huge cloud of black smoke erupt from the nose engine (we never saw it from the cockpit) and stream back. At the last moment, I came back on the yoke, *and before she reached the paved runway Annie was in the air and flying!*

I'll never understand how she could do it. My God, we'd blown two jugs in the nose engine and it was having the worst kind of mechanical spasms up there. By the time we were at the end of the runway I had three hundred feet of altitude in the bank and was cutting a tight turn to the left to stay in close to the field. Bob took over the controls and I sat back to watch and ponder this whole, incredible mess. Bob eased off on the power for a steady climb, and not until we were at four thousand feet over Merritt Island did he turn to the south. The vibration was pretty strong. You could feel it through the entire airplane. It was almost impossible to synchronize the propellers, because the engines were running up and down some insane scale of shifting power, and we played with them all the way. At 7,500 feet, I eased the throttles back to 1,600 rpm and brought the mixture to just enough lean to keep them from running too rough, and I stayed on top of those power controls every instant of the way. What kept me on my toes was the real possibility of an engine fire, but, while she was running hot on all three, they were staying within acceptable limits. I couldn't believe number three wasn't already going through her predetonation ballet. The cool air at 7,500 feet was enough of a difference so that we never did get those internal sonic booms.

The radios were working (although poorly), and the encoding altimeter and the transponder were right on the money. We called in to Miami Approach Control and had some of that back-and-forth routine of what the hell we really were, although we weren't trying for fun and games. Just north of Fort Lauderdale International, they told us to come down to two thousand feet and we pulled the plug, power full back, and let her down at an over-two-thousand-feet-a-minute rate of descent. The vibration was so wild that the instrument panel jerked about, and it got worse, and finally it was so severe we could barely read the instruments. *Annie* was shaking like a rat in a terrier's jaws, and we eased out of that descent. Terry looked as if he expected the nose engine to tear out of its mounts, it had gotten so bad. We brought in some power and that settled things down a bit, and we went to cruise power and flew directly over the center of Lauderdale International at the ordered two thousand feet. It had been one hell of a ride downstairs.

We got Miami tower, and they were sweethearts and set us up for the first in line of a bunch of airplanes. We rolled into downwind for Runway 9L, kept her in tight, and floated down the pike into a wind of twenty knots so that our ground speed was something like fifty-five miles per hour. I flared, she touched just ahead of the numbers, and I rolled off at the second intersection, standing on the left rudder and holding in some power with the right en-

gine. I immediately chopped power and let her roll past the main taxiway to an open area just beyond. Ground Control cleared us to taxi to Aero Facilities, but this was *Annie's* last gasp, and she had given us everything she had. The brakes were completely gone, things were leaking everywhere, and heat rolled over us from the engines. I nodded to Bailey. "Shut her down." Then I requested a tug from Silverio's shop, and Dan Freeman came out and they hooked up to *Annie*. Terry wasn't taking any chances with anybody or anything, and he sat in the tug while I sat on one wingtip and Bob on the other.

We rolled slowly into the big flight ramp at Aero Facilities, and a crowd gathered slowly to watch in silence. It wasn't quite a funeral procession but damned close to it. It was the end of an era. *Annie* would never fly again—the way we had brought her in here.

It was time for the resurrection.

PART FOUR

The Resurrection

I looked at *Iron Annie* within the great hangar of Aero Facilities. Bailey was taking Nick Silverio and Dan Freeman and a small army of mechanics and specialists about and under and over and through and into the airplane. Then we got together for a long session over lunch, and it was time to lay down the ground rules. The first order of business was trust—essentially, between myself and Nick Silverio. Nick ran the outfit at Aero, and he was also an airline pilot and a former executive pilot and a test pilot and he *knew* what I was talking about, so that half of our conversation went unspoken and the rest was really a long list of specific details to meet my personal wants. From that day on, Nick and I have had the closest relationship and, much more important, a deep friendship that gets better every year. The key to all this was that it went far beyond a job or a contract. *Iron Annie* to Nick was a patient that needed convalescence and complete rebuilding. We were doing everything but a bionic transplant of life, and I'm not too sure we didn't get into that as well.

Once Nick and Dan knew what we wanted, they set up their main team, and that was a great token of the future. The team came in the form of Nick Silverio, Dan Freeman, Bob Reed, John Hermann, Harold Cotton, and John Pierce, and they'd strawboss whatever other people would be working on—hold it—*rebuilding* the airplane.

Because that was my basic order. Don't repair it. Either rebuild it to new or put in what *is* new. Modify where necessary. Do whatever is necessary, but do it right, and I want a reliable airplane. Nick and Dan cautioned me that a lot of the work would be groping for a while, because they were working with an unknown.

It was June 17 when we had that meeting, and N52JU wouldn't take to the air again for another five months, but this time there wasn't any guesswork and there wasn't any patching and wiring

things together. An old-timer who'd been in the business for a hundred years by name of Jerry Dobby found us three beautiful Pratt & Whitney R1340-S1H1 engines, along with Grumman Mallard cowls, and we left the accessories up to Dan Freeman, along with the job of customizing the cowls and the exhaust stacks and systems. Paul Gaither, from Aviation Propellers, Inc., who, like Nick and Dan, became a close personal friend and who is probably the leading genius in propellers and their systems in the country, looked at the big bird and disappeared, and when he showed up again it was with diamond-studded equipment in his truck; three paddle-bladed AG-100 constant-speed props made for cropdusting. We would get maximum efficiency from those props. Working out the cable pulleys for the prop controls was going to be a marvel—and the way to start solving that problem and everything else was to completely tear apart the cockpit and start from scratch.

Every piece of wire in that airplane was to be removed. Every scrap. And all the new wiring was to be numbered, and elaborate schematics made of every line. Dan designed a new electrical control panel that went into the cabin just aft of the copilot bulkhead, and it was pure genius. It also gave us a great capacity for adding systems onto the bird as we went along. Nick ordered every electrical part of the airplane custom-made; we were all through with this nonsense of electrical hash driving us mad.

The 1340 engines hung on the mounts as if they'd been customized for the installation, which, when we thought about it, was true, since the BMWs were born from the P&Ws. The cowls were beautiful; we rerouted the wing exhausts to above the nacelle to lower noise output. The Aero Facilities team opened every panel and hatch and crawled through every inch of the airplane. New strobes and new beacons, and Cessna 421 landing

Iron Annie begins her rebirth at Aero Facilities Corporation, at Miami International Airport. She's already stripped of engines and props, one wheel, and much of her innards. AERO FACILITIES

A very happy mechanic for N52JU peers into the soul of a new engine for his big iron bird. AERO FACILITIES

The Pratt & Whitney R1340-S1H1 engines and AG-100 propellers are on the airplane; the work is going beautifully. AERO FACILITIES

The underwing skin and its look of leprosy. More important are those fuel tanks in the wing, checked out as perfect. AERO FACILITIES

lights under the belly for taxi lights. Jim Greenwood, of Gates-Learjet, sent in a Learjet landing light that we modified to fit into our underwing system. Tires were critical, and Harry Gambo, of the Pirelli Tire Company, pulled off a miracle and showed up with two brand-new tires and tubes, which went on the airplane, and Kurt Streit pulled off another miracle by finding 1943-manufactured synthetic tires and tubes (which we're holding for a museum) and had them delivered to us by Lufthansa-Condor.

We found a huge bird's nest in the tail. We found corrosion from former work where mechanics or plumbers or whatever had placed dissimilar metals one against the other, and we sought it all out and rebuilt everything. Inside the wings, we were amazed: the tanks had been skillfully sealed, and the metal and leather straps were in perfect condition. There were some leaks in the lines, but they were easily repaired. Except for the corrosion spots we identified rapidly, and some heavy corrosion inside the right wing flap, the interior metal of the airplane was incredibly clean and in excellent shape.

We had never had brakes, but we were damned well going to have them now, and they were made up of C-46 and B-17 systems, cut down to compensate for the lesser weight of the Ju-52, and they were so great in their effectiveness that Freeman finally cut down the pressure to the system. *Brakes!* Yes, Virginia, there *is* a Santa Claus. . . .

We gave ourselves a new luxury: a DC-6 fuel pump mounted within a forward belly hatch so that we could start the engines without that arm-destroying wobble pump. All we needed to do now was to throw the fuel-pump switch and a green light came on and we had pressure immediately. The inertial starters were discarded and the prop controls put in their place on the quadrant forward right section. We added quadrant starter-booster-primer switches, spring-loaded the system, added starter selector switches, eliminated the mixture system of the German design so that we were always manual lean instead of autorich when coming back on power. We put in a carbon-monoxide detector (electronic) in the cockpit because of the nose engine. Landing the Ju-52 in a heavy rain was always a suicide run, because you couldn't see through that flat windshield. Just drive a jeep at ninety miles an hour in a thunderstorm *without* wipers and you'll know what I mean. So we put in wipers, from an F-4 jet fighter, that worked off the hydraulic pump. We put in all new antennas and brought the avionics up to snuff. Freeman ordered the entire instrument panel ripped out and replaced it with a designed-to-order setup.

We stripped the fuselage down to the base—right to the bare metal—and she gleamed in the sun. As the stripper ate away the old paint, we watched in awe as layer after layer—eight layers of housepaint in all—disappeared, and there was a long moment as a gold eagle appeared on the right side of the fuselage and a huge iron cross on the left, and the big, blood-red swastika on the tail. We scoured the inside with high-pressure steam. All control surfaces were removed, and we ordered every nut, bolt, pin, and wire in that airplane to be brand-new. Nick installed new safety glass in the cockpit, ran lights through the tail cone

so we could *see* the bell cranks and cables at a glance, set up a crew call system of lights and bells, installed an intercom system for the crew. That cockpit was now a dream for night flying, with lights all over the place, and with all the new instruments, *Annie* was fully qualified for instrument flight.

The program was utter simplicity: *zero-time the airplane.* We did a couple of other things the way they should be done: We X-rayed every possible area of weakness, magnafluxed metal, dye-typed, did ultrasonic studies and whatever else was necessary so there wouldn't be any doubts in our minds as to the strength and reliability of the airplane. We stayed in constant touch with Red Gargaly and Jaime Serra and Bill Janca of the Opalocka office of the FAA, and they had a gang of FAA pilots and examiners and inspectors going through the airplane, because they were fascinated by what was going on. They never had to ask a single question, because it was all there, right in front of them, and they knew the rules: *no short cuts, no compromises; do it right.*

Where it was possible, we went to triple redundancy for every system in the airplane and gave ourselves back doors for emergencies should they ever arise. We didn't have to make a single major structural change to the airplane, and that was perhaps the most astonishing fact of all. We did another weight-and-balance and confirmed that we had removed nearly eight hundred pounds of layered old paint. Then we got the original paint scheme of the airplane from the Second World War and painted *Annie* in the colors she once flew.

We'd learned a couple of things in those long months, and Nick Silverio cautioned me that roll-out of the airplane from the Aero Facilities hangar was *not* to be considered the completed job. "When we get done, you're going to have to test the airplane. Take it out and fly her hard. Go through the stall regime and see how she handles and what's changed, and we'll find out what works well and what doesn't work, and we won't consider our job done for at least six months after your first test flight. Because you're dealing with a whole new airplane, a whole new *event* here."

Nick, baby, whatever you say . . . that's the law.

He was right, of course. We had to modify the cable pulleys for the props. Several times, we had a pressure problem inside the governors and the inside pressure blew retaining nuts clear off the en-

Tear it apart completely, rip out every piece of wire, and start over from scratch—the cockpit during restoration. AERO FACILITIES

Checking out details of new engines, props, cowls, wiring, controls—just about everything in the airplane. *Iron Annie* is rolled outside into sunlight for the first time in months. JACK KEHOE

Nick Silverio and Dan Freeman discuss a technical point during the rebirth of the phoenix at Aero Facilities. Most of the repainting by now is completed. AERO FACILITIES

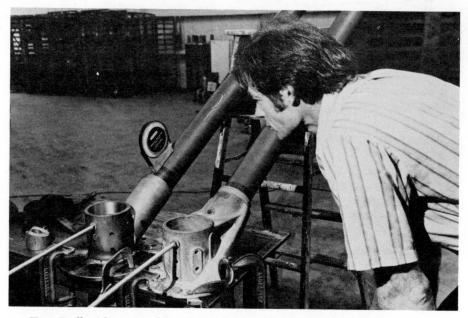

Tom Reilly (the man who makes Silly Putty out of steel) studies the new gear-axle housing for N52JU during part of the Great Restoration Program. PAUL BROWN

Miracle welder John Berndobler and his magic fire welding the units of the new gear-axle housings for *Annie*. PAUL BROWN

gines, but that was on the ground. Paul Gaither grumbled that in all his years of being in this business he'd never heard of anything like it, and even Hamilton Standard was stumped, but Paul got it all straightened out—and it didn't matter where we were, he flew in for on-the-spot, right-now repairs.

After a few weeks of testing, we settled down for some rest. But then my phone rang and it was a very unhappy mechanic on the other end. "You know the gear-axle housings? They've developed some bad cracks in them. They're old and they've been slammed around for so many years, and they're magnesium, and now we're throwing so much torque to them that they just gave way."

I took that one in silence for a while. Finally: "Can we fix them?"

"It's gonna be a bitch. We're working with magnesium and I think it goes all through the units."

Where the hell do you get gear-axle housings? We searched all through Germany and we ran into the same crap with the Spanish we had before and the clouds hung darkly over us, and then Ted Votoe came up with an idea. "Tom Reilly," he said. "In Orlando. He rebuilds planes. He plays with tough metals like they're Silly Putty. Why don't we get him on the problem?"

In the meantime, Nick had been studying various ways of doing the job. We could cast new magnesium housings or machine them out of solid aluminum blocks. The lowest estimates were three to four months and ten to fifteen thousand clams. *Oof.*

Ted Votoe—who has for three years running won our Golden Gopher Award for *always* pulling off the impossible—did it again. The airplane was in Miami and we decided to go all the way with Ted Votoe's *Plan A:* He put together a small gang consisting of Tom Reilly as honcho of the project, Rod Johnson and Ebson Spaulding as machinists, John Berndobler as the welder, Paul Brown as the photographer to record it all, Russ Votoe (Ted's son) as oil squirter and parts holder, and Ted Votoe himself as ultimate gopher and birddog. Terry Ritter watched it happen and, two weeks later, new gear-axle housings of chrome steel, modified to our design for larger end plates, came forth from the magic hands of Tom Reilly and his crew. We took them down to Miami, and Nick Silverio couldn't believe the quality of the workmanship or the fact that it had been done in two weeks. The new housings tested out to 98,000 psi, compared to the 38,000 psi of the original

units. I want to add here that after our repairs to the originals they were stronger than they had been on the airplane, but it wasn't good enough for the new standards.

The original gear-axle housings were built to a strength of 38,000 psi, and the new housings manufactured by the Reilly gang tested out to the unparalleled strength factor of 98,000 psi. Nice to know when you're riding on top of that same system. PAUL BROWN

And that warding off the inevitable? Sooner or later, we would run out of tires. That's all there was to it. We'd scoured the entire world and come up with only that one last set of synthetic tires. We looked into DC-3 tires, because the Swiss Air Force had gone in that direction, but the airplane looked dumpy with those squat, fat tires. "Let's go to C-46 tires," I decided, and Reilly huddled together and talked a lot with Nick Silverio. We then went into another major change to the bird, but one that still retained the authenticity of the airplane, because, as it turned out so conveniently, the Luftwaffe also flew a number of these airplanes with big, wide, and deeply grooved tires—which is precisely what we had with the new, C-46 tires. And they were still manufacturing them and the tubes, and you could buy the tires retreaded or brand-new, and the dark clouds went away.

Nick Silverio had been *so* right: we made our first test flight with the C-46 wheels and tires on August 1, 1977, and we considered this to be the last of the major modifications the airplane needed. Of course, during all this time, from early Novem-

Iron Annie shows off her new gear in taxi tests: new axle housings, new brakes, and those big and rugged C-46 tires. PAUL BROWN

ber of 1976 on, we had been flying *Annie* as she was intended to fly.

The love affair was again going full blast from that first test flight of the rebuilt plane. We had plans for the future. There would be cosmetic changes; we would reinstall the after-fuselage turret and put on some guns and bombs, but hell, that was *fun* time. Right now we were flying, not chained to the ground, not waiting for that inevitable crunching blow. There were all sorts of new words: confidence and sweet thunder and reliability and trust; and it had all begun on November 8, 1976, when the flock gathered in Nick's office for that first test flight.

"See? I told you the impossible would take only a little while longer. . . ." A jubilant Colonel Ted Votoe (left) sharing the joy of a perfect test flight with Martin Caidin. The new gear passed all tests with flying colors. PAUL BROWN

208

We had a lot of catching up to do on that November morning. I took the left seat and Vern Renaud was in the right seat. Our mechanic was riding shotgun as crew chief and flight engineer, and Dee Dee and Bob Bailey (whose hands were itching to get up in the front office) rode as observers. The wind was blustery and gusting to thirty knots at Miami International, but to us it was a beautiful, beautiful day. *Annie* fired up and was running on all three in just under four minutes—compared to the minimum thirty minutes, and the usual hour, it took to bring her to life before. When all the gauges were checked out in the green, I released the parking brake, brought up the throttles just a nudge, letting her roll forward, and then touched the toe brakes and we STOPPED RIGHT NOW. It was almost too much to believe.

I taxied her out carefully through the gate of Aero Facilities, turned left, and rolled to the main taxiway. We slowly worked to the west and into the run-up area for Runway 9L. The winds were so strong that the airplane was rocking on her gear, and I pondered the wisdom of a test flight under these conditions. But what the hell; the professionals had worked this airplane, and even with five months since the last time I'd had my hands on that great yoke, it all fell into place at once. We did the run-up, carefully following the new checklist I'd worked on for two solid days, and we even made a few changes as we went along, which is that old learning process. Then we were done, and after a DC-10 landed on 9R, we were cleared to the active runway and told to hold.

Then came the word to go and I went up on the power, with everyone scanning those gauges with extra care. She was soon screaming at 2,250 rpm and 36 inches. I held the yoke all the way back, let the brakes go, but kept pressure on that right rudder, and she immediately accelerated swiftly. Her song of power was like nothing I'd ever heard be-

fore. The tail came up by itself. I had full aileron into the wind and full rudder, but it was getting a bit rough holding her on the centerline. The tires were complaining with the sideloads, but we already had eighty-five and I popped the yoke sharp, just a hair, and she was instantly in the air. I let her crab, and down that runway we went, climbing at eight hundred feet a minute, and it was gorgeous. The air was rough and I couldn't have cared less, because this was the way to find it all out, baby, and *Annie* was running like the biggest damn Swiss watch with a zillion jewels you ever saw. I took her up to Pompano Beach and felt out various power settings and followed the advice from Nick and Dan and Paul and the rest of the crew and she behaved as if she'd just come out of finishing school.

She was slippery compared to before, she didn't bleed off her speed as quickly, and she demanded a whole new mental attitude in landing—because with that great big cowling out there I had a tendency to kick her into a crab before touchdown so I could see, but that's a no-no, and the first landing was a bounce off the one wheel. (We *all* did that; every pilot who flew her screwed up that first one.) I did a bunch of takeoffs and landings, and by the fourth time around the patch, I had come to *know* the airplane. I switched seats with Vern Renaud, and he was like a pianist, flexing his fingers and grinning from one ear to the other. He did three around the patch for his official checkout of the airplane for his rating in the Ju-52 as pilot-in-command, and she was honey under his hands. We stooged around some more and changed seats again and with about fifteen landings under our belt brought her back to the barn at Aero Facilities. There were about a dozen minor glitches to attend to, and the specialists stayed on the bird to attend to them before morning.

On November 9 we all piled in again. I took the

The all-new, rebuilt, restored, gleaming, and wonderful *Iron Annie* comes on down the pike for her first landing back at Miami International Airport after the test-flight program by Martin Caidin and Vern Renaud. PAUL BROWN

One picture is worth a thousand words . . . the look on Martin Caidin's face after the first test flight shows it all. NICK SILVERIO

left seat for takeoff, Bob Bailey in the right seat, and as passengers we had Vern, Larry, Dee Dee, and the irrepressible Major Frank Urbanic, who'd flown down from Patrick Air Force Base just to see how the new girl on the block performed. On the way home, we stayed at 3,000 feet for a while. I was pulling 28 inches and 1,900 rpm and we were getting a true air speed of 142 mph. You could play with combinations of manifold pressure and rpm, and if you didn't mind burning extra fuel she'd give you an honest 153 mph, but I ran the engines at what Nick said was a good working level of 1,850 rpm and 26 inches, and *Annie* would indicate 120 mph. She would do this at a thousand feet, and if you took her up to 6,500 feet she would still be indicating 120 to 125, so we were getting comfortable cross-country cruise of 145 to 150 true.

We could still boot her in the rear, which sometimes we had to do when we flew with heavy fighters in the air shows. On one huge gaggle over Lakeland at eight thousand feet they were screaming for more speed and I kept inching her up to high cruise, which was drinking fuel at a very rapid clip but still wasn't slamming the engines, and we were holding 170 mph true while the fighters flew off our wing and performed for the cameramen.

It got more and more difficult to recall what a laborious chore it had been to climb to seven thousand feet in the "old" bird. Jack Kehoe and I took her off one morning from Vero Beach for a realistic cross-country cruise climb—in other words, we wouldn't beat the engines to death but would climb at 2,100 rpm and 32 inches and indicate a steady 100 mph, thereby covering distance as well as going for altitude. It keeps the engines cool and it gets you started cross country. *Annie* went up to that 8,000 feet in 13 minutes and 41 seconds from takeoff and she wasn't even breathing hard. We let her climb on to 9,000 feet and then went to overboost, and in the climb—34 inches and 2,100 rpm—we were climbing steadily with an indicated air speed of 120 mph! That worked out to staying in the climb with an air speed of over 140 mph. Neat-o.

An old friend joins up for some escort flying northward along the Florida coastline: Don Whittington in his gleaming Messerschmitt Me-109G *Gustav*. DEE DEE CAIDIN

Bob Bailey in the front office of *Iron Annie;* he and the big iron bird had a neat way of talking with one another, and N52JU flew like a dream under his hands. VERN RENAUD

Let me digress here and move ahead for many months until the present, referring to the aircraft log to show the kind of problems we had—because they were the normal, everyday, prosaic problems of any big airplane, *and not one of them required a major fix,* and we're talking about a period of eighteen months. It shows what professional work will do and what TLC from the flight crew sustains.

In November, we had a leaking prop seal on the nose engine; repaired within three hours. In March of 1977, the radios began giving us some hash and we took the bird to Sebastian Communication, at Melbourne Regional Airport, and that avionics gang did a marvelous job. We were using Narco radios, David Clarke headsets, and Shure mikes, and the Sebastian crowd tweaked everything to the

211

A stunning example of airborne longevity: the Ju-52/3m is now N52JU, having begun its flying career in 1935—forty-three years before this picture was taken! STEVE ROCK, U. S. NAVY

Starting the flare at Merritt Island—about to touch down on home plate. KEN BUCHANAN

same impedance so that we were getting the kind of quality you expect from a 747, and our communications have been superb ever since.

There wasn't a single major discrepancy recorded from that point on, and in late July 1977, we took the airplane back to Aero Facilities for her annual inspection and new FAA papers. She passed everything with flying colors, although our departure from Miami International was fun and games. A mechanic working in the wing had unknowingly kicked open the static-line petcock, and when we took off I stared at an air-speed indicator that wasn't moving.

"Call out the air speed!" I shouted to Vern.

"You call it out! I ain't got none!" he shouted back, and he was laughing, because he'd figured out at the same moment what most likely had happened. What the hell, we knew the bird, so we took her up to fifty-five hundred and brought her into Merritt Island as if we knew what we were doing, without any air-speed indications. We repaired it in ten minutes.

On August 7, we ran into a serious problem; heavy vibration of the prop on number three, and it cracked the cowling bull ring. Paul Gaither came up and found a blade that had slipped. He took the prop back to his shop, repaired it, and it was back on the airplane in three days. Then Red Gargaly came up from Opa-locka and we went out for a toot and he had the time of his life shutting down engines one after another, and *Annie* answered the helm with only firm but gentle rudder pressure and

Red was as delighted as a kid, because this airplane was also *his* baby, and having him fly that thing around for a couple of hours was music floating down from the clouds.

September 8, 1977: Number-two engine oil-pressure gauge fluctuated badly; made precautionary landing. Faulty gauge.

October 29, 1977: Pulled the main wheels for servicing and inspection. No problems. Packed the bearings.

November 9, 1977: We had been flying the airplane *hard* and it was time for some TLC. The log entry shows: "Engine number one RPM and MP gauges replaced. Pilot and copilot altimeters changed. All three engines given 100-hour inspection—okay. Propellers given 100-hour inspection—okay. Taxi light brackets replaced and installation strengthened. Left nacelle dipstick system overhauled. Aircraft fully checked for replacement rivets, screws, and fasteners wherever necessary. All three engine cowls reinforced with anti-vibration braces. Top left and top right windshield replaced. All engines tightened for preventive maintenance."

The entry was signed off by Homer Smith, Jr., IA ⚡1265060.

Nothing is ever left to chance; N52JU flies on fuel, oil, power, and a lot of TLC from Martin Caidin (left). PAUL BROWN

It's more than a new cockpit—it's a whole new world "up front" with *Iron Annie*. And there are more goodies always being installed. KEN ROWLEY

Oberschutzer Larry von Urback and his magic transformation of the cabin of N52JU—padded, plush, and comfortable. KEN ROWLEY

November 26, 1977: Full day for aircraft TLC. Battery terminals replaced. Battery vent tube replaced. Notation that number-one engine rpm gauge was fluctuating (it was the gauge).

Then we ran into those cracked cowlings again, and the entry for December 1, 1977, reads: Repaired cracked lower cowling lip of number-one engine; patchwork, sheet-metal work performed. Joe Bean came out to Merritt Island to do the work.

And so it went—maintenance and preventive maintenance and modifications and far less than the normal load of repairs. We cut all three engine bull rings from solid units to sections of 120 degrees each to take the torque loads off the cowlings, and the vibration lessened. We removed the big T-6 spinners and some more vibration left us, and we were flying smoother than ever before. We had to replace systems, because we were using them so much. We changed the wingtip strobe power packs, replaced the expander tube of the left brake, added protective plates to the brake area, and had to repair the cable pulley for the number-two prop control in the cockpit.

We added things: The gang built a heavy new thick-gauge aluminum stairway and modified the bottom fuselage to slide it in and out smoothly and lock it into place. They added cross braces wherever we found any sign of weakening. We kept a constant check for corrosion, because the airplane rested on the ground in a high-salt environment.

We decided, in January of 1978, to start the cosmetic work. *Oberschutzer* Larry Urback—who kept insisting he was the gunner of the airplane pending the arrival of the turret and machine gun —with Ted Votoe tore out the entire cabin. They stripped it down to its intestinal framework, tore out the aluminum siding and overhead, removed the seats and stripped the *Krappenhausen.* They cleaned everything out of the cabin. They installed an eight-track tape player and a cassette player and an FM radio and eight speakers in the cabin. Then they packed fireproof glass-wool insulation all through the cabin sides and along the overhead. Over this went the aluminum sheeting, only this time it was riveted back into place instead of being screwed in. Over the aluminum went foam-rubber insulation, and over that went Naugahyde, fire-resistant, camel-colored, and gorgeous. Ted Votoe brought new carpeting for the bird.

They sandblasted and cleaned all the metalwork of the seats, primed them, repainted them. Any weak points were welded and repaired. Every window was as clear as a new-born day. The window frames were taken home by Patricia Barden and she did some impossible jobs of molding them into soft and leathery shapes, and then they went back into the airplane. The seats were returned to the bird, and when you stepped inside now it was into a clean, beautiful cabin with muffled sound and the vibration in flight damped down to less than half what it had been before.

Not everything worked out the way we wanted. We discovered that while Urback could perform miracles on his cabin restoration job, he was no expert at installing stereo systems, and after that was all done, we got Ken Rowley to come aboard and rebuild the electronic music boxes.

Eminent members of the Flying Pumphouse and Locomotive Gang: *Oberschutzer* Larry von Urback (right) with an old flying buddy of some twenty years, Martin Caidin. PAUL BROWN

There were so many other things. Smoke-oil tanks were installed in the wings and chatter pumps, so we could stream thick smoke for air shows. We put sliding safety-glass windows in the two cabin doors and another in the *Krappenhausen.* The air flows a lot better in there now. The intercom system kept getting modified until it was as nearly perfect as possible, and—

Well, that's enough for the hardware. But all these changes added up to other and far more impressive elements of the aircraft. The safety factor is a hundred times what it was before. Two-engine

Sliding down the chute and flaring out at Ti-Co Airport—a whole new airplane and a whole new ball game. PAUL BROWN

takeoffs can be performed as normal procedure, so flying on two is a breeze. We have *brakes*. We're fully equipped and certified for IFR flying, and everyone who has flown her has exclaimed about her extraordinary stability. When we start up, it's do the preflight by the book, kick the tires, climb aboard, *and just fire her up*. Those hysterical gymnastics are a thing of the past.

When we loaded up the bird before, we flew her *very* carefully. You had to, because she was so bloody heavy not only in weight but in response to the controls. No longer.

Understand that we were still flying with the same power with which this airplane flew in 1932. Don't attribute this to enormous power tacked on to N52JU. We get 600 horsepower from each of those engines, compared to 660 for the BMW 132E models, and the production transports in the last years of the war were flying with 830 horsepower in each engine. We were flying beautifully with an ancient machine with less power than it had on its

first Lufthansa routes and we were flying the hell out of it.

You don't fly big airplanes without absolute attention to weight-and-balance and your center of gravity. Aero Facilities did the job for us, and when it was all done I asked Ron Skipper as an airline captain to spell it out on another worksheet that would answer all questions on a single page. When he got through with his computer, he shook his head in delight and handed me the worksheet:

The Ju-52/3m-g8eS, N52JU, configuration as of 6 December 1976 is nearly impossible to load out of CG limits. Any reasonable effort to distribute baggage and/or cargo will yield the CG within proper limits. Only by loading the aircraft with crew, no passengers, and over 500 pounds baggage/cargo in the forward floor compartment will a CG result that is outside the forward limits (all calculations consider full fuel). Under these adverse conditions as stated, it requires only 50 pounds weight in the

216

rear baggage compartment to return the CG to proper limits. The aircraft cannot be loaded outside rear limits unless rear baggage weight restrictions are exceeded, passengers are seated in the three rearmost seats and no baggage is loaded in any forward compartments. *Ronald G. Skipper, ATR ⚹ 1429879.*

If we load the airplane with 620 gallons fuel, 60 gallons oil, 15 gallons hydraulic fluid, 12 gallons smoke oil, add twelve people with an average weight each of 170 pounds, carry 40 pounds of luggage for each passenger, add 300 pounds of tools and other equipment (and consider the heavier C-46 wheels and tires), at takeoff, with the Ju-52 stuffed, we're still a thousand pounds *below* our maximum permissible gross weight.

To get into trouble with this airplane, you'd have to work overtime—and the odds are you still couldn't do it. Just consider the permissible gross overload for a ferry flight, crew and no passengers.

The airplane is completely controllable and safe with a certified legal weight of over 25,400 pounds.

And the Germans flew them at over 30,000 pounds.

They're three years older—but the airplane is forty years younger. Martin Caidin and Sam Bothwell going over the "new" N52JU. KEN BUCHANAN

It's like *The Last Hurrah*. Ring out the old and enjoy the hell out of the new, because, damn it, *we did it*. The agony with its liberal sprinklings of ecstasy had been dragged a long way through the skies with us. It was so difficult to remember that when we flew cross country we used to ask airport personnel to drive down the runway to pick up pieces of the airplane that fell off on the takeoff roll and send them on to our final destination.

The phoenix had risen from its corrugated ashes, the scabs scraped away, the corrosion cleansed, shining new armor sprayed and baked onto the skin, and in truth the winged creature was reborn. Behind us were high times and adventure, explo-sions and fire, equipment that failed and failed and failed again. We never took off without waiting for the inevitable crunch that—

Hey, that was yesterday. A million years ago. We have a new airplane. The dream was realized; it was all true. It had been impossible and we had done the impossible. *Resurrection!*

Now was the time to *fly*. We became the barnstormers of the modern day. There were big air shows, and small ones, too, and get-togethers and bashes and hoorahs and county fairs and barbecues with bluegrass foot-stomping music, and high rendezvous with fighters and bombers and even a lot of plain old unfancy flying just for the hell of it. At

Down the home stretch for an air-show landing at the Valiant Air Command at Ti-Co Airport—history relived in the air. PAUL BROWN

Iron Annie visits the Flying Tigers Air Museum, at Kissimmee Airport, near Disney World, and gets a lot of grooming. KEN BUCHANAN

the air shows, *Annie* thundered inches over a runway and hauled up in a zoom climb at three thousand feet a minute to the swelling roar and cheers of the crowd.

We won a bunch of awards as the best-restored warbird and the best of various multiengine classics, and we appreciated those but we never went looking for them, because what we had done and the way we flew were their own reward. Larry Urback learned how to fly, and he's racked up over a hundred hours on the controls of a three-engine corrugated giant. He and *Annie* developed a language all their own, and whenever she ached or had a hurt here or there she found some way to tell him and it was given immediate attention. You never saw an airplane that thrived so well on old-fashioned TLC. We refused to do things in a hurry, because *Annie* had taken all these decades and crossed oceans and continents to get where she was, with us, and there wasn't nobody going to make us hustle to *their* tune.

We flew when we wanted, and that was that.

We flew old German pilots and Americans and Israelis and Japanese and Arabians and Cubans and Canadians and Danes and Norwegians and Poles; they came from Argentina, Australia, the Philippines, France, South Africa, and more places than I can remember, to fly in *Annie* or join me on the controls. Many of these people had once fought to kill each other and *Iron Annie* became a meeting ground—sometimes as high as ten thousand feet—for former foes, who clasped hands and banged shoulders and hugged one another in the common language of the airman.

Heinz Manthau came down from Canada. In 1937, he had earned his Luftwaffe pilot's wings and badge, and he had a silver stickpin of that badge he had carried all this time. He sat quietly in *Annie*'s cockpit for a long time, remembering when he had flown the Me-109 against our fighters and the Me-163B rocket fighter against our bombers and had had the hell knocked out of him while at the controls of a Ju-52. When he got up, he handed that Luftwaffe badge to me, and I took it to Ted Anderson, who framed it in a golden Maltese Cross and I wear it now about my neck as a great honor.

We've flown with the Thunderbirds and the Blue Angels and we've jumped the Golden Knights and a whole brace of skydivers, and astronauts have climbed into the right seat with me and grinned uncontrollably at the delight they found. Seven-four-seven captains and fighter jocks who push F-15s have taken the yoke in their hands and I've watched their eyes shine with wonder at it all. We—

Hold it. Let's do it by the numbers, by referring to the logbook to establish the dates, and sort of go with the events of each moment as they happened. Not all of them, of course, because there was so much flying done just because we wanted to and we couldn't stay ourselves from the siren call. But the highlights, and that way you can join with us as *Annie* changed the lives of so many hundreds and then thousands of people and became a new bridge to span the oceans between continents.

November 1976, and the *new Iron Annie* had six hours under her cowlings, and it was time to hie off to Kissimmee, in central Florida, for their annual whoop-to-do air show. Rick Grissom sent out the invitations, and we all went off to the manicured airfield set in the midst of lush green country. A mob of more than a hundred thousand people came out to see history re-created on the wing. We did our first takeoff before a large group of friends who remembered the "old days." We deliberately let *Annie* drag herself into the air and creep painfully over distant trees far off the runway. No one was surprised, because they expected it. I then brought *Annie* around, set her down gently, and let her roll to a stop on the runway directly before the main crowd. Larry had the flaps back to 25° and I set the trim at minus 1.5°, and while the announcer wove his spellbinding tale of this ancient winged dinosaur defying death at every movement, I stood on the brakes and we poured the coal to *Annie*. With a twenty-knot wind driving right down that runway, the tail went up while we were

Crewman atop the left wing—adding lots of go juice to the tanks. KEN BUCHANAN

Air-show takeoff at Kissimmee—eleven fighters are following. U. S. AIR
FORCE

still standing still. I popped the brakes, and Larry hit the smoke system, and within five hundred feet we were in the air and going upstairs at a healthy clip. I got ninety-five in the bank and racked her around tight. *Annie* has the ability, especially with that flap setting, of being able virtually to pivot about her center of gravity. A sort of stomp-the-rudder-and-let-her-go maneuver. She just seems to swap ends. The crowd stared in disbelief as the cow became a great swan.

We climbed to eight hundred feet and got the flaps up and Kerwin was screaming at everyone to STICK TO THE DAMNED SCHEDULE AND KEEP IT IN TIGHT, AND YOU FIGHTERS, COME AROUND AND WE ARE WAITING FOR THE T-6S AND WILL YOU GUYS MOVE IT! We used Leo as a perfect measuring device to tell how the air show was going. The louder he yelled and the more frustrated he became the better we knew we were really keeping it in there, all the way on the money. This was also the first time the T-6 drivers had flown an air show with the *new Iron Annie* and I just couldn't resist the temptation to show off.

Jack Kehoe called it out for the Jaybirds, as the crowd of T-6 and SNJ pilots had named themselves. "Okay, Ju-52, we're in position for you to

start your turn now. We'll keep our turn wide and give you lots of room."

I nodded to Larry, and he'd been waiting for this moment, and we went full bore on the props and balls to the wall on the throttles. *Annie* bellowed with power, and then I was doing what I like best in this lovable corrugated beast. To take her in tight, and I mean real tight, and at these speeds, you have to fly this airplane with all the strength you possess. That has got to be one of the greatest, the most sensational feelings in flying I've ever known. To throw all your weight and all your strength into the controls, to ram your foot against the rudder, straining until you cramp, to take the yoke in both hands and strain until your neck and shoulder muscles bulge and the sweat soaks your body, to feel that great airplane pound and hammer from the strain and hear the engines and props scream. The wind roar becomes a physical blow, and every chop of air and turbulence is magnified many times over, and you've got to fly it on the money, because you're on the deck and arrowing downward, and the fighters and T-6s are coming in tight and there are a hundred thousand people down there, and whoo-whee but *that's flying!*

The T-6s had been on my butt like a bunch of nursemaids, but they hadn't yet flown with the Sil-

221

verio special. So just as Larry answered my nod with full bore and I was stamping with everything I had on the left rudder, and pushing the yoke far over and forward, I called out as calmly as you please on the radio, "You people in those Sixes better move it. The fifty-two is coming around and we don't want to lose you."

As expected, loud guffaws and yuk-yuks followed that announcement. With her nose down, *Annie* went right through 160 and through the turn at 180, and soon the needle hung at 200 mph. It was then we heard the loveliest words of all: *"Hey, you guys! Slow down in that thing!"* and we whooped and hollered, because those were words we

Air show! Skydivers have cleared the Ju-52 to open the Valiant Air Command Air Show at Ti-Co Airport, and now the fighters and hot trainers are "roaring in for the kill." Smoke tears back from the special tanks of the left engine of *Iron Annie.* PAUL BROWN

thought we would *never* hear from a crowd of hot-rocks. We tore across the crowd line wide open and hauled *Annie* up in a wicked climb. The zoom came in at about 3,000 feet per minute and I eased her out with 100 on the gauge—my absolute minimum air speed for easing out of a pullup maneuver is that 100—and we were at a thousand feet and headed backside down the field.

Before the day was out, we were flying a strange formation with Sonny Peacock—he in his illustrious Tiger Moth, its rag biplane wings gaily adorned in RAF colors, the engine puttering and chittering away and Sonny resplendent in his leather helmet and goggles and long white scarf—and *Annie* with 25 degrees flaps down to hang in there with him.

Our last formation flight that day was strung out with a bunch of T-6s and a crowd of P-51s, Dennis Bradley from the Canadian Warplane Heritage in his gorgeous Corsair, a B-25, a B-26, that P-40N, a gaggle of T-34s, a Bearcat, and some other old war wings. George Baker came by in Doug Clark's T-33, and the Valiant Air Command was showing its stuff, on the low scale with the Tiger Moth at 50 mph and the T-33 whistling by at 500 mph. Not bad; a ten-to-one ratio in the speed game.

November 25, 1976 FAA flight. This is supposed to be work?

December 23, 1976 Air-show practice (one day of many) with smoke runs, bombing attacks, fighter co-ordination, test maneuvers, show-routine practice, and more practice. It began to rain and you never know when you're going to fly an air show in the rain, so we kept it up another two hours and finished the day hot and sweaty and muscles tight and laughing and pouring beers over heads.

New Year's Day, 1977 What better way to start off a new year? Patrick Air Force Base tower was bored stiff with nothing to do and we asked about some low passes. They said sure, so we beat up the field and used it for target practice for an hour, stopping traffic on the highway.

January 14, 1977 Bob Parke, managing editor and publisher of *Flying* magazine, went up with us on a flight down the Florida coast and he was still walking about two inches off the ground when we last saw him. . . .

January 21, 1977 On to the big air bash of the Experimental Aircraft Association, and the Warbirds of America, and the Valiant Air Command at the huge Sun 'n' Fun Fly-In at Lakeland Airport, in Florida, where *Annie* would cop a bunch of awards that were so generously bestowed by EAA. On the way over, we talked to McCoy Jetport tower at Orlando and they thought a low pass would be neat. We smoked across the runway and left everyone gaping and wandered on to Lakeland for three days of having-a-blast time. The blast was somewhat subdued by a bitter cold wave that froze everyone half to death, but there were compensations in our flying, and floating about in balloons (between which our P-40N weaved with stark attention), and a lot of air-show work and some heavy formation stuff for the TV cameras. Nick Silverio came up from Miami and that was an old home week of the first order.

Especially the last Big Formation Pass. Now we were really strung out, with the Ju-52 in the lead holding about 130 miles per hour, with the fighters way back and planning to come in with their greater speed so we'd all be bunched together as we passed directly over the field. By actual count, we had seven T-6s, five Mustangs, one B-26 and two B-25 bombers, Silberman and Hinyub in their DC-3,

Bradley in his Corsair, a couple of T-28s, and some T-34s. All told, there were about two dozen warbirds in this big damned formation. Just as we were coming onto the field perimeter I gaped.

Directly before us were four skydivers floating down into the formation, and those poor bastards were trying to snake their way frantically up their shroud lines, because there wasn't a doubt in the world they'd float right into the middle of us. They were too low to cut away their mains and come down by reserve. For a split second I just could not believe what I was seeing. Then it all happened automatically. "Emergency from the Ju-52. All fighters break immediately to the right, all trainers break to the left, bombers and transports pull up and then follow the fighters, the Ju-52 is turning left, we have jumpers in the air. Everybody form up over the lake five miles to the east. . . ." We did and we came in again and it went fine, and that afternoon those skydivers sent over a couple of cases of very cold beer for the crew of *Annie*.

Prosit!

There was a lot of other flying through February and into early March. A bunch of the guys wanted

Every air show and every appearance of the VAC gang bring out the news people and their cameras; *Annie*'s already an internationally known "star." PAUL BROWN

to have an undisturbed hearts card-playing contest, so we set up some tables and took them up to sixty-five hundred feet and the game went on for three and a half hours!

March 4, 1977 We were in Miami International taking leave of the Silverio Silver Bullet Service when the cloud deck came down low and went to broken, and Jack Kehoe sat by my side, rubbing his hands together with gleeful anticipation. "Can I file IFR, huh? Huh? Can I? Huh, huh?" I looked at this grown man, husband, father, respected business-man, outstanding pilot, a friend so close he was my brother, and he sat there grinning and drooling like the hunchback of Notre Dame, and I rolled my eyes and said, "Sure. Have at it." Jack was already checked out as pilot in the Ju-52 and he had been slavering for this moment. He got Center on the radio and filed his flight plan, and there was that long silence when he gave the specific identification of the airplane and someone in Center got snotty and Jack chortled and shot back:

"That's affirmative. Three-engine German bomber. Type is Junkers, and you pronounce that as *Yonker*. The designation is Juliet Uniform Fife Too Tree Mike Gold Ait Echo Sierra and the registration is November Fife Too Juliet Uniform."

And that, dear friends, is just how you do it with the internationally accepted phonetic alphabet. We got immediate clearance and Jack boomed out of Miami International on 9L and jumped her right into the lowest and nearest cloud he could find. The base was at eight hundred feet and went up to four thousand, with shafts of blue sky every now and then, but we simply popped right through them, and Jack Kehoe was doing everything but dance on that seat. He kept shouting that he couldn't believe the stability, and he loved the way those great wings would just absorb the turbulence in the rising cumulus. For the next hour and a half, he plunged into every cloud he could find until I finally told him it was time to go downstairs and land. How a Polack can do an Irish jig I don't know—but Jack Kehoe was the first.

March 19, 1977 There were kids who'd been thrown out of homes, there were orphans, boys and girls of all ages, and they brought them out to Melbourne Regional Airport, along with their foster parents and other kids. It was a tiring and long day, but *Iron Annie* took up one hundred and forty-one of them for the times of their lives and a tour of the coastal area and a fascinating look from the air of Cape Canaveral and the Kennedy Space Center.

March 25, 1977 Sonny Peacock has a beautiful ranch and a couple of airstrips at the Peacock Citrus and Cattle Ranch, to the west of the Fort Pierce area, and we were all on our way down to a big air show at Fort Lauderdale Executive (to assist in raising funds for a special boys' school), where the whole Valiant Air Command would meet with other warbirds and commercial acts and the Blue Angels—a thumping to-do of the first order. *Annie* had four T-6s in formation, and we went down to the deck and separated, and the T-6s fanned out and hit that ranch as if it was Battleship Row at Pearl Harbor, and everyone came running through the doors at the shattering roar, and we timed it just perfectly, for as they were looking at the T-6s pulling up, the Ju-52 came in from the opposite direction right on the deck and both engines smoking and I understand they had to replace a couple of windows and put a lot of pictures back on the walls and Sonny's housekeeper packed her bags and quit without saying so much as—well, whatever.

It was quite an air show—the Valiant Air Command helped raise more than twenty-three thousand dollars *net* for the boys' school, and I had a running list of copilots for the air work that started out with Dee Dee, whose seat was taken by her father, Chick Autry; and then Pete Sherman, who was driving a Mustang at the show, took over. Later, Sam Powell, an old friend who flew Thunderbolts in World War II, climbed into the seat, and we made some more flights. He was followed by Gerhard Hopf, a top German ace. One of our passengers was an old friend of Hopf's, the chief of Israeli Intelligence. It was quite a happy hassle.

We flew a mob of air shows and special flight presentations during the next two months, and Dee Dee had a chance to get in some good work at the controls and she wasn't white-knuckled any more when I sat back with a cigar and she went roaring down the runway. We did a lot of formation flying with Rick Thompson at the controls of his Harvard and Russ Munson, in the back seat, shooting three hours of color for a big photo spread in *Flying* magazine. We flew movie scenes for public-service television, we had a blast with Eduardo Ferrer, a captain for Eastern Airlines, who brought along one of the most gracious women I have ever met— Maria, his wife—and who became instant friends

No, it's not a wartime evacuation. Crew member rides atop the cockpit to clear the way through the crowd during a VAC air show. Smoke from exploding "bombs" and rocket blasts drifts across the runway. BOB REID

with Dee Dee's mother, Donna, and that led to Cuban dinners that had us all prostrate for two days.

There was a lot of practice work in here, flying formation with everything from a Cessna O-2, black as Hades itself, with Bill Grace on the controls, to fighters and trainers and even homemade biplanes. Practice, practice, and more practice, and you can't ever get enough of that. Early in May, we were making practice flights with the main cabin door removed from the aircraft to see how she'd behave when dropping skydivers.

I wasn't prepared for the change, and I guess it was because of the angled wing-engine installation, but even though we didn't get any real air blast inside the cabin—in fact, you could light a cigarette in the open door—*something* was acting like an air brake and it extended our takeoff roll by a good 30 per cent over that of normal. It puzzled me, but okay, I knew what she would do under those conditions and we got ready for our first jumps on the coastline of Florida. We flew to Dunn Airpark, near the space center, and about twenty-three hundred feet of that runway was usable. But that's deceptive.

This would be one of the toughest tests to which both myself and the airplane would be put. We approached from the south and the air was dead calm. There wasn't a blade of grass stirring for miles. The temperature didn't help: 96° F. And I did not like the 60-foot-high trees on the south approach to the runway, nor the power lines and houses on the opposite runway end, which you would have to face for any go-around.

I came in at only 70 mph, holding her steady, a lot of power in there because of the heat, and coming down in a steep descent. You can drop *Annie* like that and flare her *very* carefully onto her main gear with the tail low. But the combination of heat and calm was producing a husky updraft from that area of treeline, and when we hit it, to keep from gaining altitude I went even farther down with the nose. The result of all this was the first go-around I've ever done with *Annie* as we hit that small runway, indicating 110 mph and that was with full flaps. One look at what was left of the tongue depresser of a runway and I never hesitated and was full-bore on the throttles. *Annie* hit the deck and was up again so fast that observers—including my wife—thought it was a deliberate touch and go. It wasn't. I came around again, this time fishtailing from side to side to kill off the speed, and the mains grabbed runway smack on the numbers. Immediately to hard braking action and full back on

225

Lyle Goodin in perfect drop position immediately upon jumping from the Ju-52. His target, three thousand feet below, is the white dots—boats in the Indian River, during an M3 Razzle Dazzle hydroplane show.
FALLING STARS

the nose to keep from tipping down, and still *I didn't think we'd stop in time.* "Hang on!" I yelled. "There's open field to the left of the runway and I'm gonna groundloop her there!" Had it all figured out, and I must have had the world's number-one blank stare on my face when *Annie* brought her tail down and stopped at the second of three turnoffs—with eight hundred feet of runway still before us!

We took ten jumpers up to three thousand, and the takeoff was interesting. Regular short-field procedures, and I didn't like it, but everyone else who was either riding in the iron bird or watching from the ground described the moment as a spectacular climbout, with the big airplane going up like an elevator. The jumpers must have been accustomed to dragging their wheels through rooftops, because it seemed awfully low to me, but they thought the idea of rooftops three hundred feet below the wheels at the end of the runway was incredible.

Now, this first jump with Lyle Goodin and his gang had an interesting aspect to it. My friend of some twenty years Larry Urback (who flew at various times as flight engineer or gunnerless gunner and who was to rebuild the cabin) had sworn he would be the first to jump *Annie*. So he made four static-line jumps at Dunn Airpark, and then went out of a Cessna 182 for his fifth static leap—which

he concluded by breaking his leg on landing. Larry is a very determined cat, and gritting his teeth, he limped to the men's room, where he tied up his leg in masking tape and clothesline and limped back to the Cessna 182 for his first free-fall—which he made with a broken leg. He was the only one to know it, of course—Lyle would have beaten him around the head and shoulders with a two-by-four if he'd known. Larry made his sixth jump, which was his first free-fall, and landed on that busted leg.

Then he faked a big grin under his mop of red hair, lied to everyone, and laughingly cried, "I'm scared! Carry me aboard!" and all us idiots did just that, unaware he could no longer walk. At thirty-five hundred feet, irritated by a feeling he couldn't identify, Lyle okayed Larry to be first out of the Ju-52, but with a static line, and out went the red-haired Polack, *to land for the second time that day on a broken leg.* The rest of the gang went out free fall.

Annie has a strange effect on people, as this incident with Urback testifies. The Polish Prince wore a heavy cast for the next four months. . . .

May 28, 1977 Another rip-roaring air show for three days and the Valiant Air Command was out in full strength at Ti-Co Airport. *Annie* dropped skydivers, flew bomber attacks, made strafing runs, did exhibition short-field takeoffs and landings,

Warbirds of the Valiant Air Command lined up for inspection before the first flight of an air show. Living history about to take wing. PAUL BROWN

Colonel El Supremo His Magnificent Leo Kerwin, commander of the Valiant Air Command, briefs the Pumphouse Gang pilots for the exacting and demanding formation flying of an air show. STEVE ROCK, U. S. NAVY

carried over three hundred people for demonstration flights, and got torched. On our last bombing run—Mike Ross, deputy director of the Kennedy Space Center, was in the right seat with me—our pyrotechnics specialist put everything he had remaining from the show into one mighty blast, which was set off on signal as we came overhead at five hundred feet for the bombing run. The blast wave slammed us all down into our seats as the airplane was slammed in the other direction— up—and we had a wonderful view of a spectacular fireball tearing way up above us as it climbed past our wing. Very interesting. . . .

The hours kept piling up and the flying was marvelous, and then two friends, Fred Gay and Bubba Sutton, called to ask if I'd take up George Plimpton on a local flight that was designed to attract news attention to our local county. If Brevard County could survive the *Iron Annie* Pumphouse Gang, I guess it could handle George Plimpton, and at the end of our hassling the county from the air we were at five hundred feet, under Melbourne tower control, circling a balloon with apprehensive friends waving a bit timidly at us, when Plimpton asked about the switch marked SMOKE. We explained what it was to him.

"Does Bubba know about this?" he asked.

"Uh uh."

"Can we use it?"

"Sure. Let me call the tower first so they won't wonder what's going on when people phone in about a burning airplane." Melbourne tower

"Ve haff vays of makingk you vly tight vormation!" Underneath the satin shirt and silk tie, the pilot's glasses and Cherman helmet and the cigar is the usually drunken mascot of *Iron Annie*: Super Heiniedog. RUSS VOTOE

A Canadian Harvard flies formation with a "stricken" *Iron Annie*. PAUL BROWN

George Baker and Doug Clark taxi out to begin the jet fighter flight of the Valiant Air Command warbird air bash. PAUL BROWN

thought it was a neat idea, and Plimpton hit the smoke switches and Bubba swallowed his necktie, his drink, and most of his glass before he realized no one else in the airplane except himself was concerned about the thick plumes of smoke streaming back from the wing engines. He really appreciated the moment and our evil grins. We didn't appreciate the dead fish we all found in our cars that night.

August 7, 1977 Universal Studios was in the county with a mob of people shooting several segments of *The Six Million Dollar Man,* and they were working on one big scene, in which Lee Majors is supposed to drive a car off a road at high speed into a water-filled ditch. We were stooging around at two thousand feet, watching it all through binoculars, when Chick Autry, in the right seat, had it pegged. "Okay, there comes the car. Let's go get 'em."

Hey, man, it's *my* show, right? I created this bionic dude, so I figure I could take certain liberties. Everyone was concentrating like mad on the car ripping up the highway when we came in off the river, props screaming like mountain-sized buzz saws, the smoke pouring back, and we did our number just above upturned noses. We blew the car scene for them, but they said the aerial shots—not in the script—were fabulous.

It went that way for month after month, flying her by day and then going out for a lot of night work, with Vern Renaud and his silver hair and impish grin in the front office with me, and it was everything flight should be. There were more air shows and a lot of skydivers going out of the airplane, and in October of 1977 we had another one of the Kerwin Capers with a three-hour air show, all of it airborne, along the forty-eight miles of coastline of Brevard County, running up and down the damned beaches in a rainstorm that never stopped the whole time. It was another of those affairs dreamed up by the cockamamie team of Fred Gay and Bubba Sutton, and we set some sort of record for air shows, which was capped off by George Baker doing the whole county right off the beach on the deck at better than five hundred miles per hour.

October 30, 1977 We tried something new at an air show at Venice, on the west coast of Florida. *Annie* started down the runway with flaps set for jump takeoff, and we had a T-6 on each side and trailing us, and the idea was, see, for us to get off quickly while the T-6s continued straight ahead and we would climb up and out to our right, getting up the flaps and starting an immediate turn to come back down the field. Dennis McDonald was in the right seat with me (Kerwin had stolen his airplane), and we had gone through another of those hot-pants routines with the T-6 drivers who were going to give us "lots of time and room to make your turn." We boomed up and I never got a straight-and-level moment but had the nose down as soon as Larry shouted, "Flaps up!" and it was one of those swapping-ends maneuvers, because

Annie just *pivoted* and we were going the other way and the T-6s got there just in time to join us for the pullup, at the far end of the runway.

December 3, 1977 We jumped Major Richard Tifts, leader of the Army's Golden Knights skydiving team, and a couple of his gang, during a visit to Kissimmee. Fun-and-games time. The next day, Grace "The Ace" Page, one of the world's greatest air-show performers and who holds the world's record for spins (for her J-3 Cub), flew *Annie*, and those two were just made for one another. I capped off this day by flying Grace and her friends down the Florida coast and managed the artful job of landing at the wrong airport.

December 13, 1977 Bubba Sutton brought an old friend—without telling me beforehand—to the airplane, and it was sheer magic to have astronaut Wally Schirra in the right seat as we toured Cape Canaveral at five hundred feet and visited the Mercury, Gemini, and Apollo launch pads, from where Wally had ripped into orbit at eighteen thousand miles an hour. He'd never seen his launch pads from this altitude, and then we went up to the Kennedy Space Center and did the same thing—with clearance from the White House for the flight

Penny the Wolf gets her bovine thighbone gift from Martin Caidin as a disbelieving Red Gargaly looks on. DEE DEE CAIDIN

230

—with Wally keying his microphone and playing songs on a solid-gold kazoo, to the bewilderment of the tower crew at Patrick Air Force Base. . . .

December was a crazy month. On the twenty-seventh we caught the Goodyear Blimp over the Indian River, chatted with them on their frequency, and got invited to do a bunch of aerial attacks so they—and we—could take movies. In the right seat this wintry day was Karl Frensch, who'd been in a Ju-52 cockpit for the invasion of Holland in 1940, and the pictures of *Annie* getting Good-year are framed in his den.

The next day, we had a *very* special delivery mission. Red Gargaly has a huge wolf—name of Penny—for a pet. Dee Dee and I bought a huge thighbone from a cow, called Susan and Joy, Red's daughters, and got them to wrangle Red out to Lauderdale Executive with Penny but not really knowing *why*. Three hundred other people knew, however, and the pictures of that thighbone delivery, to a delighted Penny and a head-shaking Red Gargaly, are among our more precious mementos.

"You mean you flew that big damn' airplane all the way down here to deliver a bone to my dog?" Red insisted.

"Wolf," we corrected. "We wouldn't have done it for a dog. But look at how Penny is starving. She—"

"She's on a diet!" Red yelled. "You ever try to keep a timber wolf on a diet?"

"Not any more she ain't. C'mon, you got the privilege of buying lunch." Penny came along with her thighbone, and when the day was done, I sat back and let Dee Dee take the big bird home.

And so it went, and so it goes. We flew honor flights over the funerals of friends who had flown with us and had gone west. We continued flying our air shows, and did formation work, and sent skydivers leaping happily into space from our big, open door. We had our marvelous meetings with Kurt Weil, who had helped to create and design this same airplane fifty years before. We had one air show with a low pass down the runway at a requested one hundred feet, with Dennis Sherman off my right wing in a T-6 and John Silberman and Jay Hinyub off the left wing in an AT-11 with an all-glass nose, and we looked up in stark disbelief as a bunch of jet fighters came head on at us, also at the same one hundred feet. They'd gotten the numbers messed up and there was only one way to go and that was *down*, and it's the way we went,

Kurt Streit—"The Master"—inspects N52JU with Martin Caidin before their first flight together. RUSS VOTOE

A well-deserved and long-awaited reflective moment: Kurt Streit at the controls of a Ju-52 for the first time in thirty-three years! *Iron Annie* is three thousand feet over central Florida. RUSS VOTOE

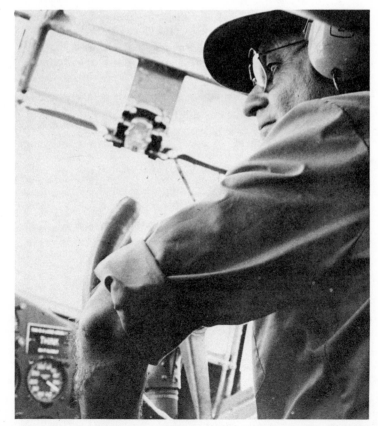

and the mob of airplanes crossed in a great blur and everything was cool, man, except for that grove of trees that appeared suddenly ahead of us. Abrupt maneuvers are not the answer when you're in formation and on the deck, and I eased her up as the last jet flashed overhead, and we did a little tree-topping with the wheels, but those massive wheels and gear weren't even bothered, although Pat Coyle, in the cabin, lost his cookies when he saw the branches flying by, and John Silberman said he would have given ten thousand dollars for ten seconds of film of that particular sight. He gave us his first Annual Treemower Award that night.

And then it was May 31, 1978, and a moment for which I had been waiting for years. National Airlines delivered to Florida a man we'd waited for all this time: Kurt Streit himself, former IFR instructor for the Luftwaffe, test pilot for Junkers, master of combat survival through Africa and Europe and Stalingrad—and a man I was meeting for the first time face to face but whom I felt I had known for a hundred years.

There's no way to describe the next several days of our flying, because I don't have the words. It was everything it should be, it was everything I hoped it would be, it was more than everything I had imagined. Kurt could hardly believe *Iron Annie,* and with a group of German engineers and pilots, he crawled all through the Ju-52 and pronounced her as good as the day she left the factory.

Two old masters meeting quietly beneath the wing of *Iron Annie:* Eastern Air Lines Captain Vern Renaud (left) and Kurt Streit, who flew the Ju-52 for both Lufthansa and the Luftwaffe. RUSS VOTOE

"No; *better,*" Kurt corrected himself, "because of the changes you have made. She is incredible. She flies as if her power were twice what you have, and she is . . . she is so smooth and responsive it is difficult to believe." He patted me on the shoulder. "All airplanes talk to their pilots, no? And *Annie,* I can see you and she have learned well to talk with one another."

The moment.

Kurt Streit in the right seat of N52JU, and thundering out of our home field, and the sun bright and warm and the air like pure satin, and God, but we *flew.* She lifted her nose and hung high and then slid off on a wing and swooped like a great golden eagle earthward and then came up and around again, and it was music and bright sunlight and the sweet thunder of those radials.

In the evenings, we exchanged old memories, and with all I knew about the lineage and the history and the records of the Ju-52, it seems there is always something else to learn, something new, even astonishing, and in my home in Cocoa Beach late that night of our first flights together, Kurt told me about two Ju-52s of which only a few men ever knew and which have never seen print in either detail or photograph.

"They were hush-hush," Kurt said, "and only two of these very special 52s were built, and from top to bottom and wing across wing they were absolutely black, without a single mark of any kind on them. Each machine was powered with three BMW 801e supercharged engines of 1,500 horsepower each, plus special constant-speed propellers. The modifications were done at the Dessau plant, and I went there in 1943, after Stalingrad, to check out the airplane. The normal fuel capacity was doubled, and they had installed in them a special oxygen system for operating at extreme altitudes.

"It was not possible for a Ju-52 to fly as this airplane could fly. We went to an advanced airfield and we loaded up with special agents for a top-secret flight. We flew to a highly secret airfield far behind the Russian lines, and from there we operated on special missions. Our agents spoke perfect Russian, and their job was to get to big tank factories in the Ural Mountains and blow them up, and then they would rush back to where the black Ju-52 waited for them with engines already running.

"It was a hell of an aircraft. With 100 per cent power, you moved ahead as if you were shot from a catapult, and you held the yoke all the way back and in three hundred feet, no more, the machine was off the ground and you kept hard back on the yoke and she climbed at better than three thousand feet a minute. The airplanes would outclimb almost all of the Russian fighters and they rarely flew at night anyway, so once they were off the ground they would keep climbing to over thirty thousand feet and return to friendly territory.

"What was just as interesting was that all these modifications were made without a single structural change to either the wings or the fuselage. They didn't need any. The airplane is simply that strong. In fact, the Dessau engineers did a study that indicated you could put engines of two thousand horsepower each on the Ju-52 and you wouldn't need to make a single change to the machine."

Kurt Streit and I flew for two more days. He is a warm and sensitive human being, and I personally consider the greatest moment in all my years of flying that time when we went into the cockpit and he took the right seat and he nodded to me, and we didn't have to say one word, and for our first flight we didn't, we had full communication without words, and it wasn't until we had been in the air for twenty minutes that he took a long and deep breath, and then we had some talk from one pilot to another.

It had been a long road for both of us.

August 30, 1978 We flew to Langley Air Force Base, in Virginia, to put on a Valiant Air Command show for the Air Force and NASA. It was one of the best aerial demonstrations ever. The good feelings it left did not last long, though, for two days later, while on a cross-country flight, Pete and Glynes Sherman's *Lightning* crashed, killing them both. We lost some of the best ever.

———◆———

Well, I've thought a great deal about how to end this book, but it doesn't work. There isn't any ending, really, because *Iron Annie* flies like a dream and there are more great moments in her future.

We're building the after-fuselage gun turret, and when it's all done we'll install the turret and connect the lines back there and put in the right kind of machine gun: the kind that makes noise and spits fire but doesn't have any ammunition and doesn't hurt anyone. There's a whole stack of new

Two of the leading madmen of the Dr. Strangelove Team of the Pumphouse and Locomotive Gang: Ted Votoe (left) and Larry Urback with two huge bombs they've just "liberated" in a moonlight requisition for the rearming of *Iron Annie*. RUSS VOTOE

Every seat filled, flaps down, *Iron Annie* slides down final approach at Langley Air Force Base. MAJOR VERN ALEXANDER, U. S. AIR FORCE

Holding formation in a T-34 flown by Leo Kerwin, the photographer catches the Ju-52 at the exact moment of touchdown on the Langley Air Force Base runway. MAJOR VERN ALEXANDER, U. S. AIR FORCE

Two T-6s hold position as Martin Caidin brings the Ju-52 in for a high-speed, low-altitude pass down the Langley Air Force Base runway. STEVE ROCK, U. S. NAVY

A rare picture indeed. The Ju-52 leads a formation of three T-6s (upper) and, below, left to right, a P-38L, a T-28A, and an F4F-4. STEVE ROCK, U. S. NAVY

Kommandant Martin von Caidin in the office he prefers to all others: the captain's seat of the Ju-52. MAJOR VERN ALEXANDER, U. S. AIR FORCE

These pictures were the last ever taken of the Lockheed P-38L Lightning fighter owned and flown by Pete Sherman, of the Valiant Air Command, during the Langley Air Show of the command. Two days later, the Lightning crashed, killing Pete and Glynes Sherman. This, then, was their last air show. STEVE ROCK, U. S. NAVY

avionics waiting to go into N52JU: ILS and Lo-calizer systems, and digital ADF and DME, and still more. We'll probably redesign the entire panel from scratch in the interests of greater efficiency. There's some new carpeting we're getting to like pretty much, and perhaps the metal in those original seats is weary and they're ready for replacement with new and modern equipment. The seats don't really matter; it's where they take you that counts.

And there are some engines that fascinate us. Twelve hundred horsepower each and big, three-bladed, constant-speed props so that we'll take off in four or five hundred feet any time and in cruise shut down the nose engine and feather the prop, or even fly her on the nose engine alone if we have to do that, and we've got some ideas about an external sound system, and we're looking at some bombs to hang beneath the wings (with coolers for beer, naturally), and then there are the headphones we'd like to put by each seat so that whoever flies with us can listen in to everything that's going on between the flight crew and the tower and air-traffic center, and when we're in there tight during the air shows, ripping downstairs with the fighters, they can share that, too, and I guess I've found that closing statement, after all.

TO BE CONTINUED . . .

A man and his airplane. They've come a long way together and, if Fate deals her cards kindly, they have a long way to go. CECIL STOUGHTON